# CSET Physics
## Teacher Certification Exam

**215**
**220**

**By:** Sharon A. Wynne, M.S.

**XAMonline, Inc.**
Boston

Copyright © 2018 XAMonline, Inc.
All rights reserved. No part of the material protected by this copyright notice may be reproduced or utilized in any form or by any means, electronic or mechanical, including photocopying, recording or by any information storage and retrievable system, without written permission from the copyright holder.

To obtain permission(s) to use the material from this work for any purpose including workshops or seminars, please submit a written request to:

XAMonline, Inc.
21 Orient Avenue
Melrose, MA 02176
Toll Free 1-800-301-4647
Email: info@xamonline.com
Web www.xamonline.com

Library of Congress Cataloging-in-Publication Data
Wynne, Sharon A.

    CSET Physics (215, 220): Teacher Certification / Sharon A. Wynne.
    ISBN 978-1-60787-651-9

1. Physics      2. Study Guides.      3. CSET
4. Teachers' Certification & Licensure.      5. Careers

**Disclaimer:**
The opinions expressed in this publication are the sole works of XAMonline and were created independently from the National Education Association,
Educational Testing Service, or any State Department of Education, National Evaluation Systems or other testing affiliates.

Between the time of publication and printing, state specific standards as well as testing formats and website information may change that is not included in part or in whole within this product. XAMonline developed the sample test questions and the questions reflect similar content as on real tests; however, they are not former tests. XAMonline assembles content that aligns with state standards but makes no claims nor guarantees teacher candidates a passing score. Numerical scores are determined by testing companies such as NES or ETS and then are compared with individual state standards. A passing score varies from state to state.

**Printed in the United States of America**
CSET: Physics (215, 220)
ISBN: 978-1-60787-651-9

# TEACHER CERTIFICATION STUDY GUIDE

## SUBAREA II.      CONSERVATION OF ENERGY AND MOMENTUM

### COMPETENCY 2.1 CONSERVATION OF ENERGY AND MOMENTUM

Skill 2.1a    Use conservation of energy to characterize kinetic-potential energy systems such as oscillating systems, projectile motion, and roller coasters ............ 31

Skill 2.1b    Analyze elastic and inelastic collisions and solve for unknown values ..... 32

Skill 2.1c    Solve problems involving linear and rotational motion in terms of conservation of momentum and energy ............ 33

Skill 2.1d    Recognize relationships between energy/momentum conservation principles and Newton's Laws ............ 36

Skill 2.1e    Examine the impact of friction on conservation principles ............ 37

Skill 2.1f    Interpret force-versus-time and force-versus-distance graphs to find, for example, work done or impulse on a system ............ 37

## SUBAREA III.      HEAT AND THERMODYNAMICS

### COMPETENCY 3.1 HEAT AND THERMODYNAMICS

Skill 3.1a    Solve problems involving the laws of thermodynamics using the relationships among work, heat flow, energy, and entropy ............ 40

Skill 3.1b    Define and correctly apply thermodynamic properties of materials such as specific heat, heats of fusion, heat of vaporization, thermal conductivity, and thermal expansion to solve problems ............ 42

Skill 3.1c    Solve problems for ideal gas systems ............ 46

Skill 3.1d    Interpret graphs showing phase changes and graphs of cyclic processes ............ 49

Skill 3.1e    Solve problems involving cyclic processes, including calculations of work done, heat gain/loss, and entropy change ............ 53

Skill 3.1f    Describe a plasma, state its characteristic properties, and contrast it with an ideal gas ............ 57

# TEACHER CERTIFICATION STUDY GUIDE

# Table of Contents

### PART I. UNDERSTANDING AND SKILL IN PHYSICS

## SUBAREA I.                                              MOTION AND FORCES

### COMPETENCY 1.1 MOTION AND FORCES

| | | |
|---|---|---|
| Skill 1.1a | Discuss and apply Newton's laws | 1 |
| Skill 1.1b | Solve problems using Newton's Second Law | 3 |
| Skill 1.1c | Define pressure and relate it to fluid flow and buoyancy | 4 |
| Skill 1.1d | Describe the relationships among position, distance, displacement, speed, velocity, acceleration, and time, and perform simple calculations using these variables for both linear and circular motion | 7 |
| Skill 1.1e | Construct and analyze simple vector and graphical representations of motion and forces | 10 |
| Skill 1.1f | Generate and understand functional relationships of graphs showing distance, velocity, and acceleration versus time | 13 |
| Skill 1.1g | Recognize relationships among variables for linear motion and rotational motion | 14 |
| Skill 1.1h | Solve 2-dimensional problems involving vector analysis of motion and forces, including projectile motion, uniform circular motion, and statics | 16 |
| Skill 1.1i | Identify the separate forces that act on a body and describe the net force on the body | 18 |
| Skill 1.1j | Construct appropriate free-body diagrams of many-body problems | 21 |
| Skill 1.1k | Solve periodic motion problems | 23 |
| Skill 1.1l | Solve problems involving linear and rotational motion in term of forces and torques | 25 |
| Skill 1.1m | Identify fundamental forces, including gravity, nuclear forces, and electromagnetic forces, and explain their roles in nature | 27 |
| Skill 1.1n | Explain and calculate mechanical advantages for levers, pulleys, and inclined planes | 29 |

**PHYSICS**

# TEACHER CERTIFICATION STUDY GUIDE

## SUBAREA IV.                          WAVES

### COMPETENCY 4.1 WAVES

Skill 4.1a      Compare the characteristics of sound, light, and seismic waves.............. 58

Skill 4.1b      Explain that energy is transferred by waves without mass transfer and provide examples................................................................................................ 59

Skill 4.1c      Explain how lenses are used in simple optical systems, including the camera, telescope, microscope, and the eye............................................. 60

Skill 4.1d      Explain and apply the laws of reflection and refraction ........................... 62

Skill 4.1e      Compare transmission, reflection, and absorption of light in matter ................................................................................................................ 64

Skill 4.1f      Relate wave propagation to properties of materials................................ 65

Skill 4.1g      Describe, distinguish, and solve both conceptual and numerical problems involving interference, diffraction, refraction, reflection, Doppler effect, polarization, dispersion, and scattering ....................................................................... 66

## SUBAREA V.                          ELECTROMAGNETISM

### COMPETENCY 5.1 ELECTROMAGNETISM

Skill 5.1a      Describe and provide examples of electrostatic and magnetostatic phenomena 71

Skill 5.1b      Predict charges or poles based on attraction/repulsion observations....... 72

Skill 5.1c      Build a simple compass and use it to determine direction of magnetic fields, including the Earth's magnetic field ......................................................... 73

Skill 5.1d      Analyze electric and magnetic forces, charges, and fields using Coulomb's law, the Lorentz force, and the right-hand rule ................................................ 75

Skill 5.1e      Relate electric currents to magnetic fields and describe the application of these relationships, such as in electromagnets, electric current generators, motors, and transformers ........................................................................................ 79

Skill 5.1f      Solve problems involving the relationships between electric and magnetic phenomena ............................................................................................. 84

Skill 5.1g      Define and calculate power, voltage differences, current, and resistance in simple circuits................................................................................................... 86

Skill 5.1h      Design and interpret simple series and parallel circuits ........................... 88

Skill 5.1i      Apply energy principles to analyze problems in electricity, magnetism, and circuit theory involving capacitors, resistors, and inductors ............................... 90

Skill 5.1j      Calculate power, voltage changes, current, and resistance in multiloop circuits involving capacitors, resistors, and inductors........................................... 93

**PHYSICS**

# TEACHER CERTIFICATION STUDY GUIDE

| | | |
|---|---|---|
| Skill 5.1k | Interpret and design mixed series and parallel circuits involving capacitors, resistors, and inductors | 97 |
| Skill 5.1l | Explain properties of transistors, diodes, and semiconductors | 99 |

## SUBAREA 6. QUANTUM MECHANICS AND THE STANDARD MODEL OF PARTICLES

### COMPETENCY 6.1 QUANTUM MECHANICS AND THE STANDARD MODEL OF PARTICLES

| | | |
|---|---|---|
| Skill 6.1a | Distinguish the four fundamental forces of nature, describe their ranges, and identify their force carriers | 101 |
| Skill 6.1b | Evaluate the assumptions and relevance of the Bohr model of the atom | 101 |

## PART II. SKILLS AND ABILITIES APPLICABLE TO THE CONTENT DOMAINS IN SCIENCE

## SUBAREA I. INVESTIGATION AND EXPERIMENTATION

### COMPETENCY 1.1 QUESTION FORMULATION

| | | |
|---|---|---|
| Skill 1.1a. | Formulate and evaluate a viable hypothesis | 103 |
| Skill 1.1b. | Recognize the value and role of observation prior to question formulation | 103 |
| Skill 1.1c. | Recognize the iterative nature of questioning | 104 |
| Skill 1.1d. | Given an experimental design, identify possible hypotheses that it may test | 104 |

### COMPETENCY 1.2. PLANNING A SCIENTIFIC INVESTIGATION

| | | |
|---|---|---|
| Skill 1.2a. | Given a hypothesis, formulate an investigation or experimental design to test that hypothesis | 105 |
| Skill 1.2b. | Evaluate an experimental design for its suitability to test a given hypothesis | 105 |
| Skill 1.2c. | Distinguish between variable and controlled parameters | 106 |

# TEACHER CERTIFICATION STUDY GUIDE

## COMPETENCY 1.3 OBSERVATION AND DATA COLLECTION

Skill 1.3a. Identify changes in natural phenomena over time without manipulating the phenomena. ................................................................................................ 107

Skill 1.3b. Analyze the locations, sequences, and time intervals that are characteristic of natural phenomena ................................................................. 108

Skill 1.3c. Select and use appropriate tools and technology to perform tests, collect data, analyze relationships, and display data. ................................. 109

Skill 1.3d. Evaluate the precision, accuracy, and reproducibility of data ................. 110

Skill 1.3e. Identify and analyze possible reasons for inconsistent results, such as sources of error or uncontrolled conditions ............................................... 110

Skill 1.3f. Identify and communicate sources of unavoidable experimental error .. 111

Skill 1.3g. Recognize the issues of statistical variability and explain the need for controlled tests ................................................................................................ 111

Skill 1.3h. Know and evaluate the safety issues when designing an experiment and implement appropriate solutions to safety problems ............................... 111

Skill 1.3i. Appropriately employ a variety of print and electronic resources to collect information and evidence as part of a research project ........................... 113

Skill 1.3j. Assess the accuracy validity and reliability of information gathered from a variety of sources ...................................................................................... 113

## COMPETENCY 1.4 DATA ANALYSIS/GRAPHING

Skill 1.4a. Construct appropriate graphs from data and develop qualitative and quantitative statements about relationships between variables ................. 114

Skill 1.4b. Recognize the slope of the linear graph as the constant in the relationship $y=kx$ and apply this principle in interpreting graphs constructed from data ................................................................................................................... 115

Skill 1.4c. Apply simple mathematical relationships to determine a missing quantity in an algebraic expression, given the two remaining terms ............................ 115

Skill 1.4d. Determine whether a relationship on a given graph is linear or non- linear and determine the appropriateness of extrapolating the data ................................................................................................................... 116

Skill 1.4e. Solve scientific problems by using quadratic equations and simple trigonometric, exponential, and logarithmic functions ..................................................... 117

**PHYSICS**

## COMPETENCY 1.5 DRAWING CONCLUSIONS AND COMMUNICATING EXPLANATIONS

Skill 1.5a. Draw appropriate and logical conclusions from data ............................. 120

Skill 1.5b. Communicate the logical connection among hypotheses, science concepts, tests conducted, data collected, and conclusions drawn from the scientific evidence 120

Skill 1.5c. Communicate the steps and results of an investigation in written reports and oral presentations................................................................................... 120

Skill 1.5d. Recognize whether evidence is consistent with a proposed explanation ............................................................................................................... 120

Skill 1.5e. Construct appropriate visual representations of scientific phenomenon and processes............................................................................................ 120

Skill 1.5f. Read topographic and geologic maps for evidence provided on the maps and construct and interpret a simple scale map ............................................ 120

## SUBAREA II.                                                                    NATURE OF SCIENCE

## COMPETENCY 2.1. SCIENTIFIC INQUIRY

Skill 2.1a. Distinguish among the terms hypothesis, theory, and prediction as used in scientific investigations ............................................................................. 121

Skill 2.1b. Evaluate the usefulness, limitations, and interdisciplinary and cumulative nature of scientific evidence as it relates to the development of models and theories as representations of reality .................................................................... 122

Skill 2.1c. Recognize that when observations do not agree with an accepted scientific theory, either the observations are mistaken or fraudulent, or the accepted theory is erroneous or incorrect................................................................. 122

Skill 2.1d. Understand that reproducibility of data is critical to the scientific endeavor ............................................................................................................... 123

Skill 2.1e. Recognize that science is a self- correcting process that eventually identifies misconceptions and experimental biases................................................ 123

Skill 2.1f. Recognize that an inquiring mind is at the heart of the scientific method and that doing science involves thinking critically about the evidence presented, the usefulness of models, and the limitations of theories.............................. 123

Skill 2.1g. Recognize that theories are judged by how well they explain observations and predict results and that when they represent new ideas that are counter to mainstream ideas they often encounter vigorous criticism..................... 124

Skill 2.1h. Recognize that when observations, data, or experimental results do not agree, the unexpected results are not necessarily mistakes................................... 124

#### TEACHER CERTIFICATION STUDY GUIDE

Skill 2.1i. Know why curiosity, honesty, openness, and skepticism are so highly regarded in science and how they are incorporated into the way science is carried out...125

## COMPETENCY 2.2 SCIENTIFIC ETHICS

Skill 2.2a. Understand that honesty is at the core of scientific ethics; first and foremost is the honest and accurate reporting of procedures used and data collected.. 126

Skill 2.2b. Know that all scientists are obligated to evaluate the safety of an investigation and ensure the safety of those performing the experiment............................. 127

Skill 2.2c. Know the procedures for respectful treatment of all living organisms in experimentation and other investigations ................................................. 127

## COMPETENCY 2.3 HISTORICAL PERSPECTIVES

Skill 2.3a. Discuss the cumulative nature of scientific evidence as it relates to the development of models and theories...................................................... 128

Skill 2.3b. Recognize that as knowledge in science evolves, when observations do not support an accepted scientific theory, the observations are reconsidered to determine if they are mistaken or fraudulent, or if the accepted theory is erroneous or incomplete........................................................................................ 129

Skill 2.3c. Recognize and provide specific examples that scientific advances sometimes result in profound paradigm shifts in scientific theories ................................................................................................ 129

## SUBAREA III.                                                       SCIENCE AND SOCIETY

## COMPETENCY 3.1 SCIENCE LITERACY

Skill 3.1a. Recognize that science attempts to make sense of how the natural and the designed world function ........................................................................ 131

Skill 3.1b. Demonstrate the ability to apply critical and independent thinking to weigh alternative explanations of events ............................................................ 131

Skill 3.1c. Apply evidence, numbers, patterns, and logical arguments to solve problems..131

Skill 3.1d. Understand that, although much has been learned about the objects, events and phenomena in nature, there are many unanswered questions, i.e., science is a work in progress ................................................................................ 131

Skill 3.1e. Know that the ability of science and technology to resolve societal problems depends on the scientific literacy of a society ......................................... 133

**PHYSICS**

# TEACHER CERTIFICATION STUDY GUIDE

## COMPETENCY 3.2 DIVERSITY

Skill 3.2a. Identify examples of women and men of various social and ethnic backgrounds with diverse interests, talents, qualities and motivations who are, or who have been, engaged in activities of science and related fields ............ 134

## COMPETENCY 3.3 SCIENCE, TECHNOLOGY, AND SOCIETY

Skill 3.3 a. Identify and evaluate the impact of scientific advances on society ......... 135

Skill 3.3 b. Recognize that scientific advances may challenge individuals to reevaluate their personal beliefs ............ 136

## COMPETENCY 3.4 SAFETY

Skill 3.4a. Choose appropriate safety equipment for a given activity ............ 137

Skill 3.4b. Discuss the safe use, storage, and disposal of commonly used chemicals and biological specimens ............ 137

Skill 3.4c. Assess the safety conditions needed to maintain a science laboratory . 138

Skill 3.4d. Read and decode MSDS/OSHA labels on laboratory supplies and equipment 139

Skill 3.4e. Discuss key issues in the disposal of hazardous materials in either the laboratory or the local community ............ 140

Skill 3.4f. Be familiar with standard safety procedures such as those outlined in the Science Safety Handbook for California Schools (1999) ............ 140

Sample Test ............ 141

Answer Key ............ 160

Rigor Analysis Table ............ 161

Rationales with Sample Questions ............ 162

# TEACHER CERTIFICATION STUDY GUIDE

## Great Study and Testing Tips!

*What* to study in order to prepare for the subject assessments is the focus of this study guide but equally important is *how* you study.

You can increase your chances of truly mastering the information by taking some simple, but effective steps.

## Study Tips:

**1. Some foods aid the learning process.** Foods such as milk, nuts, seeds, rice, and oats help your study efforts by releasing natural memory enhancers called CCKs (*cholecystokinin*) composed of *tryptophan*, *choline*, and *phenylalanine*. All of these chemicals enhance the neurotransmitters associated with memory. Before studying, try a light, protein-rich meal of eggs, turkey, and fish. All of these foods release the memory enhancing chemicals. The better the connections, the more you comprehend.

Likewise, before you take a test, stick to a light snack of energy boosting and relaxing foods. A glass of milk, a piece of fruit, or some peanuts all release various memory-boosting chemicals and help you to relax and focus on the subject at hand.

**2. Learn to take great notes.** A by-product of our modern culture is that we have grown accustomed to getting our information in short doses (i.e. TV news sound bites or USA Today style newspaper articles.)

Consequently, we've subconsciously trained ourselves to assimilate information better in neat little packages. If your notes are scrawled all over the paper, it fragments the flow of the information. Strive for clarity. Newspapers use a standard format to achieve clarity. Your notes can be much clearer through use of proper formatting. A very effective format is called *"Cornell Method."*

> Take a sheet of loose-leaf lined notebook paper and draw a line all the way down the paper about 1-2" from the left-hand edge.
>
> Draw another line across the width of the paper about 1-2" up from the bottom. Repeat this process on the reverse side of the page.

Look at the highly effective result. You have ample room for notes, a left hand margin for special emphasis items or inserting supplementary data from the textbook, a large area at the bottom for a brief summary, and a little rectangular space for just about anything you want.

**PHYSICS**

# TEACHER CERTIFICATION STUDY GUIDE

3. **Get the concept then the details**. Too often we focus on the details and don't gather an understanding of the concept. However, if you simply memorize only dates, places, or names, you may well miss the whole point of the subject.

A key way to understand things is to put them in your own words. If you are working from a textbook, automatically summarize each paragraph in your mind. If you are outlining text, don't simply copy the author's words.

*Rephrase* them in your own words. You remember your own thoughts and words much better than someone else's, and subconsciously tend to associate the important details to the core concepts.

4. **Ask Why?** Pull apart written material paragraph by paragraph and don't forget the captions under the illustrations.

Example: If the heading is "Stream Erosion", flip it around to read "Why do streams erode?" Then answer the questions.

If you train your mind to think in a series of questions and answers, not only will you learn more, but it also helps to lessen the test anxiety because you are used to answering questions.

5. **Read for reinforcement and future needs**. Even if you only have 10 minutes, put your notes or a book in your hand. Your mind is similar to a computer; you have to input data in order to have it processed. *By reading, you are creating the neural connections for future retrieval.* The more times you read something, the more you reinforce the learning of ideas.

Even if you don't fully understand something on the first pass, *your mind stores much of the material for later recall.*

6. **Relax to learn so go into exile**. Our bodies respond to an inner clock called biorhythms. Burning the midnight oil works well for some people, but not everyone.

If possible, set aside a particular place to study that is free of distractions. Shut off the television, cell phone, and pager and exile your friends and family during your study period.

If you really are bothered by silence, try background music. Light classical music at a low volume has been shown to aid in concentration over other types. Music that evokes pleasant emotions without lyrics is highly suggested. Try just about anything by Mozart. It relaxes you.

**7. Use arrows not highlighters.** At best, it's difficult to read a page full of yellow, pink, blue, and green streaks. Try staring at a neon sign for a while and you'll soon see that the horde of colors obscure the message.

A quick note, a brief dash of color, an underline, and an arrow pointing to a particular passage is much clearer than a horde of highlighted words.

**8. Budget your study time.** Although you shouldn't ignore any of the material, *allocate your available study time in the same ratio that topics may appear on the test.*

# TEACHER CERTIFICATION STUDY GUIDE

## Testing Tips:

**1. Get smart, play dumb. Don't read anything into the question.** Don't make an assumption that the test writer is looking for something else than what is asked. Stick to the question as written and don't read extra things into it.

**2. Read the question and all the choices *twice* before answering the question.** You may miss something by not carefully reading, and then re-reading both the question and the answers.

If you really don't have a clue as to the right answer, leave it blank on the first time through. Go on to the other questions, as they may provide a clue as to how to answer the skipped questions.

If later on, you still can't answer the skipped ones . . . **Guess.** The only penalty for guessing is that you *might* get it wrong. Only one thing is certain; if you don't put anything down, you will get it wrong!

**3. Turn the question into a statement.** Look at the way the questions are worded. The syntax of the question usually provides a clue. Does it seem more familiar as a statement rather than as a question? Does it sound strange?

By turning a question into a statement, you may be able to spot if an answer sounds right, and it may also trigger memories of material you have read.

**4. Look for hidden clues.** It's actually very difficult to compose multiple-foil (choice) questions without giving away part of the answer in the options presented. In most multiple-choice questions you can often readily eliminate one or two of the potential answers. This leaves you with only two real possibilities and automatically your odds go to Fifty-Fifty for very little work.

**5. Trust your instincts.** For every fact that you have read, you subconsciously retain something of that knowledge. On questions that you aren't really certain about, go with your basic instincts. **Your first impression on how to answer a question is usually correct.**

**6. Mark your answers directly on the test booklet.** Don't bother trying to fill in the optical scan sheet on the first pass through the test.

*Just be very careful not to miss-mark your answers when you eventually transcribe them to the scan sheet.*

**7. Watch the clock!** You have a set amount of time to answer the questions. Don't get bogged down trying to answer a single question at the expense of 10 questions you can more readily answer.

**PHYSICS**

TEACHER CERTIFICATION STUDY GUIDE

# PART I. UNDERSTANDING AND SKILL IN PHYSICS

## SUBAREA I. MOTION AND FORCES

### COMPETENCY 1.1 MOTION AND FORCES

**Skill 1.1a    Discuss and apply Newton's laws (i.e., first, second, third, and law of universal gravitation)**

**Newton's first law of motion:** "An object at rest tends to stay at rest and an object in motion tends to stay in motion with the same speed and in the same direction unless acted upon by an unbalanced force". This tendency of an object to continue in its state of rest or motion is known as **inertia**. Note that, at any point in time, most objects have multiple forces acting on them. If the vector addition of all the forces on an object results in a zero net force, then the forces on the object are said to be **balanced**. If the net force on an object is non-zero, an **unbalanced** force is acting on the object.

Prior to Newton's formulation of this law, being at rest was considered the natural state of all objects because at the earth's surface we have the force of gravity working at all times which causes nearly any object put into motion to eventually come to rest. Newton's brilliant leap was to recognize that an unbalanced force changes the motion of a body, whether that body begins at rest or at some non-zero speed.

We experience the consequences of this law everyday. For instance, the first law is why seat belts are necessary to prevent injuries. When a car stops suddenly, say by hitting a road barrier, the driver continues on forward due to inertia until acted upon by a force. The seat belt provides that force and distributes the load across the whole body rather than allowing the driver to fly forward and experience the force against the steering wheel.

**Newton's second law of motion:** "The acceleration of an object as produced by a net force is directly proportional to the magnitude of the net force, in the same direction as the net force, and inversely proportional to the mass of the object".
In the equation form, it is stated as $F = ma$, force equals mass times acceleration. It is important, again, to remember that this is the net force and that forces are vector quantities. Thus if an object is acted upon by 12 forces that sum to zero, there is no acceleration. Also, this law embodies the idea of inertia as a consequence of mass. For a given force, the resulting acceleration is proportionally smaller for a more massive object because the larger object has more inertia.

The first two laws are generally applied together via the equation **F=ma**. The first law is largely the conceptual foundation for the more specific and quantitative second law.

PHYSICS

The **weight** of an object is the result of the gravitational force of the earth acting on its mass. The acceleration due to Earth's gravity on an object is 9.81 m/s². Since force equals mass * acceleration, the magnitude of the gravitational force created by the earth on an object is

$$F_{Gravity} = m_{object} \cdot 9.81 \, m/s^2$$

**Newton's third law of motion**: "For every action, there is an equal and opposite reaction". This statement means that, in every interaction, there is a pair of forces acting on the two interacting objects. The size of the force on the first object equals the size of the force on the second object. The direction of the force on the first object is opposite to the direction of the force on the second object.

**1. The propulsion/movement of fish through water:** A fish uses its fins to push water backwards. The water pushes back on the fish. Because the force on the fish is unbalanced the fish moves forward.
**2. The motion of car:** A car's wheels push against the road and the road pushes back. Since the force of the road on the car is unbalanced the car moves forward.
**3. Walking:** When one pushes backwards on the foot with the muscles of the leg, the floor pushes back on the foot. If the forces of the leg on the foot and the floor on the foot are balanced, the foot will not move and the muscles of the body can move the other leg forward.

**Newton's universal law of gravitation** states that any two objects experience a force between them as the result of their masses. Specifically, the force between two masses $m_1$ and $m_2$ can be summarized as

$$F = G \frac{m_1 m_2}{r^2}$$

where G is the gravitational constant ($G = 6.672 \times 10^{-11} \, Nm^2 / kg^2$), and r is the distance between the two objects.

Important things to remember:

1. The gravitational force is proportional to the masses of the two objects, but *inversely* proportional to the *square of the distance* between the two objects.
2. When calculating the effects of the acceleration due to gravity for an object above the earth's surface, the distance above the surface is ignored because it is inconsequential compared to the radius of the earth. The constant figure of 9.81 m/s² is used instead.

Problem: Two identical 4 kg balls are floating in space, 2 meters apart. What is the magnitude of the gravitational force they exert on each other?

Solution:

$$F = G\frac{m_1 m_2}{r^2} = G\frac{4 \times 4}{2^2} = 4G = 2.67 \times 10^{-10} N$$

**Skill 1.1b   Solve problems using Newton's Second Law (e.g., problems involving time, velocity, and space-dependent forces)**

**Problems involving constant force**

1. For the arrangement shown, find the force necessary to overcome the 500 N force pushing to the left and move the truck to the right with an acceleration of 5 m/s².

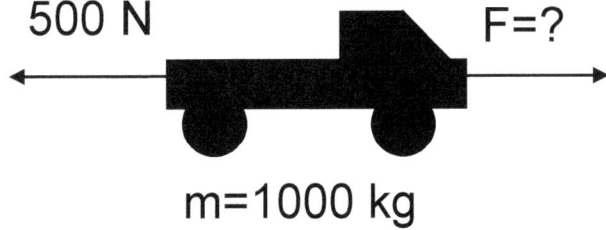

Since we know the acceleration and mass, we can calculate the net force necessary to move the truck with this acceleration. Assuming that to the right is the positive direction we sum the forces and get
F−500N = 1000kg x 5 m/s². Solving for F, we get 5500 N.

2. A 30 kg woman is in a car accident. She was driving at 50m/s when she had to hit the brakes to avoid hitting the car in front of her.
   a. The automatic tensioning device in her seatbelt slows her down to a stop over a period of one half second. How much force does it apply?

$$F = m \cdot \frac{\Delta v}{t} \rightarrow F = 30 \cdot \frac{50}{.5} = 3000 N$$

   b. If she hadn't been wearing a seatbelt, the windshield would have stopped her in .001 seconds. How much force would have been applied there?

$$F = m \cdot \frac{\Delta v}{t} \rightarrow F = 30 \cdot \frac{50}{.001} = 1500000 N$$

## Problems involving varying force

1. A falling skydiver of mass 75 Kg experiences a drag force due to air resistance that is proportional to the square of his velocity and is given by $f_{drag} = -\frac{1}{2}C\rho A v^2$ where the drag coefficient C=0.5 and the density of air is given by $\rho = 1.29 Kg/m^3$. If the cross-sectional area of the skydiver is approximately 0.7 sq.m, what is his terminal velocity?

   As the skydiver falls, his velocity increases and so does the drag force which is proportional to the square of the velocity. When the drag force reaches a value equal to the weight of the skydiver, the net force on him is zero and the velocity remains at a constant value known as the terminal velocity. Thus, if $v_t$ is the terminal velocity, the net force on the skydiver at that point is given by

   $$mg - \frac{1}{2}C\rho A v_t^2 = 0$$

   Thus, $v_t = \sqrt{\dfrac{2mg}{C\rho A}} = \sqrt{\dfrac{2 \times 75 \times 9.8}{0.5 \times 1.29 \times 0.7}} = 57 m/s$

2. The restoring force on an object attached to a spring is given by Hooke's law $F = -kx$ and is dependent on the displacement of the object. Since the acceleration of the mass is given by $a = \dfrac{d^2x}{dt^2}$, using Newton's second law of motion we get $ma = -kx$ or $m\dfrac{d^2x}{dt^2} + kx = 0$.

   For a solution to the motion of the mass-spring system see **Skill 1.1k**.

### Skill 1.1c   Define pressure and relate it to fluid flow and buoyancy (e.g., heart valves, atmospheric pressure)

The weight of a column of fluid creates hydrostatic pressure. Common situations in which we might analyze hydrostatic pressure include tanks of fluid, a swimming pool, or the ocean. Also, **atmospheric pressure** is an example of hydrostatic pressure. Because hydrostatic pressure results from the force of gravity interacting with the mass of the fluid or gas, for an incompressible fluid it is governed by the following equation:

$$P = \rho g h$$

where P=hydrostatic pressure
$\rho$=density of the fluid
g=acceleration of gravity
h=height of the fluid column

Example: How much pressure is exerted by the water at the bottom of a 5 meter swimming pool filled with water?

Solution: We simply use the equation from above, recalling that the acceleration due to gravity is 9.8m/s² and the density of water is 1000 kg/m³.

$$P = \rho g h = 1000 \frac{kg}{m^3} \times 9.8 \frac{m}{s^2} \times 5m = 49,000 Pa = 49 kPa$$

**Archimedes' Principle** states that, for an object in a fluid, "the upthrust is equal to the weight of the displaced fluid". Today, we call Archimedes' "upthrust" **buoyancy**. Buoyancy is the force produced by a fluid on a fully or partially immersed object. The buoyant force ($F_{buoyant}$) is found using the following equation:

$$F_{bouyant} = \rho V g$$

    where $\rho$=density of the fluid
        V=volume of fluid displaced by the submerged object
        g=the acceleration of gravity

Notice that the buoyant force opposes the force of gravity. For an immersed object, a gravitational force (equal to the object's mass times the acceleration of gravity) pulls it downward, while a buoyant force (equal to the weight of the displaced fluid) pushes it upward.

Also note that, from this principle, we can predict *whether* an object will sink or float in a given liquid. We can simply compare the density of the material from which the object is made to that of the liquid. If the material has a lower density, it will float; if it has a higher density it will sink. Finally, if an object has a density equal to that of the liquid, it will neither sink nor float.

Example: Will gold ($\rho$=19.3 g/cm³) float in water?

Solution: We must compare the density of gold with that of water, which is 1 g/cm³.

$$\rho_{gold} > \rho_{water}$$

So, gold will sink in water.

Example: Imagine a 1 m³ cube of oak (530 kg/m³) floating in water. What is the buoyant force on the cube and how far up the sides of the cube will the water be?

Solution: Since the cube is floating, it has displaced enough water so that the buoyant force is equal to the force of gravity. Thus the buoyant force on the cube is equal to its weight 1X530X9.8 N = 5194 N.

To determine where the cube sits in the water, we simply the find the ratio of the wood's density to that of the water:

$$\frac{\rho_{oak}}{\rho_{water}} = \frac{530\,kg/m^3}{1000\,kg/m^3} = 0.53$$

Thus, 53% of the cube will be submerged. Since the edges of the cube must be 1m each, the top 0.47m of the cube will appear above the water.

Much of what we know about fluid flow today was originally discovered by Daniel Bernoulli. His most famous discovery is known as **Bernoulli's Principle** which states that, if no work is performed on a fluid or gas, an increase in velocity will be accompanied by a decrease in pressure. The mathematical statement of the Bernoulli's Principle for incompressible flow is:

$$\frac{v^2}{2} + gh + \frac{p}{\rho} = \text{constant}$$

where $v$ = fluid velocity
$g$ = acceleration due to gravity
$h$ = height
$p$ = pressure
$\rho$ = fluid density

Though some physicists argue that it leads to the compromising of certain assumptions (i.e., incompressibility, no flow motivation, and a closed fluid loop), most agree it is correct to explain "lift" using Bernoulli's principle. This is because Bernoulli's principle can also be thought of as predicting that the pressure in moving fluid is less than the pressure in fluid at rest. Thus, there are many examples of physical phenomenon that can be explained by Bernoulli's Principle:

- The lift on airplane wings occurs because the top surface is curved while the bottom surface is straight. Air must therefore move at a higher velocity on the top of the wing and the resulting lower pressure on top accounts for lift.
- The tendency of windows to explode rather than implode in hurricanes is caused by the pressure drop that results from the high speed winds blowing across the

outer surface of the window. The higher pressure on the inside of the window then pushes the glass outward, causing an explosion.
- The ballooning and fluttering of a tarp on the top of a semi-truck moving down the highway is caused by the flow of air across the top of the truck. The decrease in pressure causes the tarp to "puff up."
- A perfume atomizer pushes a stream of air across a pool of liquid. The drop in pressure caused by the moving air lifts a bit of the perfume and allows it to be dispensed.

Flow of incompressible fluids is also governed by the **equation of continuity** $v_1 A_1 = v_2 A_2$ which arises from the conservation of mass and states that the product of the cross-sectional area of a pipe and the velocity of the fluid flowing through it must be constant. This means that the fluid will flow faster in the narrower portions of the pipe and more slowly in the wider regions.

The equation of continuity, along with Bernoulli's equation, may be used to explain blood flow characteristics in artificial heart valves. As blood flows through the narrow area in a valve, the velocity of flow increases (equation of continuity) and results in a pressure drop (Bernoulli's equation). Artificial valves are designed to minimize this effect. Other potential problems with artificial valves may also be modeled using fluid dynamics.

**Skill 1.1d    Describe the relationships among position, distance, displacement, speed, velocity, acceleration, and time, and perform simple calculations using these variables for both linear and circular motion**

Kinematics is the part of mechanics that seeks to understand the motion of objects, particularly the relationship between position, velocity, acceleration and time.

The above figure represents an object and its displacement along one linear dimension.

First we will define the relevant terms:

**1. Position or Distance** is usually represented by the variable *x*. It is measured relative to some fixed point or datum called the origin in linear units, meters, for example.

**2. Displacement** is defined as the change in position or distance which an object has moved and is represented by the variables D, d or $\Delta x$. Displacement is a vector with a magnitude and a direction.

**3. Velocity** is a vector quantity usually denoted with a V or v and defined as the rate of change of position. Typically units are distance/time, m/s for example. Since velocity is a vector, if an object changes the direction in which it is moving it changes its velocity even if the speed (the scalar quantity that is the magnitude of the velocity vector) remains unchanged.

**i) Average velocity:** $\vec{v} \equiv \frac{\Delta d}{\Delta t} = d_1 - d_0 / t_1 - t_0$.

The ratio, $\Delta d / \Delta t$ is called the average velocity. Average here denotes that this quantity is defined over a period $\Delta t$.

**ii) Instantaneous velocity** is the velocity of an object at a particular moment in time. Conceptually, this can be imagined as the extreme case when $\Delta t$ is infinitely small.

**5. Acceleration,** represented by *a*, is defined as the rate of change of velocity and the units are $m/s^2$. Both an average and an instantaneous acceleration can be defined similarly to velocity.

From these definitions we develop the kinematic equations. In the following, subscript i denotes initial and subscript f denotes final values for a time period. Acceleration is assumed to be constant with time.

$$v_f = v_i + at \qquad (1)$$

$$d = v_i t + \frac{1}{2}at^2 \qquad (2)$$

$$v_f^2 = v_i^2 + 2ad \qquad (3)$$

$$d = \left(\frac{v_i + v_f}{2}\right)t \qquad (4)$$

Problem:
Leaving a traffic light a man accelerates at 10 m/s². a) How fast is he going when he has gone 100 m? b) How fast is he going in 4 seconds? C) How far does he travel in 20 seconds.

Solution:
a) Use equation 3. He starts from a stop so $v_i=0$ and $v_f^2 = 2 \times 10 m/s^2 \times 100 m = 2000\ m^2/s^2$ and $v_f = 45$ m/s.
b) Use equation 1. Initial velocity is again zero so $v_f = 10 m/s^2 \times 4s = 40$ m/s.
c) Use equation 2. Since initial velocity is again zero, $d = 1/2 \times 10\ m/s^2 \times (20s)^2 = 2000$ m

Motion on an arc can also be considered from the view point of the kinematic equations. Linear motion is measured in rectangular coordinates. Rotational motion is measured differently, in terms of the angle of displacement. There are three common ways to measure rotational displacement; degrees, revolutions, and radians. Degrees and revolutions have an easy to understand relationship, one revolution is 360°. Radians are slightly less well known and are defined as $\frac{arc\ length}{radius}$. Therefore 360°=2π radians and 1 radian = 57.3°.

The major concepts of linear motion are duplicated in rotational motion with linear displacement replaced by **angular displacement** $\theta$.

**Angular velocity** $\omega$ = rate of change of angular displacement.
**Angular acceleration** $\alpha$ = rate of change of angular velocity.

The kinematic equations for circular motion with constant angular acceleration are exactly analogous to the linear equations and are given by

$$\omega_f = \omega_i + \alpha t$$
$$\theta = \omega_i t + \frac{1}{2}\alpha t^2$$
$$\omega_f^2 = \omega_i^2 + 2\alpha\theta$$

Problem:
A wheel is rotating at the rate of 1 revolution in 8 seconds. If a constant deceleration is applied to the wheel it stops in 7 seconds. What is the deceleration applied to the wheel?

Solution:
Initial angular velocity = 2π/8 radians/sec = 0.25π radians/sec.
Final angular velocity = 0 radians/sec.
Using the rotational kinematic equations, angular acceleration applied to the wheel = (0 - 0.25x3.14)/7 = -0.11 radian/ (sec.sec)

**Skill 1.1e  Construct and analyze simple vector and graphical representations of motion and forces (e.g., distance, speed, time)**

Vectors are used in representing any quantity that has both magnitude and direction. This is why both velocities and forces are expressed as vector quantities. It is not sufficient, for example, to describe a car as traveling south; we must know that it is traveling south at 50 miles per hour to fully describe its motion. Similarly, we must know not only that the force of gravity has a magnitude of 9.8 m/s² times the mass of an object, but that it is directed toward the center of the earth.

When we wish to analyze a physical situation involving vector quantities such as force and velocity, the first step is typically the creation of a diagram. The objects involved are drawn and arrows are used to represent the vector quantities, which are labeled appropriately. In precise diagrams drawn to scale on graph paper, the magnitude of each force is indicated by the length of the arrow and the exact angles between the vectors will be depicted. Otherwise, angles and magnitudes may simply be noted on the diagram.

To add two vectors graphically, the base of the second vector is drawn from the point of the first vector as shown below with vectors **A** and **B**. The sum of the vectors is drawn as a dashed line, from the base of the first vector to the tip of the second. As illustrated, the order in which the vectors are connected is not significant as the endpoint is the same graphically whether **A** connects to **B** or **B** connects to **A**. This principle is sometimes called the parallelogram rule.

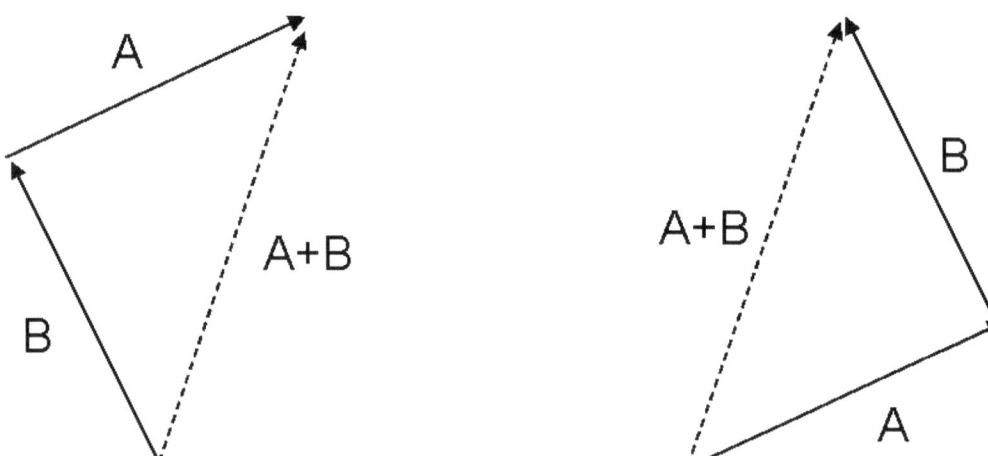

If more than two vectors are to be combined, additional vectors are simply drawn in accordingly with the sum vector connecting the base of the first to the tip of the final vector.

To add two vectors using trigonometric methods, the vectors must be broken down into their orthogonal components using sine, cosine, and tangent functions. Add both x components to get the total x component of the sum vector, then add both y components to get the y component of the sum vector. Use the Pythagorean Theorem and the three trigonometric functions to the get the size and direction of the final vector.

Example: Here is a diagram showing the x and y-components of a displacement vector D1:

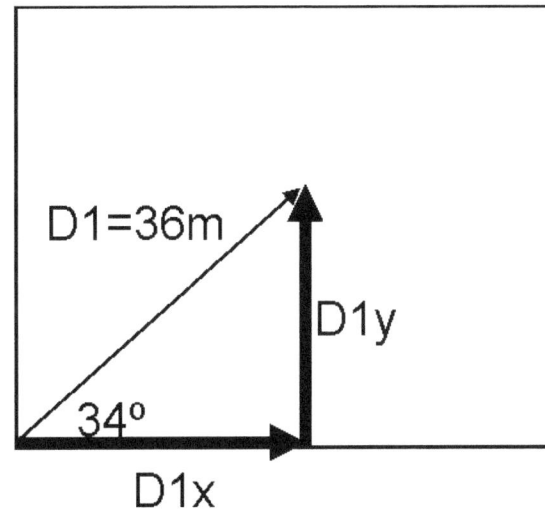

Notice that the x-component D1x is adjacent to the angle of 34 degrees.

Thus D1x=36m (cos34) =29.8m

The y-component is opposite to the angle of 34 degrees.

Thus D1y =36m (sin34) = 20.1m

A second displacement vector D2 is broken up into its components in the diagram below using the same techniques. We find that D2y=9.0m and D2x=-18.5m.

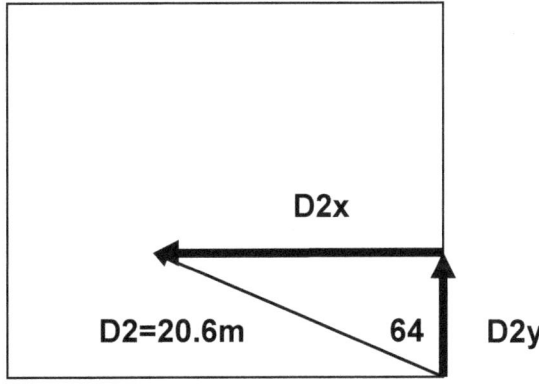

To find the sum of the vectors D1 and D2, we add the x components and the y components to get DTotal x =11.3 m   and   DTotal y =29.1 m.

Now we have to use the Pythagorean theorem to get the total magnitude of the final vector and the arctangent function to find the direction.
DTotal=31.2m; tan θ= DTotal y / DTotal x = 29.1m / 11.3 =2.6   θ=69 degrees

As a further example, let's use vectors to diagram the movement of a boat as it crosses a river. The velocities involved are the velocity at which the person in the boat paddles ($V_p$), the velocity of the river current ($v_r$), and the net velocity of the boat ($v_b$). Suppose that we know the river is running due east and the boat begins on the south shore and travels to the north shore. This gives us directions for the vectors. Now, if we also know the magnitude we can complete our diagram. Let's say the person paddles at 4 miles/ hour (mph) and the current travels at 12 mph. Drawing the vectors roughly to scale, we can produce the diagram at right. The dashed arrow shows the net velocity of the boat. To solve the problem, we could combine the vectors using graphical or trigonometric methods.

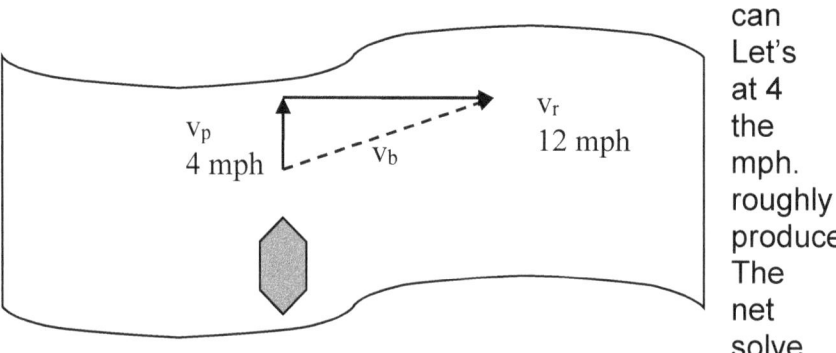

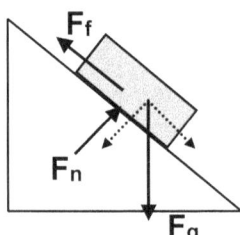

We can similarly diagram and solve problems involving force vectors. For instance, the diagram at left shows a block sliding down an inclined ramp. The relevant forces are shows: the force of friction ($F_f$), the normal force ($F_n$), and the force of gravity ($F_g$). As in the problem above, we can specify magnitudes and solve the problem to find the resultant force on this block.

See **Skills 1.1i** and **1.1j** for vector analysis of different kinds of forces. **Skill 1.1f** discusses graphical representations of distance, velocity and acceleration as a function of time.

**Skill 1.1f    Generate and understand functional relationships of graphs showing distance, velocity, and acceleration versus time**

The relationship between time, position or distance, velocity and acceleration can be understood conceptually by looking at a graphical representation of each as a function of time. Simply, the velocity is the slope of the position vs. time graph and the acceleration is the slope of the velocity vs. time graph. If you are familiar with calculus then you know that this relationship can be generalized: velocity is the first derivative and acceleration the second derivative of position. Here are three examples:

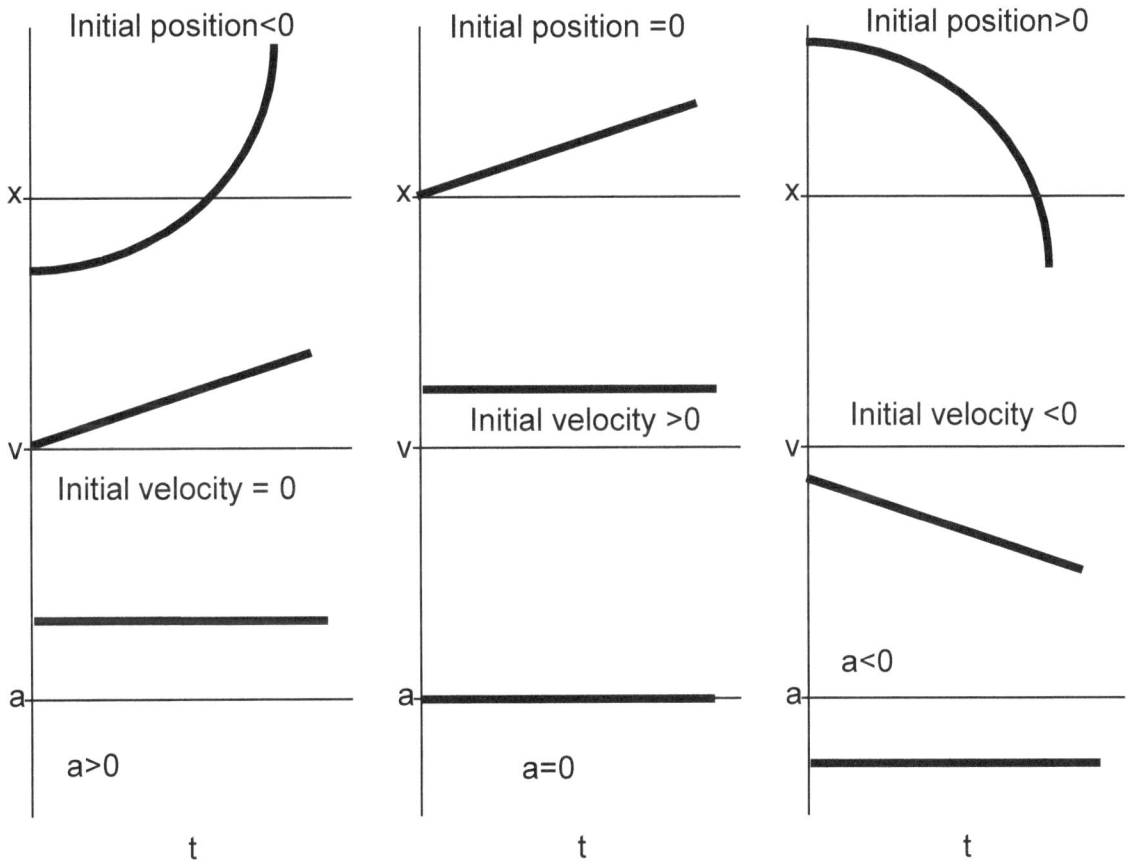

There are three things to notice:
1) In each case acceleration is constant. This isn't always the case, but a simplification for this illustration.
2) A non-zero acceleration produces a position curve that is a parabola.
3) In each case the initial velocity and position are specified separately. The acceleration curve gives the shape of the velocity curve, but not the initial value and the velocity curve gives the shape of the position curve but not the initial position.

## Skill 1.1g  Recognize relationships among variables for linear motion and rotational motion

As pointed out earlier, displacement, velocity and acceleration are all vector quantities, i.e. they have magnitude (the speed is the magnitude of the velocity vector) and direction. This means that if one drives in a circle at constant speed one still experiences an acceleration that changes the direction. We can define a couple of parameters for objects moving on circular paths and see how they relate to linear motion.

**1. Tangential speed:** The tangent to a circle or arc is a line that intersects the arc at exactly one point. If you were driving in a circle and instantaneously moved the steering wheel back to straight, the line you would follow would be the tangent to the circle at the point where you moved the wheel. The tangential speed then is the instantaneous magnitude of the velocity vector as one moves around the circle.

**2. Tangential acceleration:** The tangential acceleration is the component of acceleration that would change the tangential speed and this can be treated as a linear acceleration if one imagines that the circular path is unrolled and made linear.

**3. Centripetal acceleration:** Centripetal acceleration corresponds to the constant change in the direction of the velocity vector necessary to maintain a circular path. Always acting toward the center of the circle, centripetal acceleration has a magnitude proportional to the tangential speed squared divided by the radius of the path.

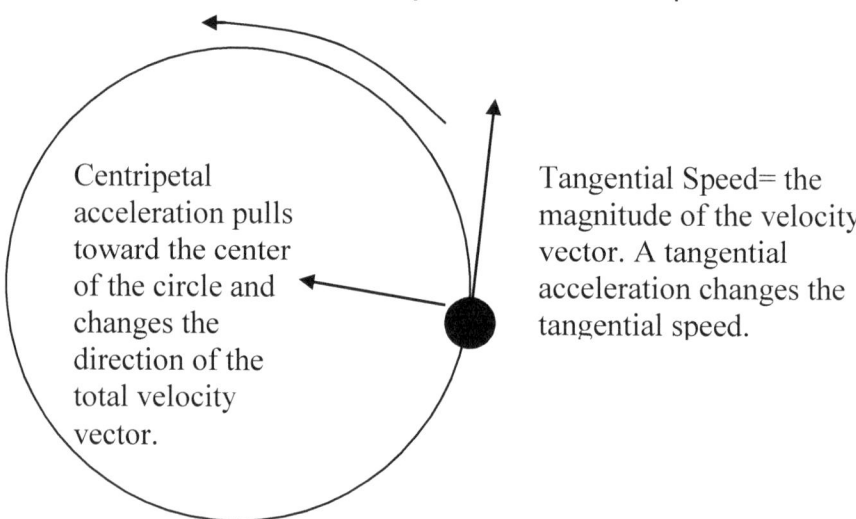

Centripetal acceleration pulls toward the center of the circle and changes the direction of the total velocity vector.

Tangential Speed= the magnitude of the velocity vector. A tangential acceleration changes the tangential speed.

The linear tangential velocity $v$ of an object moving in a circular path can be written as $v = r\omega$ and the linear tangential acceleration as $a = r\alpha$. For centripetal acceleration see **Skill 1.1h**.

Though the kinematic equations for rotational motion are analogous to those for linear motion (**Skill 1.1d**) and a rotational version of Newton's second law of motion can be written, an important difference in the equations relates to the use of mass in rotational systems. In rotational problems, not only is the mass of an object important but also its location. In order to include the spatial distribution of the mass of the object, a term called **moment of inertia** is used, $I = m_1 r_1^2 + m_2 r_2^2 + \cdots + m_n r_n^2$. The moment of inertia is always defined with respect to a particular axis of rotation.

Example:

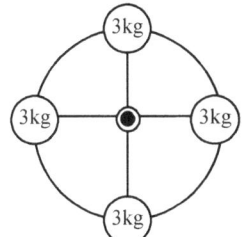

If the radius of the wheel on the left is 0.75m, what is its moment of inertia about an axis running through its center perpendicular to the plane of the wheel?

$$I = 3 \cdot 0.75^2 + 3 \cdot 0.75^2 + 3 \cdot 0.75^2 + 3 \cdot 0.75^2 = 6.75$$

Note: $I_{Sphere} = \frac{2}{5} mr^2$, $I_{Hoop/Ring} = mr^2$, $I_{disk} = \frac{1}{2} mr^2$

The rotational analog of Newton's second law of motion is given in terms of **torque** $\tau$, moment of inertia $I$, and angular acceleration $\alpha$:

$$\tau = I\alpha$$

where the torque $\tau$ is the rotational force on the body. In simple terms, the torque $\tau$ produced by a force F acting at a distance r from the point of rotation is given by the product of r and the component of the force that is perpendicular to the line joining the point of rotation to the point of action of the force.

A concept related to the moment of inertia is the **radius of gyration** ($k$), which is the average distance of the mass of an object from its axis of rotation, i.e., the distance from the axis where a point mass $m$ would have the same moment of inertia.

$k_{Sphere} = \sqrt{\frac{2}{5}} r$, $k_{Hoop/Ring} = r$, $k_{disk} = \frac{r}{\sqrt{2}}$. As you can see $I = mk^2$

This is analogous to the concept of center of mass, the point where an equivalent mass of infinitely small size would be located, in the case of linear motion.

**Angular momentum (L)**, and **rotational kinetic energy (KE$_r$)**, are therefore defined as follows: $L = I\omega$, $KE_r = \frac{1}{2} I\omega^2$

**Skill 1.1h Solve 2-dimensional problems involving vector analysis of motion and forces, including projectile motion, uniform circular motion, and statics**

In a previous section, we discussed the relationships between distance, velocity, acceleration and time and the four simple equations that relate these quantities when acceleration is constant (e.g. in cases such as gravity). In two dimensions the same relationships apply, but each dimension must be treated separately.

The most common example of an object moving in two dimensions is a projectile. A projectile is an object upon which the only force acting is gravity. Some examples:
i) An object dropped from rest.
ii) An object thrown vertically upwards at an angle
iii) A canon ball.

Once a projectile has been put in motion (say, by a canon or hand) the only force acting it is gravity, which near the surface of the earth implies it experiences a=g=9.8m/s$^2$.

This is most easily considered with an example such as the case of a bullet shot horizontally from a standard height at the same moment that a bullet is dropped from exactly the same height. Which will hit the ground first? If we assume wind resistance is negligible, then the acceleration due to gravity is our only acceleration on either bullet and we must conclude that they will hit the ground at the same time. The horizontal motion of the bullet is not affected by the downward acceleration.

Problem:
I shoot a projectile at 1000 m/s from a perfectly horizontal barrel exactly 1 m above the ground. How far does it travel before hitting the ground?

Solution:
First figure out how long it takes to hit the ground by analyzing the motion in the vertical direction. In the vertical direction, the initial velocity is zero so we can rearrange kinematic equation 2 from the previous section to give:

$t = \sqrt{\dfrac{2d}{a}}$ . Since our displacement is 1 m and a=g=9.8m/s$^2$, t=0.45 s.

Now use the time to hitting the ground from the previous calculation to calculate how far it will travel horizontally. Here the velocity is 1000m/s and there is no acceleration. So we simple multiply velocity with time to get the distance of 450m.

**Uniform circular motion** describes the motion of an object as it moves in a circular path at constant speed. There are many everyday examples of this behavior though we may not recognize them if the object does not complete a full circle. For example, a car rounding a curve (that is an arc of a circle) often exhibits uniform circular motion. Since the motion is uniform, the *magnitude* of the mass's velocity (v) is constant. Thus the tangential acceleration is zero. However, the velocity's direction is always tangent to the circle and so always changing. Therefore a centripetal acceleration is acting on the mass. This acceleration is directed toward the center of the circular path and is always perpendicular to the velocity, as shown below:

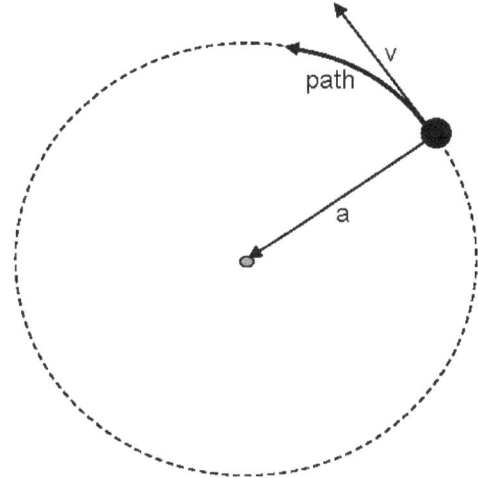

Centripetal acceleration is mathematically expressed as:

$$a = \frac{v^2}{r} = \omega^2 r$$

where $\omega = vr$ is the angular velocity of the mass and $r$ is the radius of the circular path.

The force (F) experienced by the mass (m) is known as centripetal force and is always directed towards the center of the circular path. It has constant magnitude given by the following equation:

$$F = ma = m\frac{v^2}{r} = m\omega^2 r$$

Problem:

A car travels round a curve of radius 100m at a speed of 90 Km/h. What is the magnitude of its centripetal acceleration?

Solution:
$$90 Km/h = \frac{90 \times 10^3}{60 \times 60} m/s = 25 m/s$$

$$a = \frac{v^2}{r} = \frac{(25)^2}{100} = 6.25 m/s^2$$

There are situations where multiple forces are acting on an object but the object remains at rest. In cases like this we say that the object is in **static equilibrium**. The following are examples of this type of problem.

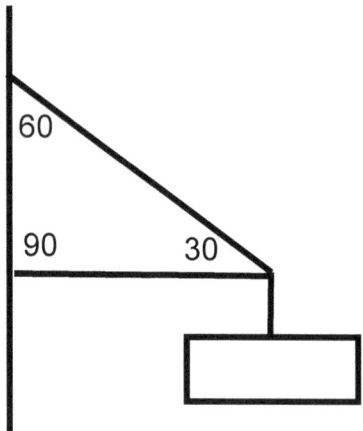

Problem: A sign hangs outside a building supported as shown in the diagram. The sign has a mass of 50 kg. Calculate the tension in the cable.

Solution: Since there is only one upward pulling cable it must balance the weight. The sign exerts a downward force of 490 N. Therefore, the cable pulls upwards with a force of 490 N. It does so at an angle of 30 degrees. To find the total tension in the cable:

$$F_{total} = 490 \text{ N} / \sin 30°$$
$$F_{total} = 980 \text{ N}$$

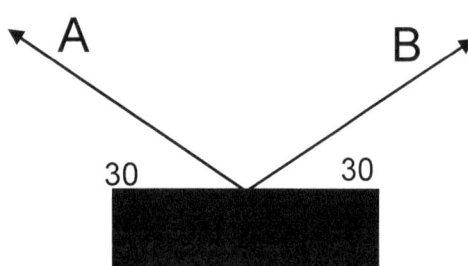

Problem: A block is held in static equilibrium by two cables. Suppose the tension in cables A and B are measured to be 50 Newtons each. The angle formed by each cable with the horizontal is 30 degrees. Calculate the weight of the block.

Solution: We know that the upward pull of the cable must balance the downward force of the weight of the block and the right pulling forces must balance the left pulling forces.

Using trigonometry we know that the y component of each cable can be calculated as:
$$F_y = 50 \text{ N} \sin 30°$$
$$F_y = 25 \text{ N}$$

Since there are two cables supplying an upward force of 25 N each, the overall downward force supplied by the block must be 50 N.

**Skill 1.1i    Identify the separate forces that act on a body (e.g., gravity, pressure, tension/compression, normal force, friction) and describe the net force on the body**

Some of the common forces that act on a body are the following:

## Gravity

This is the force that pulls a body towards the center of the earth, i.e. downwards, and is also called the weight of the body. It is given by

$$W = mg$$

Where $m$ is the mass of the body and $g=9.81$ m/s² is the acceleration due to gravity.

## Normal force

When a body is pressed against a surface it experiences a reaction force that is perpendicular to the surface and in the direction away from the surface. For instance, an object resting on a table experiences an upward reaction force from the table that is equal and opposite to the force that the object exerts on the table. When the table is horizontal and no additional force is being applied to the object, the normal force is equal to the weight of the object.

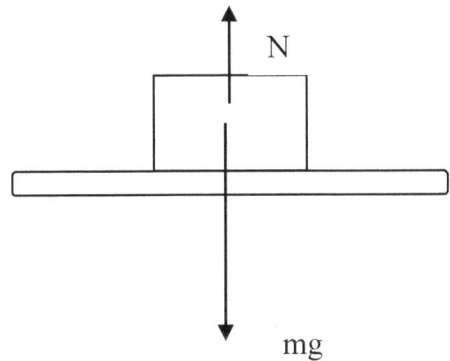

## Friction

Friction is the force on a body that opposes its sliding over a surface. This force is due to the bonding between the two surfaces and is greater for rough surfaces.
It acts in the direction opposite to the force attempting to move the object. When the object is at rest, the frictional force is known as **static friction**. The frictional force on an object in motion is known as **kinetic friction**.

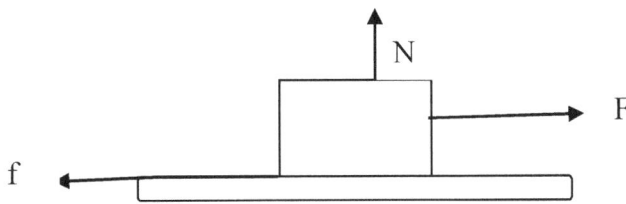

The frictional force is usually directly proportional to the normal force and can be calculated as **F**$_f$ = $\mu$ **F**$_n$ where $\mu$ is either the coefficient of static friction or kinetic friction depending on whether the object is at rest or in motion.

## Tension/Compression

Tension is the force that acts in a rope, cable or rod that is attached to something and is being pulled. Tension acts along the cord. When a hand pulls a rope attached to a box, for instance, the tension T in the rope acts to pull the rope apart while it works on the box and the hand in the opposite direction as shown below:

Compression is the opposite of tension in that the force acts to shorten a rigid body instead of pulling it apart.

## Pressure

For a description of fluid pressure and the force of buoyancy see **Skill 1.1c.**

## Net force

The forces that act on a body come from many different sources. Their effect on a body, however, is the same; a change in the state of motion of the body as given by Newton's laws of motion. Therefore, once we identify the magnitude and direction of each force acting on a body, we can combine the effect of all the forces together using vector addition and find the net force.

Problem:

Find the net force on a 5 Kg box sliding down an inclined surface at an angle of $30°$ with the horizontal if the coefficient of friction of the surface is 0.5.

Solution:

There are three forces acting on the box, gravity, the normal force and the frictional force. We can resolve these forces along the inclined plane and perpendicular to the plane and find the net force in each direction.

*Perpendicular to the plane:*

The component of the gravitational force perpendicular to the plane = mgcos30 = 5 x 9.8 x 0.87 = 42.6N
The normal force acting on the box is equal and opposite to the perpendicular component of the gravitational force. Thus the net force on the box perpendicular to the plane is zero.

*Along the inclined plane:*

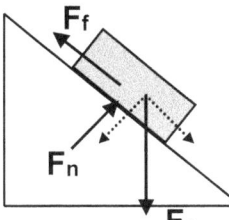

The component of the gravitational force down the plane = mgsin30 = 5 x 9.8 x 0.5 = 24.5N
The force of friction up the plane = μ **Fn** = 0.5 x 42.6 = 21.3N
Thus the net force on the box acts down the plane and is equal to 24.5 – 21.3 = 3.2N

**Skill 1.1j    Construct appropriate free-body diagrams of many-body problems (e.g., two or more coupled masses)**

When a system is composed of two or more bodies, we can analyze the forces on each body and find the net force on each separately. A free-body diagram is a diagram showing all the forces on a body. The body is represented by a point for simplicity.

Example:

A force $F$ is applied to two bodies of mass $M$ and $m$ in contact on a smooth surface. The forces on the mass $M$ include the applied force $F$, the upward normal force $N_M$ exerted by the table, the horizontal normal contact force $N$ between the two bodies and the force of gravity $Mg$. The forces on the mass m are the weight of the body $mg$, the normal force $N_m$ and the contact force N between the two bodies.

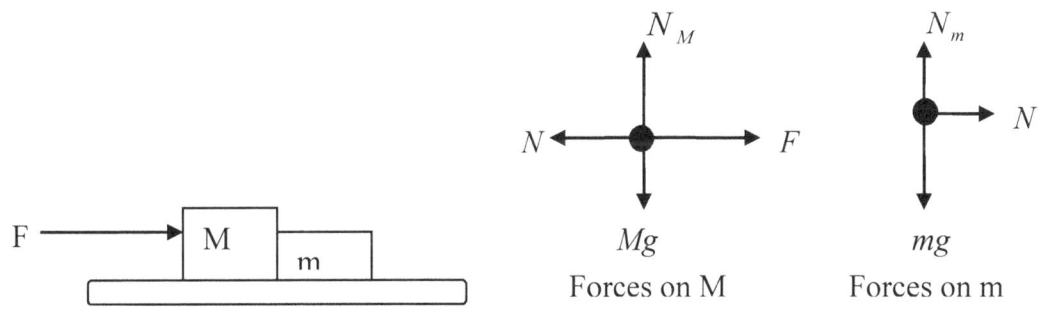

Example: A massless rope attached to a mass *M* on a rough table goes over a pulley and has a mass *m* attached to the other end as shown in the figure below. The forces on *M* are its weight, the normal force exerted by the table, the force of friction *f* and the tension T in the rope.

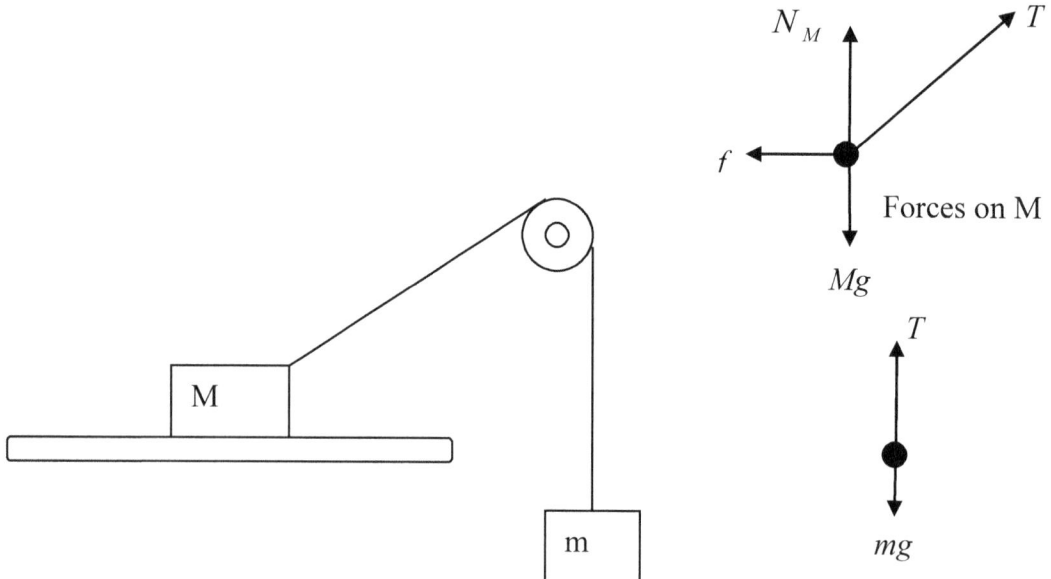

The forces on *m* are its weight and the tension *T* in the rope.

Example: Masses m1, m2 and m3 are connected by massless ropes and suspended from a ceiling. The forces on m1 are its weight, the tension T1 in the top rope acting upwards and the tension T2 in the middle rope acting downwards. The forces on m2 are its weight, the tension T2 in the middle rope acting upwards and the tension T3 in the bottom rope acting downwards. The forces on mass m3 are its weight and the tension T3 in the bottom rope acting upwards.

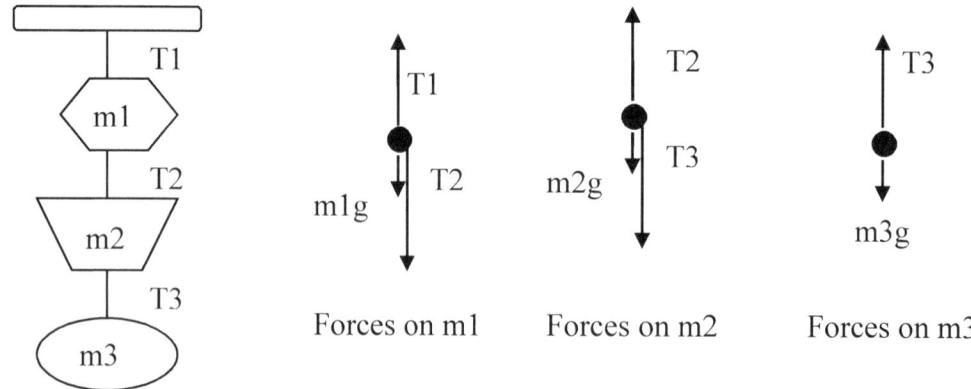

**Skill 1.1k   Solve periodic motion problems**

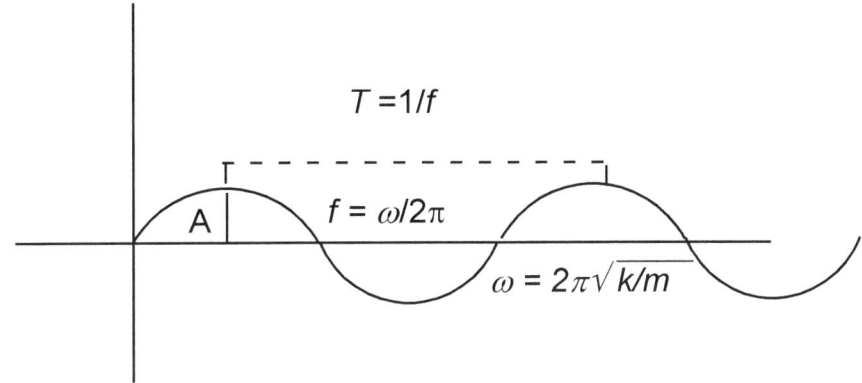

The above diagram depicts the various elements of simple harmonic motion. The displacement of a simple harmonic oscillator varies sinusoidally with time and is given by

$$x = A\cos(\omega t + \delta)$$

where A is the maximum displacement or amplitude, $\omega$ is the angular frequency and $\delta$ is the phase constant which is zero in the diagram. We can see from the equation that the displacement goes through a full cycle at time intervals given by the period $T = 2\pi/\omega$. The **frequency** $f$ is the number of cycles per second or the number of vibrations made per unit of time. The unit of frequency is the **hertz** (Hz). The **displacement** $x$ is the distance a vibrating object is moved from its normal resting position.

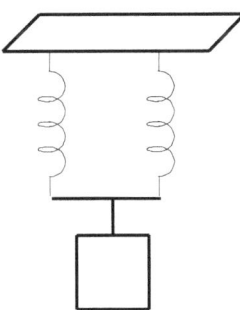

The above diagram is an example of a **Hookean system** (a spring, wire, rod, etc.) where the spring returns to its original configuration after being displaced and then released. When the spring is stretched a distance $x$, the restoring force exerted by the spring is expressed by Hooke's Law

$$F = -kx$$

The minus sign indicates that the restoring force is always opposite in direction to the displacement. The variable $k$ is the spring constant and measures the stiffness of the spring in N/m.

The period of simple harmonic motion for a Hookean spring system is dependent upon the mass (m) of the spring and the stiffness of the spring (k) and is given by

$$T = \frac{1}{f} = \frac{1}{\frac{\omega}{2\pi}} = \frac{2\pi}{\omega} = \frac{2\pi}{\sqrt{\frac{k}{m}}} = 2\pi\sqrt{\frac{m}{k}}$$

Problem:

Each spring in the above diagram has a stiffness of $k = 20 N/m$. The mass of the object connected to the spring is 2 kg. Ignoring friction forces, find the period of motion.

Solution:

Utilizing Hooke's Law, the net restoring force on the spring would be

$$F = -(20 N/m)x - (20 N/m)x = -(40 N/m)x$$

Comparison with $F = -kx$ shows the equivalent $k$ to be 40 N/m.

Using the above formula for our problem, we have

$$T = 2\pi\sqrt{\frac{m}{k}} = 2\pi\sqrt{\frac{2 kg}{40 N/m}} = 2(3.14)\sqrt{0.05} = 1.4s$$

The period of a simple pendulum depends upon the length of the string or rod and the value, $g$, of the acceleration due to gravity and is given by:

$$T = 2\pi\sqrt{\frac{L}{g}}$$

Problem: What is the length in meters of a pendulum, which has a period of 1.2s?

PHYSICS

$$T = 2\pi\sqrt{\frac{L}{g}}$$

Solution:
$$1.2s = 2(3.14)\sqrt{\frac{L}{9.8 m/s}}$$
$$1.44s = (6.28)^2 \left(\frac{L}{9.8 m/s}\right)$$
$$1.44s = \frac{39.44L}{9.8 m/s}$$
$$14.112m = 39.44L$$
$$.358m$$

## Skill 1.1l  Solve problems involving linear and rotational motion in term of forces and torques

For problems involving linear motion in terms of forces see **Skill 1.1b**. The relationship between angular acceleration $\alpha$, moment of inertia $I$, and torque $\tau$ in any situation is given by the rotational analog of Newton's second law of motion:

$$\tau = I\alpha$$

Problem:

The angular velocity of a disc changes steadily from 0 to 6 rad/s in 200 ms. If the moment of inertia of the disc is 10 $Kgm^2$ what is the torque applied to the disc?

Solution:

The constant angular acceleration of the disc = $\frac{6}{200 \times 10^{-3}} = 30 rad/s^2$

Thus torque applied = $10 \times 30 = 300 N.m$.

Problem: A disk of mass 2 Kg and Radius 0.5m is mounted on a horizontal frictionless axle. A block of mass 1.5 Kg is hung from a massless string wrapped around the disk that does not slip. Find the acceleration of the block, the tension in the string and the angular acceleration of the disk.

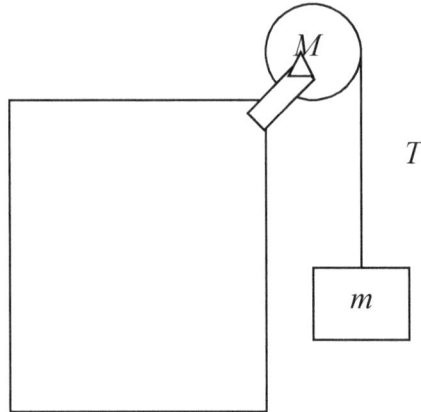

Solution: The forces on the block are the tension $T$ in the string and the weight of the block. The acceleration $a$ of the block is given by Newton's second law:
$$mg - T = ma$$

The torque on the disk of radius R is TR and the moment of inertia of the disk is $\frac{1}{2}MR^2$.

Thus, applying Newton's second law in angular form we get
$$TR = \frac{1}{2}MR^2\left(\frac{a}{R}\right)$$

since the string does not slip and the linear acceleration of the disk is the same as the acceleration of the block. Combining both equations,
$$a = \frac{2T}{M} = \frac{2(mg - ma)}{M}; \Rightarrow a(M + 2m) = 2mg; \Rightarrow a = \frac{2mg}{M + 2m} = \frac{2 \times 1.5}{2 + 1.5 \times 2} \times 9.8 = 5.9 m/s^2$$

Using the second equation, the tension in the string is given by
$$T = \frac{1}{2}Ma = 0.5 \times 2 \times 5.9 = 5.9 N$$

The angular acceleration of the disk is given by
$$\alpha = \frac{a}{R} = \frac{5.9}{0.5} = 11.8 rad/s^2$$

**Skill 1.1m    Identify fundamental forces, including gravity, nuclear forces, and electromagnetic forces (magnetic and electric), and explain their roles in nature, such as the role of gravity in maintaining the structure of the universe**

There are four fundamental forces that control the behavior of all matter and describe all physical phenomena; gravity, weak interaction, electromagnetism, and strong interaction. Amazingly these same forces control the tiniest sub-nuclear particles, all the life forms on Earth, and the movement of all the planets in the universe. Most physicists believe that we will ultimately be able to understand even these forces as one single, fundamental interaction. Electricity and magnetism were once thought to be separate forces, but we now know that they are parts of a single theory of electromagnetism. Electroweak theory has helped to tie weak interactions with electromagnetism. Likewise, we may eventually combine all four fundamental forces into a single relationship. Note that, while they are called forces, these interactions are not forces in the classic Newtonian sense.

The four forces interact on largely different scales and using different mediators, as will be shown below. They are listed from weakest to strongest; if we assigned gravity a relative strength of 1, then the weak interaction would be $10^{25}$ times stronger, the electromagnetic by a factor of $10^{36}$, and the strong interaction by a factor of $10^{38}$.

**Gravity**: Though gravity is the weakest interaction, it has infinite range and affects all masses. Thus, it is responsible for the structure of galaxies, the orbits of planets, and the expansion of the universe as well as everyday phenomena such as the falling of objects. Gravity is mediated by elementary particles known as gravitons and is currently understood through the theory of General Relativity.

The formation of our sun and solar system as well as other objects in the universe is due to the attractive nature of the gravitational interaction. Large clouds of gas and dust slowly coalesced into these structures under the pull of gravity. The round shape of each object is also due to this attraction towards the center. The more massive an object, the greater its gravitational pull. Gravity also acts more strongly on other objects that are close by. Thus we see planets orbiting around stars and moons orbiting around planets.

**Weak interaction**: Despite the name, weak interactions are much stronger than gravity but with a much smaller range. They are responsible for certain phenomena occurring in the atomic nucleus, including beta decay, and other occurrences on this size scale. Weak interactions are mediated by bosons and understood through the Electroweak Theory.

Since weak interactions have a very short range their effect is ordinarily negligible. There are cases, however, where weak interactions allow processes that violate conservation laws that are strictly maintained by electromagnetic and strong interactions. Quark flavors can change only through weak interactions. This allows radioactive decays such as beta decay in which, for instance, a neutron (two down and one up quark) is replaced by a proton (two up and one down quark) and an electron.

**Electromagnetism**: This force acts on charged particles and, like gravity, has a large enough range that we can observe its effect in everyday occurrences. Electromagnetism is responsible for a wide range of phenomena ranging from rainbows and sound to lasers and the structure of metal. It is mediate by photons and understood through the theory of Quantum Electrodynamics (QED).

We observe the effects of electromagnetism in practically everything we do. Electromagnetic forces acting on protons and electrons within atoms hold atoms together. These forces also give rise to the intermolecular forces within objects. This gives us the sense of solidity through the resistance we feel when we grasp an object. The electromagnetic interactions between electron orbitals are responsible for all chemical phenomena. Light, our fundamental means of perceiving the universe, is itself an electromagnetic wave in addition to other familiar waves such as radio waves, microwaves and x-rays.

**Strong interactions**: Strong interactions work primarily on sub-atomic particles though their range is theoretically infinite. They are responsible for holding protons and neutrons together. Nuclear force, which holds the nucleus together, is a byproduct of strong interactions. This demonstrates the large strength of these interactions, since electromagnetic forces would otherwise cause the protons in the nucleus to repel one another. Nuclear fission and fusion processes occur due to strong interactions. Strong interactions are mediated by gluons and understood through the theory of Quantum Chromodynamics.

**TEACHER CERTIFICATION STUDY GUIDE**

**Skill 1.1n    Explain and calculate mechanical advantages for levers, pulleys, and inclined planes**

Mechanical advantage is the multiplication of a force by a certain mechanism such as a lever or a pulley. Using such a device, a smaller force may be used to lift or move a heavier object.

The mechanical advantage of a lever is the ratio of the distance from the applied force (effort) to the fulcrum to the distance from the resistance force (load) to the fulcrum.

Example:

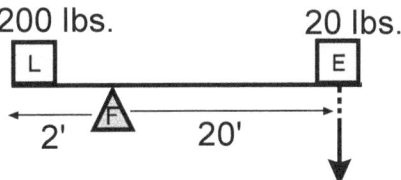

In the above diagram, the mechanical advantage would be $\frac{20}{2}$ or 10:1. Therefore, an applied force of 20 lbs. will balance a resistance force of 200 lbs but only because it is applied at a distance 10 times greater from the fulcrum than the load.

The mechanical advantage of a pulley is equal to the number of ropes that support the pulley with each end of the rope counted as a separate rope.

Example:

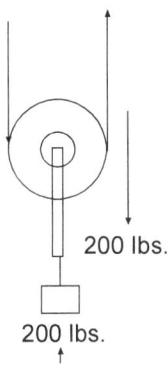

In the above diagram, there are two rope ends supporting the pulley. Therefore, the mechanical advantage of the pulley is 2 and an effort force of 100 lbs will lift a load of 200 lbs.

The mechanical advantage of an inclined plane is equal to the length of the slope divided by the height of the inclined plane. (This is true as long as the effort is applied parallel to the slope of the plane.)

Example:

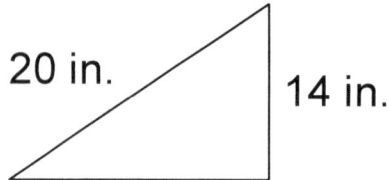

For the inclined plane in the above diagram, the mechanical advantage would be

$$\frac{S}{H} = \frac{20}{14} = 1.43$$

An inclined plane produces a mechanical advantage by increasing the distance through which the force must move. In this example, the object moved 20 in. along the slope in order to increase the vertical distance by 14 in.

## SUBAREA II. CONSERVATION OF ENERGY AND MOMENTUM

## COMPETENCY 2.1 CONSERVATION OF ENERGY AND MOMENTUM

**Skill 2.1a** Use conservation of energy to characterize kinetic-potential energy systems such as oscillating systems (pendulums and springs), projectile motion, and roller coasters

Though we know total energy is always conserved, there are many physical everyday examples in which we can see how kinetic energy is lost when it is converted to potential energy and vice versa. Recall that kinetic energy is energy possessed by an object due to motion and potential energy is that stored by an object due to position associated with a force.

Total energy must always be conserved, but in an oscillating system, that energy is alternately in the form of kinetic and potential energy. Imagine, for instance, a mass connected to a spring. As the spring is compressed, elastic potential energy is stored within the spring. Specifically, when the spring is maximally compressed, it also has maximum potential energy and minimum kinetic energy (zero kinetic energy). When the spring is released, this potential energy converts back into kinetic energy as the mass travels outward. This conversions happens several more times as the spring oscillates.

We can further demonstrate this using the following equations for a mass on a spring. Remember that k= the spring constant, A= amplitude, ω= angular frequency, t= time, and Φ=phase:

$$\text{Kinetic energy} = \tfrac{1}{2} k A^2 \sin^2(\omega_0 t + \Phi)$$
$$\text{Potential energy} = \tfrac{1}{2} k A^2 \cos^2(\omega_0 t + \Phi)$$
$$\text{Total energy} = \tfrac{1}{2} k A^2$$

We know that sine and cosine are 180° out of phase. Thus, this is a mathematical statement that when potential energy is maximal, kinetic energy is minimum. Further, kinetic energy plus potential energy is always equal to a constant, that is, total energy in the system is always conserved.

The preceeding example was one involving elastic potential energy, but there are others involving other types of potenial energy. For example, chemical potential energy is converted to kinetic energy in the combustion reactions that move the pistons in modern engines. Conversion of gravitational potential energy is also very familiar. For instance, a ball rolling down a hill or a roller coaster descending a track are converting potential energy to kinetic energy. Their gravitational potential energies are largest when they are furthest from the earth. As they accelerate toward the ground, potential energy decreases and kinetic energy (and speed) increases. Once again, we see that total energy is conserved during these conversions of energy.

## Skill 2.1b  Analyze elastic and inelastic collisions and solve for unknown values

The law of **conservation of linear momentum** states that the total momentum of an *isolated system* (not affected by external forces and not having internal dissipative forces) always remains the same. For instance, in any collision between two objects in an isolated system, the total momentum of the two objects after the collision will be the same as the total momentum of the two objects before the collision. In other words, any momentum lost by one of the objects is gained by the other.

A collision may be **elastic** or **inelastic**. In a totally elastic collision, the kinetic energy is conserved along with the momentum. In a totally inelastic collision, on the other hand, the kinetic energy associated with the center of mass remains unchanged but the kinetic energy relative to the center of mass is lost. An example of a totally inelastic collision is one in which the bodies stick to each other and move together after the collision. Most collisions are neither perfectly elastic nor perfectly inelastic and only a portion of the kinetic energy relative to the center of mass is lost.

Imagine two carts rolling towards each other as in the diagram below

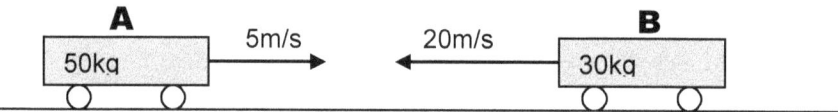

Before the collision, cart **A** has 250 kg m/s of momentum, and cart **B** has –600 kg m/s of momentum. In other words, the system has a total momentum of –350 kg m/s of momentum.

After the inelastic collision, the two cards stick to each other, and continue moving. How do we determine how fast, and in what direction, they go?

We know that the new mass of the cart is 80kg, and that the total momentum of the system is –350 kg m/s. Therefore, the velocity of the two carts stuck together must be $\dfrac{-350}{80} = -4.375 \, m/s$

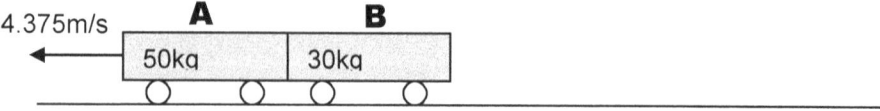

Conservation of momentum works the same way in two dimensions, the only change is that you need to use vector math to determine the total momentum and any changes, instead of simple addition.

Imagine a pool table like the one below. Both balls are 0.5 kg in mass.

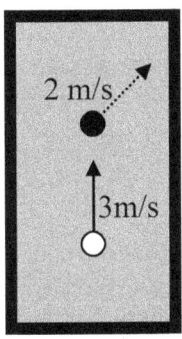

Before the collision, the white ball is moving with the velocity indicated by the solid line and the black ball is at rest. After the collision the black ball is moving with the velocity indicated by the dashed line (a 135° angle from the direction of the white ball).

With what speed, and in what direction, is the white ball moving after the collision?

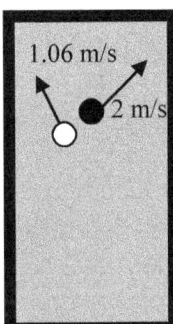

$p_{white/before} = .5 \cdot (0,3) = (0,1.5)$   $p_{black/before} = 0$   $p_{total/before} = (0,1.5)$

$p_{black/after} = .5 \cdot (2\cos 45, 2\sin 45) = (0.71, 0.71)$

$p_{white/after} = (-0.71, 0.79)$

i.e. the white ball has a velocity of $v = \sqrt{(-.71)^2 + (0.79)^2} = 1.06 m/s$

and is moving at an angle of $\theta = \tan^{-1}\left(\dfrac{0.79}{-0.71}\right) = -48°$ from the horizontal

**Skill 2.1c    Solve problems involving linear and rotational motion in terms of conservation of momentum and energy**

The work-energy theorem states that the amount of work done on an object is equal to its change in mechanical energy (kinetic or potential energy). Specifically, in systems where multiple forces are at work, the energy change of the system is the work done by the *net* force on the object. Problems dealing with the work-energy theorem may look at changes in kinetic energy, changes in potential energy, or some combination of the two. It is also important to remember that only external forces can cause changes in an object's total amount of mechanical energy. Internal forces, such as spring force or gravity, only lead to conversions between kinetic and potential energy rather than changes in the total level of mechanical energy.

Example:

1. A woman driving a 2000 kg car along a level road at 30 m/s takes her foot off the gas to see how far her car will roll before it slows to a stop. She discovers that it takes 150m. What is the average force of friction acting on the car?

$$W = \Delta KE$$
$$f \cdot s \cos \theta = \tfrac{1}{2} mv_{final}^2 - \tfrac{1}{2} mv_{initial}^2$$
$$f \cdot 150 \cdot (-1) = \tfrac{1}{2} \cdot 2000 \cdot 0^2 - \tfrac{1}{2} \cdot 2000 \cdot 30^2$$
$$-150 f = -900000$$
$$f = 6000 N$$

According to the work-energy theorem, the amount of work done on the car is equal to the change in its mechanical energy which in this case is its change in kinetic energy. Since the only force acting on the car is friction, all the work can be attributed to the frictional force. It is important to realize, for this problem, that the force of friction is against the direction of motion, and thus cosθ = -1.

Example:

A 20kg child lifts his .5 kg ball off the floor to put it away on his bookshelf 1.5 meters above the ground. How much work has he done?

$$W = \Delta PE$$
$$W = mgh_{final} - mgh_{initial}$$
$$W = mg(h_{final} - h_{initial}) = .5 \cdot 9.8 \cdot 1.5 = 7.35 J$$

Example:

A uniform ball of radius *r* and mass *m* starts from rest and rolls down a frictionless incline of height *h*. When the ball reaches the ground, how fast is it going?

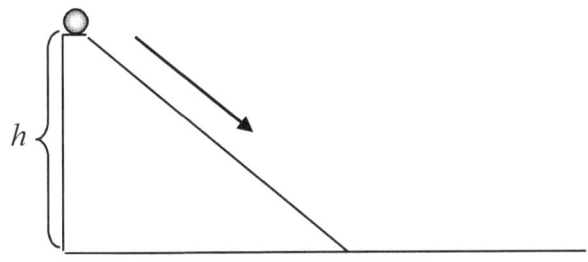

$$PE_{initial} + KE_{rotational\ initial} + KE_{linear/initial} = PE_{final} + KE_{rotational\ final} + KE_{linear/final}$$

$$mgh + 0 + 0 = 0 + \frac{1}{2}I\omega_{final}^2 + \frac{1}{2}mv_{final}^2 \rightarrow mgh = \frac{1}{2} \cdot \frac{2}{5}mr^2\omega_{final}^2 + \frac{1}{2}mv_{final}^2$$

$$mgh = \frac{1}{5}mr^2(\frac{v_{final}}{r})^2 + \frac{1}{2}mv_{final}^2 \rightarrow mgh = \frac{1}{5}mv_{final}^2 + \frac{1}{2}mv_{final}^2$$

$$gh = \frac{7}{10}v_{final}^2 \rightarrow v_{final} = \sqrt{\frac{10}{7}gh}$$

Similarly, unless a net torque acts on a system, the angular momentum remains constant in both magnitude and direction. This can be used to solve many different types of problems including ones involving satellite motion.

Example:
A planet of mass *m* is circling a star in an orbit like the one below. If its velocity at point A is 60,000m/s, and $r_B = 8\ r_A$, what is its velocity at point B?

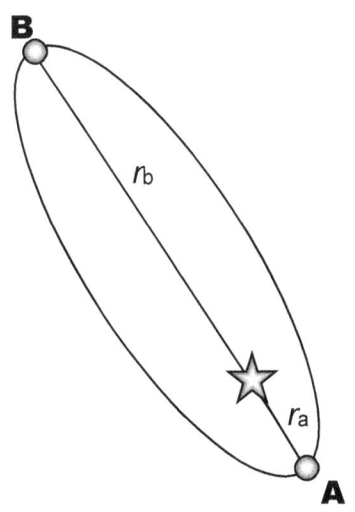

$$I_B\omega_B = I_A\omega_A$$
$$mr_B^2\omega_B = mr_A^2\omega_A$$
$$r_B^2\omega_B = r_A^2\omega_A$$
$$r_B^2\frac{v_B}{r_B} = r_A^2\frac{v_A}{r_A}$$
$$r_Bv_B = r_Av_A$$
$$8r_Av_B = r_Av_A$$
$$v_B = \frac{v_A}{8} = 7500 m/s$$

**Skill 2.1d** **Recognize relationships between energy/momentum conservation principles and Newton's Laws**

Newton's three laws of motion are:

1. Every object in a state of uniform motion tends to remain in that state of motion unless an external force is applied to it.
2. The relationship between an object's mass, $m$, its acceleration, $a$, and the applied force $F$ is $F = ma$.
3. For every action, there is an equal and opposite reaction.

The law of conservation of energy implies that energy can be neither created nor destroyed, but it can be changed from one from into another. Conservation of linear momentum states that a body or system of bodies in motion retains its total momentum, unless an external force is applied to it. Conservation of angular momentum is similar to the conservation of linear momentum in that a body or system that is rotating continues to rotate at the same rate unless a torque is applied to it.

Newton's laws deal with force and mass. Force is the time derivative of momentum. In a situation where particles interact by way of instantaneously transmitted forces, Newton's second law may be viewed as a definition of force and the third law can be derived from conservation of momentum. However, this is a special case and things in nature do not always work this way. In situations where the forces do not directly impact the material particles, Newton's second law would not apply. However, conservation of momentum always applies.

Another example involves electromagnetic fields. Conservation of angular momentum holds true for electromagnetic fields and their interactions with material particles. However, Newton's laws do not apply and his third law is invalid even in the case of static electrical and magnetic interactions. Conservation of energy was discovered long after Newton's lifetime because it involved an understanding of invisible and microscopic forms of energy.

These three conservation laws derive from Newton's laws. The laws of conservation can be applied more generally than Newton's laws as Newton was not aware of light and momentum and energy undetectable by the human eye. Unlike Newton's laws, which can only be applied to classical physics, the laws of conservation can be applied to both modern and classical physics.

# TEACHER CERTIFICATION STUDY GUIDE

**Skill 2.1e   Examine the impact of friction on conservation principles**

The principle of conservation of energy states that an isolated system maintains a constant total amount of energy despite the fact that the energy may change forms. To put it another way, energy cannot be created or destroyed but can be changed from one form to another. For example, friction can turn kinetic energy into thermal energy. Here the total energy would be conserved but mechanical energy would not.

A **conservative** force is one that conserves mechanical energy (kinetic + potential energy), i.e. there is no change in mechanical energy when a conservative force acts on an object. Consider a mass on a spring on a frictionless surface. This is a closed loop system. If conservative forces alone act on the mass during each cycle, the velocity of the mass at the beginning and the end of the cycle must be the same for the mechanical energy to have been conserved. In this way, the force has done no work. At any point in the cycle of motion, the total mechanical energy of the system remains constant even though the energy moves back and forth between kinetic and potential forms. If work is done on the mass, then the forces acting on the mass are **nonconservative**. In a real system there will be some dissipative forces that will convert some of the mechanical energy to thermal energy. Conservative forces are independent of path the object takes, while nonconservative forces are path dependent.

Friction is a nonconservative force. If a box is pushed along a rough surface from one side of the room to the other and back, friction opposes the movement in both directions; so the work done by friction cannot be equal to zero. This example also helps illustrate how nonconservative forces are path dependent. More work is done by friction if the path is tortuous rather than straight, even if the start and end points are the same. Let's try an example with a small box of mass 5 kg. The box moves in a circle 2 meters in diameter. The coefficient of kinetic friction between the box and the surface it rests on is 0.2. How much work is done by friction during one revolution?

The force exerted by friction is calculated by
$$F_k = \mu_k F_n = (0.2)(5 \text{ kg})(9.8 \text{ m/s}^2) = 9.8 \text{ N}$$

The force opposes the movement of the box during the entire distance of one revolution, or approximately 6.3 meters ($2\pi r$).
The total work done by friction is
$$W = F \times \cos \theta = (9.8 \text{ N})(6.3 \text{ m})(\cos 180) = -61.7 \text{ Joules}$$
As expected, the work is not zero since friction is not a conservative force. Since it does negative work on an object, it reduces the mechanical energy of the object even though the total energy of the system is conserved.

**Skill 2.1f   Interpret force-versus-time and force-versus-distance graphs to find, for example, work done or impulse on a system**

PHYSICS

In physics, work done by a constant force is defined as force times distance $W = F \cdot s$. Work is a scalar quantity, it does not have direction, and it is usually measured in Joules ($N \cdot m$). It is important to remember, when doing calculations about work, that the only part of the force that contributes to the work is the part that acts in the direction of the displacement. Therefore, sometimes the equation is written as $W = F \cdot s \cos\theta$, where θ is the angle between the force and the displacement.

When the force applied to an object varies over the distance moved, the total work done in moving from a point $x_1$ to a point $x_2$ is given by $W = \int_{x_1}^{x_2} F_x dx$ where $F_x$ is the force applied to the object, in the direction of movement, at any point $x$.

The area under a force-distance graph equals the work done on the object.

Example:

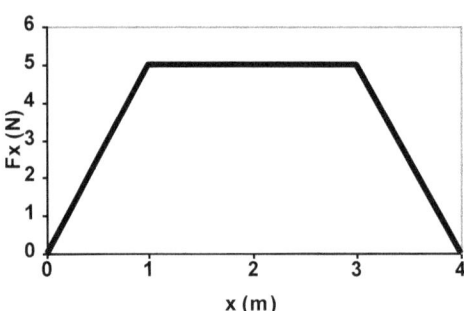

In the above diagram, the x-directed force that acts on an object is shown as a function of x. The area under the curve equals
$$\frac{1}{2}(1)(5) + (2)(5) + \frac{1}{2}(1)(5) = 2.5 + 10 + 2.5 = 15$$
Therefore, the work done equals 15 J.

An impulse is defined as a force acting over a period of time (integral of force over time), and any impulse acting on the system is equivalent to a change in its momentum, as you can see from the equations below:

$$F = m \cdot a \rightarrow F = m \cdot \frac{\Delta v}{t} \rightarrow F \cdot t = m \cdot \Delta v$$

As long as the direction of the force producing the impulse is constant, the area under a force-versus-time graph can be used to determine the impulse.

Example:

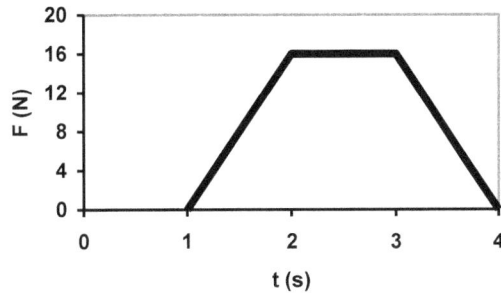

The force shown on the above graph is applied to an object in the direction of motion. The impulse imparted to the object equals the change in the object's momentum. On a force-versus-time graph, impulse is also the area under the graph, which in this case equals 32 kg m/s.

TEACHER CERTIFICATION STUDY GUIDE

**SUBAREA III.**                                           **HEAT AND THERMODYNAMICS**

**COMPETENCY 3.1 HEAT AND THERMODYNAMICS**

**Skill 3.1a**    Solve problems involving the laws of thermodynamics using the relationships among work, heat flow, energy, and entropy

**The first law of thermodynamics** is a restatement of conservation of energy, i.e. the principle that energy cannot be created or destroyed. It also governs the behavior of a system and its surroundings. The change in heat energy supplied to a system (Q) is equal to the sum of the change in the internal energy (U) and the change in the work (W) done by the system against internal forces.

The internal energy of a material is the sum of the total kinetic energy of its molecules and the potential energy of interactions between those molecules. Total kinetic energy includes the contributions from translational motion and other components of motion such as rotation. The potential energy includes energy stored in the form of resisting intermolecular attractions between molecules.

Mathematically, we can express the relationship between the heat supplied to a system, its internal energy and work done by it as

$$\Delta Q = \Delta U + \Delta W$$

Let us examine a sample problem that relies upon this law.

Problem: A closed tank has a volume of 40.0 m³ and is filled with air at 25°C and 100 kPa. We desire to maintain the temperature in the tank constant at 25°C as water is pumped into it. How much heat will have to be removed from the air in the tank to fill the tank ½ full?

Solution: The problem involves isothermal compression of a gas, so $\Delta U_{gas}=0$. Consulting the equation above, $\Delta Q = \Delta U + \Delta W$, it is clear that the heat removed from the gas must be equal to the work done by the gas.

$$Q_{gas} = W_{gas} = P_{gas}V_1 \ln\left(\frac{V_2}{V_T}\right) = P_{gas}V_T \ln\left(\frac{\tfrac{1}{2}V_T}{V_T}\right) = P_{gas}V_T \ln \tfrac{1}{2}$$

$$= (100 kPa)(40.0 m^3)(-0.69314) = -2772.58 kJ$$

Thus, the gas in the tank must lose 2772.58 kJ to maintain its temperature.

To understand the **second law of thermodynamics**, we must first understand the concept of entropy. Entropy is the transformation of energy to a more disordered state and is the measure of how much energy or heat is available for work. The greater the entropy of a system, the less energy is available for work. The simplest statement of the second law of thermodynamics is that the entropy of an isolated system not in equilibrium tends to increase over time. The entropy approaches a maximum value at equilibrium. Below are several common examples in which we see the manifestation of the second law.

- The diffusion of molecules of perfume out of an open bottle
- Even the most carefully designed engine releases some heat and cannot convert all the chemical energy in the fuel into mechanical energy
- A block sliding on a rough surface slows down
- An ice cube sitting on a hot sidewalk melts into a little puddle; we must provide energy to a freezer to facilitate the creation of ice

When discussing the second law, scientists often refer to the "arrow of time". This is to help us conceptualize how the second law forces events to proceed in a certain direction. To understand the direction of the arrow of time, consider some of the examples above; we would never think of them as proceeding in reverse. That is, as time progresses, we would never see a puddle in the hot sun spontaneously freeze into an ice cube or the molecules of perfume dispersed in a room spontaneously re-concentrate themselves in the bottle. The above-mentioned examples are **spontaneous** as well as **irreversible**, both characteristic of increased entropy. Entropy change is zero for a complete cycle in a **reversible process**, a process where infinitesimal quasi-static changes in the absence of dissipative forces can bring a system back to its original state without a net change to the system or its surroundings. All real processes are irreversible. The idea of a reversible process, however, is a useful abstraction that can be a good approximation in some cases.

A quantitative measure of entropy S is given by the statement that the change in entropy of a system that goes from one state to another in an isothermal and reversible process is the amount of heat absorbed in the process divided by the absolute temperature at which the process occurs.

$$\Delta S = \frac{\Delta Q}{T}$$

Stated more generally, the entropy change that occurs in a state change between two equilibrium states A and B via a reversible process is given by

$$\Delta S_{A \to B} = \int_A^B \frac{dQ}{T}$$

Problem: What is the change in entropy of a cube of ice of mass 30g which melts at temperature 0C? The latent heat of fusion of ice is 334 KJ/Kg.

Solution: The amount of heat absorbed by the ice cube = $30 \times 10^{-3} \times 334 KJ = 10020 J$.

Thus change in entropy = $(10020/273) J/K$ = 36.7 J/K

**Skill 3.1b    Define and correctly apply thermodynamic properties of materials such as specific heat (heat capacity), heats of fusion, heat of vaporization, thermal conductivity, and thermal expansion to solve problems**

**Specific heat and latent heat**

A substance's **molar heat capacity** is the heat required to **change the temperature of one mole of the substance by one degree**. Heat capacity has units of joules per mol-kelvin or joules per mol-°C. The two units are interchangeable because we are only concerned with differences between one temperature and another. A Kelvin degree and a Celsius degree are the same size. The **specific heat** of a substance (also called specific heat capacity) is the heat required to **change the temperature of one gram or kilogram by one degree**. Specific heat has units of joules per gram-°C or joules per kilogram-°C.

These terms are used to solve problems involving a change in temperature by applying the formula:
$q = n \times C \times \Delta T$   where $q \Rightarrow$ heat added (positive) or evolved (negative)

$n \Rightarrow$ amount of material

$C \Rightarrow$ molar heat capacity if $n$ is in moles, specific heat if $n$ is a mass

$\Delta T \Rightarrow$ change in temperature $T_{final} - T_{initial}$

When a material is undergoing a phase change (e.g. from solid to liquid), however, it absorbs or releases heat without a corresponding change in temperature. When a material is heated and experiences a phase change, the thermal energy is used to break the intermolecular bonds holding the material together. Similarly, bonds are formed with the release of thermal energy when a material changes its phase during cooling. The heat absorbed or emitted in these cases is known as the latent heat of fusion or vaporization.

## TEACHER CERTIFICATION STUDY GUIDE

Example:
What is the change in energy of 10 g of gold at 25 °C when it is heated beyond its melting point to 1300 °C. You will need the following data for gold:

Solid heat capacity: 28 J/mol-K
Molten heat capacity: 20 J/mol-K
Enthalpy of fusion: 12.6 kJ/mol
Melting point: 1064 °C

Solution: First determine the number of moles used: $10 \text{ g} \times \dfrac{1 \text{ mol}}{197 \text{ g}} = 0.051 \text{ mol}$.

There are then three steps. 1) Heat the solid. 2) Melt the solid. 3) Heat the liquid. All three require energy so they will be positive numbers.

1) Heat the solid:

$$q_1 = n \times C \times \Delta T = 0.051 \text{ mol} \times 28 \, \dfrac{\text{J}}{\text{mol-K}} \times (1064 \, °C - 25 \, °C)$$

$$= 1.48 \times 10^3 \text{ J} = 1.48 \text{ kJ}$$

2) Melt the solid:

$$q_2 = n \times \Delta H_{fusion} = 0.051 \text{ mol} \times 12.6 \, \dfrac{\text{kJ}}{\text{mol}}$$

$$= 0.64 \text{ kJ}$$

3) Heat the liquid:

$$q_3 = n \times C \times \Delta T = 0.051 \text{ mol} \times 20 \, \dfrac{\text{J}}{\text{mol-K}} \times (1300 \, °C - 1064 \, °C)$$

$$= 2.4 \times 10^2 \text{ J} = 0.24 \text{ kJ}$$

The sum of the three processes is the total change in energy of the gold:

$$q = q_1 + q_2 + q_3 = 1.48 \text{ kJ} + 0.64 \text{ kJ} + 0.24 \text{ kJ} = 2.36 \text{ kJ}$$
$$= 2.4 \text{ kJ}$$

## Thermal conduction

The amount of heat transferred by conduction through a material depends on several factors. It is directly proportional to the temperature difference $\Delta T$ between the surface from which the heat is flowing and the surface to which it is transferred. Heat flow $H$ increases with the area $A$ through which the flow occurs and also with the time duration $t$. The thickness of the material reduces the flow of heat. The relationship between all these variables is expressed as

$$H = \frac{k.t.A.\Delta T}{d}$$

where the proportionality constant $k$ is known as the **thermal conductivity**, a property of the material. Thermal conductivity of a good conductor is close to 1 (0.97 cal/cm.s.$^0 C$ for silver) while good insulators have thermal conductivity that is nearly zero (0.0005 cal/cm.s.$^0 C$ for wood).

Problem: A glass window pane is 50 cm long and 30 cm wide. The glass is 1 cm thick. If the temperature indoors is $15^0 C$ higher than it is outside, how much heat will be lost through the window in 30 minutes? The thermal conductivity of glass is 0.0025 cal/cm.s.$^0 C$.

Solution: The window has area $A$ = 1500 sq. cm and thickness $d$ = 1 cm. Duration of heat flow is 1800 s and the temperature difference $\Delta T = 15^0 C$. Therefore heat loss through the window is given by

$$H = (0.0025 \times 1800 \times 1500 \times 15)/1 = 101250 \text{ calories}$$

## Thermal expansion

Most solid and liquid materials expand when heated with a change in dimension proportional to the change in temperature. A notable exception to this is water between $0^0 C$ and $4^0 C$.

If we consider a long rod of length $L$ that increases in length by $\Delta L$ when heated, the fractional change in length $\Delta L / L$ is directly proportional to the change in temperature $\Delta T$.

$$\Delta L / L = \alpha . \Delta T$$

The constant of proportionality $\alpha$ is known as the **coefficient of linear expansion** and is a property of the material of which the rod is made.

# TEACHER CERTIFICATION STUDY GUIDE

Problem: The temperature of an iron rod 10 meters long changes from $-3^0C$ to $12^0C$. If iron has a coefficient of linear expansion of 0.000011 per $^0C$, by how much does the rod expand?

Solution: The length of the rod $L$ = 10 meters.
Change in temperature $\Delta T = 12^0C - (-3^0C) = 15^0C$
Change in length of the rod $\Delta L = 0.000011 \times 10 \times 15 = .00165$ meters

If instead of a rod, we consider an area $A$ that increases by $\Delta A$ when heated, we find that the fractional change in area is proportional to the change in temperature $\Delta T$. The proportionality constant in this case is known as the **coefficient of area expansion** and is related to the coefficient of linear expansion as demonstrated below.

If $A$ is a rectangle with dimensions $L_1$ and $L_2$, then

$$A + \Delta A = (L_1 + \Delta L_1)(L_2 + \Delta L_2)$$
$$= (L_1 + \alpha L_1 \Delta T)(L_2 + \alpha L_2 \Delta T)$$
$$= L_1 L_2 + 2\alpha L_1 L_2 \Delta T + \alpha^2 (\Delta T)^2$$

Ignoring the higher order term for small changes in temperature, we find that

$$\Delta A = 2\alpha A \Delta T = \gamma A \Delta T$$

Thus the coefficient of area expansion $\gamma = 2\alpha$.

Following the same procedure as above, we can show that the change in volume of a material when heated may be expressed as

$$\Delta V = 3\alpha V \Delta T = \beta V \Delta T$$

where the **coefficient of volume expansion** $\beta = 3\alpha$.

Problem: An aluminum sphere of radius 10cm is heated from $0^0C$ to $25^0C$. What is the change in its volume? The coefficient of linear expansion of aluminum is 0.000024 per $^0C$.

Solution: Volume $V$ of the sphere = $\frac{4}{3}\Pi r^3 = \frac{4}{3} \times 3.14 \times 1000 cm^3 = 4186.67 cm^3$
Change in volume of the sphere = $3 \times 0.000024 \times 4186.67 \times 25 = 7.54 cm^3$

PHYSICS

**Skill 3.1c   Solve problems for ideal gas systems**

The relationship between **kinetic energy** and **intermolecular forces** determines whether a collection of molecules will be a gas, liquid, or solid. In a gas, the energy of intermolecular forces is much weaker than the kinetic energy of the molecules. Kinetic molecular theory is usually applied to gases and is best applied by imagining ourselves shrinking down to become a molecule and picturing what happens when we bump into other molecules and into container walls.

Gas **pressure** results from molecular collisions with container walls. The **number of molecules** striking an **area** on the walls and the **average kinetic energy** per molecule are the only factors that contribute to pressure. A higher **temperature** increases speed and kinetic energy. There are more collisions at higher temperatures, but the average distance between molecules does not change, and thus density does not change in a sealed container.

Kinetic molecular theory explains why the pressure and temperature of **ideal gases** behave the way they do by making a few assumptions, namely:

1) The energies of intermolecular attractive and repulsive forces may be neglected.
2) The average kinetic energy of the molecules is proportional to absolute temperature.
3) Energy can be transferred between molecules during collisions and the collisions are elastic, so the average kinetic energy of the molecules doesn't change due to collisions.
4) The volume of all molecules in a gas is negligible compared to the total volume of the container.

Strictly speaking, molecules also contain some kinetic energy by rotating or experiencing other motions. The motion of a molecule from one place to another is called **translation**. Translational kinetic energy is the form that is transferred by collisions, and kinetic molecular theory ignores other forms of kinetic energy because they are not proportional to temperature.

The pressure, temperature and volume relationships for an ideal gas (a gas described by the assumptions of the kinetic molecular theory listed above) are given by the following gas laws:

**Boyle's law** states that the volume of a fixed amount of gas at constant temperature is inversely proportional to the gas pressure, or:

$$V \propto \frac{1}{P}, \text{ or } PV = \text{constant}$$

Problem: A 15 liter container contains gas at a pressure of 5 atmospheres. If the volume of the container is reduced to 3 liters and the temperature remains unchanged, what will be the pressure in the container?

Solution: Since PV is constant by Boyle's law, the product of the initial pressure and volume is equal to the product of the final pressure and volume, i.e.
$$P_1 V_1 = P_2 V_2$$

Therefore, $P_2 = P_1 V_1 / V_2 = 15 \times 5 / 3 \, atm. = 25 \, atm.$

**Gay-Lussac's law** states that the pressure of a fixed amount of gas in a fixed volume is proportional to absolute temperature, or:
$$P \propto T.$$

**Charles' law** states that the volume of a fixed amount of gas at constant pressure is directly proportional to absolute temperature, or:
$$V \propto T.$$

Problem: A container has 25 liters of gas at $0°C$. What will the volume of the gas be if the temperature is raised to $100°C$ at constant pressure?

Solution: From Charles' law we know that $V_1 / T_1 = V_2 / T_2$.

Thus $V_2 = V_1 T_2 / T_1 = 25 \times 373 / 273 = 34.2 \, liters$.

The **combined gas law** uses the above laws to determine a proportionality expression that is used for a constant quantity of gas:
$$V \propto \frac{T}{P}.$$
The combined gas law is often expressed as an equality between identical amounts of an ideal gas at two different states ($n_1 = n_2$):
$$\frac{P_1 V_1}{T_1} = \frac{P_2 V_2}{T_2}.$$

**Avogadro's hypothesis** states that equal volumes of different gases at the same temperature and pressure contain equal numbers of molecules. **Avogadro's law** states that the volume of a gas at constant temperature and pressure is directly proportional to the quantity of gas, or $V \propto n$ where $n$ is the number of moles of gas.

Avogadro's law and the combined gas law yield $V \propto \frac{nT}{P}$. The proportionality constant $R$--the **ideal gas constant**--is used to express this proportionality as the **ideal gas law**:
$$PV = nRT.$$

# TEACHER CERTIFICATION STUDY GUIDE

The ideal gas law is useful because it contains all the information of Charles's, Avogadro's, Boyle's, and the combined gas laws in a single expression.

Solving ideal gas law problems is a straightforward process of algebraic manipulation. **Errors commonly arise from using improper units**, particularly for the ideal gas constant $R$. An absolute temperature scale must be used—never °C—and is usually reported using the Kelvin scale, but volume and pressure units often vary from problem to problem.

If pressure is given in atmospheres and volume is given in liters, a value for $R$ of **0.08206 L-atm/(mol-K)** is used. If pressure is given in pascal (newtons/m$^2$) and volume in m$^3$, then the SI value for $R$ of **8.314 J/(mol-K)** may be used because a joule is defined as a newton-meter or a pascal-m$^3$. A value for $R$ of **8.314 Pa-m$^3$/(mol-K)** is identical to the ideal gas constant using joules.

The ideal gas law may also be rearranged to determine gas molar density in moles per unit volume (molarity):

$$\frac{n}{V} = \frac{P}{RT}.$$

**Gas density** $d$ in grams per unit volume is found after multiplication by the molecular weight $M$:

$$d = \frac{nM}{V} = \frac{PM}{RT}.$$

**Molecular weight** may also be determined from the density of an ideal gas:\

$$M = \frac{dV}{n} = \frac{dRT}{P}.$$

Example:

Determine the molecular weight of an ideal gas that has a density of 3.24 g/L at 800 K and 3.00 atm.

Solution:

$$M = \frac{dRT}{P} = \frac{\left(3.24 \ \frac{g}{L}\right)\left(0.08206 \ \frac{L\text{-atm}}{mol\text{-}K}\right)(800 \ K)}{3.00 \ atm} = 70.9 \ \frac{g}{mol}.$$

Tutorials for gas laws may be found online at: http://www.chemistrycoach.com/tutorials-6.htm. A flash animation tutorial for problems involving a piston may be found at http://www.mhhe.com/physsci/chemistry/essentialchemistry/flash/gasesv6.swf.

PHYSICS

# TEACHER CERTIFICATION STUDY GUIDE

**Skill 3.1d  Interpret graphs showing phase changes and graphs of cyclic processes**

The temperature of a material rises when heat is transferred to it and falls when heat is removed from it. When the material is undergoing a phase change (e.g. from solid to liquid), however, it absorbs or releases heat without a corresponding change in temperature. A **temperature vs. heat graph** can demonstrate these relationships visually. One can also calculate the specific heat or latent heat of phase change for the material by studying the details of the graph.

Example: The plot below shows heat applied to 1g of ice at -40C. The horizontal parts of the graph show the phase changes where the material absorbs heat but stays at the same temperature. The graph shows that ice melts into water at 0C and the water undergoes a further phase change into steam at 100C.

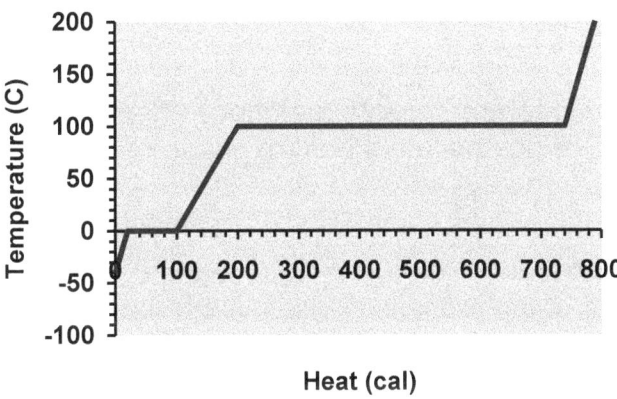

Heat (cal)

The specific heat of ice, water and steam and the latent heat of fusion and vaporization may be calculated from each of the five segments of the graph.

For instance, we see from the flat segment at temperature 0C that the ice absorbs 80 cal of heat. The latent heat $L$ of a material is defined by the equation $\Delta Q = mL$ where $\Delta Q$ is the quantity of heat transferred and $m$ is the mass of the material. Since the mass of the material in this example is 1g, the latent heat of fusion of ice is given by $L = \Delta Q / m = 80$ cal/g.

The next segment shows a rise in the temperature of water and may be used to calculate the specific heat $C$ of water defined by $\Delta Q = mC\Delta T$, where $\Delta Q$ is the quantity of heat absorbed, m is the mass of the material and $\Delta T$ is the change in temperature. According to the graph, $\Delta Q$ = 200-100 =100 cal and $\Delta T$ = 100-0=100C. Thus, C = 100/100 = 1 cal/gC.

Problem: The plot below shows the change in temperature when heat is transferred to 0.5g of a material. Find the initial specific heat of the material and the latent heat of phase change.

PHYSICS 49

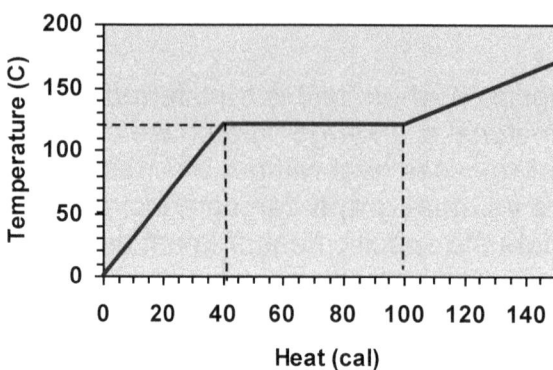

Solution:

Looking at the first segment of the graph, we see that $\Delta Q = 40$ cal and $\Delta T = 120$ C. Since the mass $m = 0.5$g, the specific heat of the material is given by $C = \Delta Q / (m\Delta T) = 40/(0.5 \times 120) = 0.67$ cal/gC.

The flat segment of the graph represents the phase change. Here $\Delta Q = 100 - 40 = 60$ cal. Thus, the latent heat of phase change is given by $L = \Delta Q / m = 60/(0.5) = 120$ cal/g.

Cyclic processes are those in which a thermodynamic system is returned to its initial starting point at the end of the process. Since the internal energy of the system depends only on its state and not on the processes it undergoes, the **net change in internal energy for a cyclic process is zero**. Work done by or on the system and the heat the system exchanges with its surroundings, however, are not independent of the path and may have non-zero values for a cyclic process. Since the net change in internal energy is zero, according to the first law of thermodynamics $\Delta Q = \Delta W$, i.e. the net work done by the system is equal to the quantity of heat supplied to it.

Cyclic processes form the basis of heat engines and heat pumps and may be represented on a PV diagram. For a gas in a state of equilibrium, the pressure $P$, volume $V$ and temperature $T$ are related through an equation of state. For a **quasi-static process** in which the gas remains close to equilibrium at all times, any two of these variables can characterize the state of the gas at a point in time. On a PV diagram, the state of a gas at any point is represented by its pressure $P$ and volume $V$. Since $P$, $V$ and $T$ are related, when the volume changes through expansion or compression, either the pressure or temperature or both of these variables must change.

For a process represented in a clockwise direction (as shown in the figure below) on the PV diagram, the net work done is positive and is given by the enclosed area. This is a heat engine. For a process represented in the counter-clockwise direction, work is done on the system and not by the system. This is a heat pump or refrigerator.

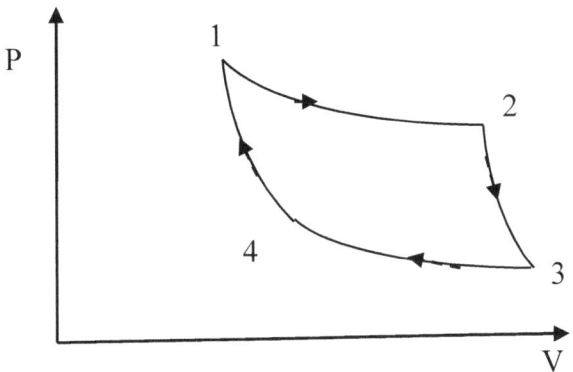

A typical thermodynamic cycle involves expansion and compression of the working substance as well as heat intake and heat outflow with a net output of work (e.g. conversion of thermal energy to mechanical energy) with each cycle. Each segment of a cycle represents a process that takes place in one of several different ways defined below.

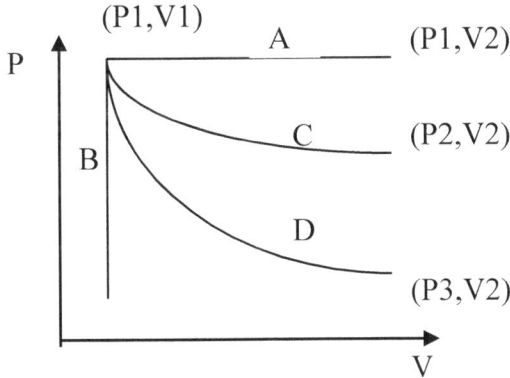

Processes where pressure remains constant are known as **isobaric** (A) processes. These are represented by horizontal straight lines on a PV diagram.

Processes in which volume remains constant are **isochoric** (B) processes represented by vertical lines on a PV diagram.

**Isothermal** (C) processes are those in which the temperature of the gas remains the same throughout. For an ideal gas $PV = nRT$ = constant. Thus the PV curve is a hyperbola. Since the temperature does not change, the internal energy of the gas remains constant and the heat $Q$ absorbed by the gas is equal to the work $W$ done by the gas.

During an **adiabatic** process no heat flows in or out of the gas. Thus the work done by the gas equals the decrease in internal energy of the gas and the temperature falls as the gas expands. The decrease in temperature leads to a greater decrease in pressure than in the case of isothermal expansion. As a result, the PV curve for adiabatic expansion of a gas is steeper than that for isothermal expansion.

Carnot described an ideal reversible engine, the Carnot engine, that works between two heat reservoirs in a cycle known as the **Carnot cycle** which consists of two isothermal (12 and 34) and two adiabatic processes (23 and 41) as shown in the diagram below.

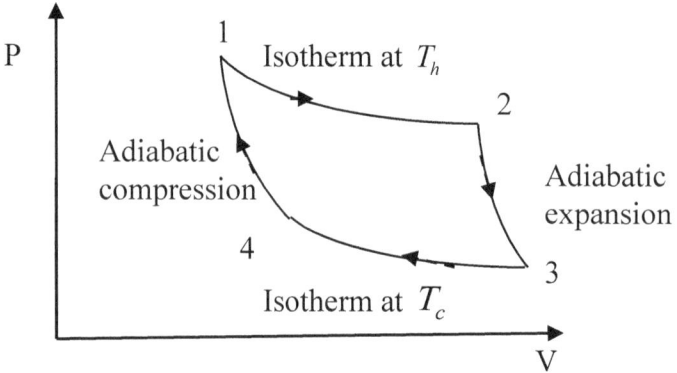

The Carnot engine absorbs heat while expanding from a hot reservoir at temperature $T_h$, undergoes an adiabatic expansion, contracts while rejecting heat $Q_c$ to a cold reservoir at a lower temperature $T_c$ and then contracts adiabatically.

The **Otto cycle** is used in four stroke engines and consists of two isochoric segments and two adiabatic segments. Adiabatic compression (12) is followed by heat absorption at constant volume (23), adiabatic expansion (34) and heat rejection (41) at constant volume.

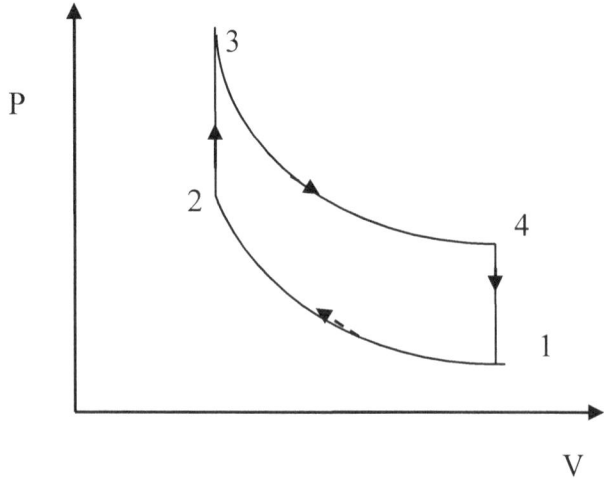

There are many other types of thermodynamic cycles. In each case the work done by or on the system is given by the area enclosed within closed curve.

**Skill 3.1e  Solve problems involving cyclic processes, including calculations of work done, heat gain/loss, and entropy change**

The work done by the gas or on the gas can be calculated from its PV diagram, i.e. the plot of the gas pressure vs. volume.

Consider a gas confined in a cylinder with a frictionless piston. In a quasi-static process, the piston moves very slowly without acceleration. If the area of the piston is A and it moves a distance dx, then the force exerted by the gas on the piston is PA and the work done by the gas is PAdx.

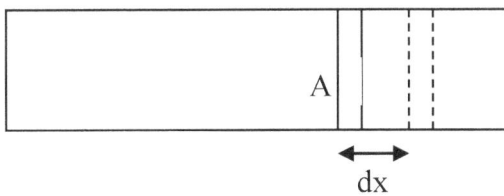

Since the change in volume of the gas $dV = Adx$, the work done by the gas is given by $dW = PAdx = PdV$. If the gas expands quasi-statically from volume V1 to volume V2, the total work done is $W = \int_{V1}^{V2} PdV$. In a PV diagram, this expression represents the area under the pressure vs. volume curve.

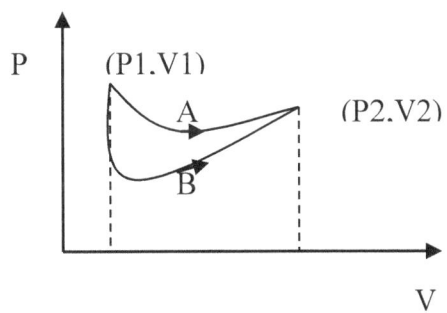

The work done by a gas is not determined only by its initial and final states but by the path through which the gas expands in the PV space. In the example diagram displayed above, a gas starts at pressure P1 and volume V1 and expands to volume V2 at pressure P2. It is clear that if the gas expands through the path A, the area under the curve and the work done by the gas will be greater than the case where the gas expands through the path B.

Problem: If a gas expands from 1 liter to 2 liters at a constant pressure of 3 atmospheres, what is the work done by the gas?

Solution: Since pressure is constant, $W = P\int_{V1}^{V2} dV = P(V2 - V1) = 3(2-1) = 3$ L.atm.

Given that $1L = 10^{-3} m^3$ and 1 atm = $101.3 \times 10^3 N/m^2$, $W = 303.9 J$.

Problem: A sample of gas expands from $2m^3$ to $5m^3$ along the path Y shown in the PV diagram below. It is then compressed back to $2m^3$ along the path X or the path Z. What is the net work done by the gas in each case?

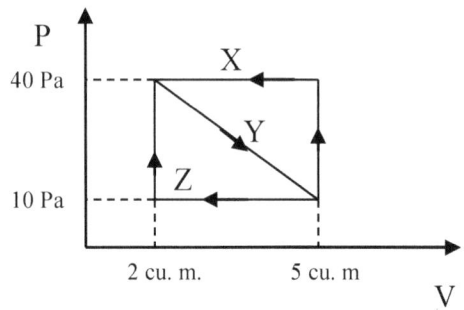

Solution: The work done by the gas in the expansion of the gas along path Y (given by the area under Y) = 0.5 (40 + 10) x 3 J = 75 J.

The work done by the gas is negative when it is compressed.

When the gas is compressed along path X work done = -40x3J = -120J.
When the gas is compressed along path Z work done = -10x3J = -30J.

Net work done by the gas in the YX cycle = 75 – 120J = -45J.
Net work done by the gas in the YZ cycle = 75 – 30J = 45J.

Problem: 1 mol of an ideal monatomic gas goes through the cycle shown below in a heat engine. Process Z is isobaric or constant pressure, process X is isochoric or constant volume and process Y is adiabatic, i.e. no heat is absorbed or released by the gas.

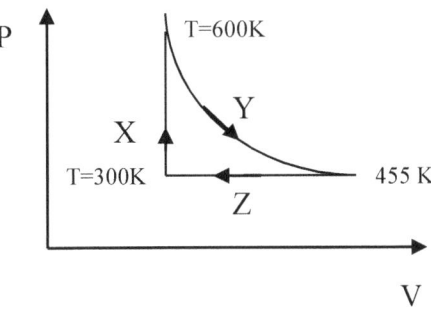

What is the heat absorbed or released, the change in internal energy, and the work done for each of the three processes and the whole cycle?

Solution:

For process X: Internal energy for 1 mol of a monatomic ideal gas = $\frac{3}{2}nRT$ = 12.47 x T Joules where R is the ideal gas constant (8.314 J/mol.K) and T is the temperature of the gas.
Thus change in internal energy = 12.47x (600 – 300) = 3741J.
Since there is no change in volume, work done = 0J.
Thus, by the first law of thermodynamics, heat absorbed = 3741J.

For process Y: Since this process is adiabatic, heat absorbed = 0J.
Change in internal energy of process Y = 12.47 (455-600) J = -1808J
Since heat absorbed is zero, by the first law of thermodynamics work done =1808J

For process Z: Change in internal energy = 12.47 (300-455) = -1933J

For an ideal monatomic gas, the specific heat at constant pressure = 2.5R = 20.78 J/mol.K. Thus, heat absorbed by the gas = 20.78 (300-455) = -3221J
Work done by the gas = -3221J + 1933J = -1288J

For the entire cycle: Heat absorbed = 3741 + 0 - 3221J = 520J
Change in internal energy = 3741-1808-1933 = 0J
Work done by the gas = 0 + 1808 -1288J = 520J

Problem: One mole of an ideal monatomic gas goes through the cycle shown below. How much work is done as the gas expands along the path xyz? How does the internal energy and entropy change in the process yz? What is the change in internal energy and entropy over the whole cycle? Give the answers in terms of p, v and the temperature T at the point x.

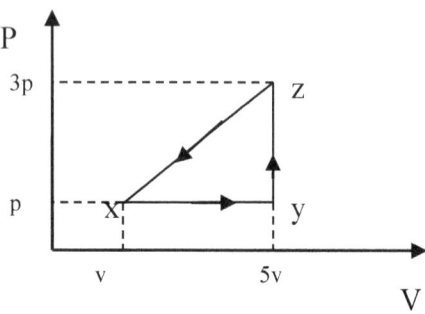

Solution: The work done along the path xy = p(5v – v) = 4pv. The work done along the path yz is zero since there is no change in the volume. Thus, the net work done along the path xyz = 4pv.

Using the ideal gas law, at point x  pv = RT.
The temperature at point y = px5v/R=5T.
The temperature at point z = 3px5v/R = 15T.

Since the internal energy of a mole of monatomic gas at temperature T is given by 1.5RT, the change in internal energy along the path yz = 1.5R (15T-5T) = 15RT.

Change in entropy along path yz = $\int \frac{dQ}{T} = \int_{5T}^{15T} \frac{C_v dT}{T} = \frac{3}{2} R \ln 3$ since the specific heat at constant volume for a mole of monatomic gas $C_v = \frac{3}{2} R$.

For the entire cycle both change in internal energy and entropy are zero since both are state variables that depend only on the state of the system and not on the path followed throughout the cycle.

**Skill 3.1f  Describe a plasma, state its characteristic properties, and contrast it with an ideal gas**

Plasma is a physical state of matter. A material that has been heated to a temperature where the molecules are unstable is a plasma; for example, a spark. In a plasma state, a material is a mixture of neutral molecules, atoms, clusters of atoms, ions, and free electrons. Plasmas respond to magnetic fields and are highly electrically conductive.

An ideal gas describes the behavior approached by a gas as the pressure nears zero. It is assumed that intermolecular forces are zero in an ideal gas. No substances actually achieve the state of "ideal" gas, but some come close. Plasmas behave differently than ideal gases because the atoms in plasmas exist as charged ions and therefore interact with each other. In addition, in a plasma, the electrons have been excited so much by the increased heat that they completely escape the molecules and move independently. A low density or weakly charged plasma in which particles move about relatively freely may be treated as an ideal gas.

# SUBAREA IV. WAVES

## COMPETENCY 4.1 WAVES

**Skill 4.1a** Compare the characteristics of sound, light, and seismic waves (e.g., transverse/longitudinal, travel through various media, relative speed)

Waves propagate energy through space. Commonly observed waves such as water waves or waves in a stretched string are mechanical waves that travel through a medium. Even though the disturbance is propagated, the medium itself moves only locally, either back and forth in the direction of propagation or perpendicular to the direction of propagation.

**Longitudinal waves** are created by oscillations in the direction in which the wave travels. Thus, if we imagine a longitudinal waveform moving down a tube, particles will move back and forth parallel to the sides of the tube. Sound is one of the most important types of longitudinal waves and travels through various media such as air or water through compressions and rarefactions of the media. When the particles of the medium are drawn close together it is called compression. When the particles of the medium are spread apart it is called rarefaction. The properties of a medium determine the speed of sound in it (see **Skill 4.1f)**. The speed of sound in air at $0^\circ C$ 331 m/s.

**Transverse waves**, on the other hand, oscillate in a direction perpendicular to the direction of wave travel. So let's imagine the same tube, this time with a transverse wave traveling down it. In this case, the particles oscillate up and down or side to side within the tube. Particle displacement in a transverse wave can also be easily visualized in the vibration of a taut string.

Excellent videos that demonstrate the movement of individual particles are available at the following web address:
http://www.kettering.edu/~drussell/Demos/waves/wavemotion.html

Mechanical waves differ from electromagnetic waves in that they need a medium through which to travel. Electromagnetic waves such as visible light and X-rays travel in vacuum and are created through transverse oscillations of electric and magnetic fields. The speed of light in vacuum is $3 \times 10^8 m/s$.

**Seismic waves** are of several types, both transverse and longitudinal. Seismic compressional or P waves are longitudinal while the shear or S waves are transverse. Both of these are known as **body waves** and are propagated through the earth's interior. The difference in arrival times of P waves and S waves help scientists calculate the location of an earthquake. The other two types of waves are Love waves and Rayleigh waves that are **surface waves** which travel close to the surface of the earth. Love waves are transverse with particles moving horizontally perpendicular to direction of travel. Rayleigh waves are created by particles that move both up and down and side to side in elliptical paths.

Seismic waves typically travel several Kilometers every second. The exact speed is determined by the composition of the rocks as well as temperature and pressure. P waves are the fastest, traveling 1 to 14 Km/s. S waves are slower with speeds ranging from 1 to 8 Km/s. Velocities of Love waves range from 2 to 6 Km/s. Rayleigh waves are the slowest and propagate with speeds between 1 to 5 Km/s.

### Skill 4.1b  Explain that energy is transferred by waves without mass transfer and provide examples

A disturbance can move from one end of a medium to another end through a wave without the transfer of matter. The individual particles of the medium are temporarily displaced but eventually return to their equilibrium positions. This is in contrast to energy transfer, which involves the transfer of matter, such as the hitting of a tennis ball. In order for the tennis ball to move, the player must transfer energy from herself to the ball by swinging through with the racquet and hitting the ball.

When a wave moves in the ocean, energy is transferred through the wave, but the wave returns to its resting position. No matter is transferred. This is proven by the fact that the amount of water in the middle of the ocean remains the same. Another example would be a sound wave. When one person speaks to another, energy in the form of sound is transferred from one person's mouth to the ear of the other person. However, the air molecules, which are the particles of the medium, return to their original position after the transfer.

# TEACHER CERTIFICATION STUDY GUIDE

## Skill 4.1c  Explain how lenses are used in simple optical systems, including the camera, telescope, microscope, and the eye

A lens is a device that causes electromagnetic radiation to converge or diverge. The most familiar lenses are made of glass or plastic and designed to concentrate or disperse visible light. Two of the most important parameters for a lens are its thickness and it's focal length. Focal length is a measure of how strongly light is concentrated or dispersed by a lens. For a convex or converging lens, the focal length is the distance from the center of the lens to the point at which a beam of light will be focused to a single spot. Conversely, for a concave or diverging lens, the focal length is the distance to the point from which a beam appears to be diverging.

The images produced by lenses can be either virtual or real. A virtual image is one that is created by rays of light that appear to diverge from a certain point. Virtual images cannot be seen on a screen because the light rays do not actually meet at the point where the image is located. If an image and object appear on the same side of a converging lens, that image is defined as virtual. For virtual images, the image location will be negative and the magnification positive. Real images, on the other hand, are formed by light rays actually passing through the image. Thus, real images are visible on a screen. Real images created by a converging lens are inverted and have a positive image location and negative magnification.

### Simple magnifier
A simple magnifier is a convex or converging lens that allows a user to place an object closer to the eye than the near point (the distance within which objects become blurry, assumed to be approximately 25 cm) and view an enlarged virtual image. The magnification achieved is given by 25/f where f is the focal length of the magnifying lens.

### Telescope
A telescope is a device that has the ability to make distant objects appear to be much closer. Most telescopes are one of two varieties, a refractor which uses lenses or a reflector which uses mirrors. Each accomplishes the same purpose but in totally different ways. The basic idea of a telescope is to collect as much light as possible, focus it, and then magnify it. The objective lens or primary mirror of a telescope brings the light from an object into focus. An eyepiece lens takes the focused light and "spreads it out" or magnifies it using the same principle as a magnifying glass using two curved surfaces to refract the light.

## Microscope

Microscopes are used to view objects that are too small to be seen with the naked eye. A microscope usually has an objective lens that collects light from the sample and an eyepiece which brings the image into focus for the observer. It also has a light source to illuminate the sample. Typical optical microscopes achieve magnification of up to 1500 times.

## Eye

The eye is a very complex sensory organ. Although there are many critical anatomical features of the eye, the lens and retina are the most important for focusing and sensing light. Light passes through the cornea and through the lens. The lens is attached to numerous muscles that contract and relax to move the lens in order to focus the light onto the retina. The pupil also contracts and relaxes to allow more or less light in the eye as required. The eye relies on refraction to focus light onto the retina. Refraction occurs at four curved interfaces; between the air and the front of the cornea, the back of the cornea and the aqueous humor, the aqueous humor at the front of the lens, and the back of the lens and the vitreous humor. When each of these interfaces are working properly the light arrives at the retina in perfect focus for transmission to the brain as an image.

## Eye Glasses

When all the parts of the eye are not working together correctly, corrective lenses or eyeglasses may be needed to assist the eye in focusing the light onto the retina. The surfaces of the lens or cornea may not be smooth causing the light to refract in the wrong direction. This is called astigmatism. Another common problem is that the lens is not able to change its curvature appropriately to match the image. The cornea can also be misshaped resulting in blurred vision.

Corrective lenses consist of curves pieces of glass which bend the light in order to change the focal point of the light. A nearsighted eye forms images in front of the retina. To correct this, a minus lens consisting of two concave prisms is used to bend light out and move the image back to the retina. A farsighted eye creates images behind the retina. This is corrected using plus lenses that bend light in and bring the image forward onto the retina. The worse the vision, the farther out of focus the image is on the retina. Therefore the stronger the lens the further the focal point is moved to compensate.

**Camera**

A camera is another device that utilizes the lens' ability to refract light to capture and process an image. As with the eye, light enters the lens of a camera and focuses the light on the other side. Instead of focusing on the retina, the image is focused on the film to create a film negative. This film negative is later processed with chemicals to create a photograph. A camera uses a converging or convex lens. This lens captures and directs light to a single point to create a real image on the surface of the film. To focus a camera on an image, the distance of the lens from the film is adjusted in order to ensure that the real image converges on the surface of the film and not in front of or behind it.

Different lenses are available which capture and bend the light to different degrees. A lens with more pronounced curvature will be able to bend the light more acutely causing the image to converge more closely to the lens. Conversely a flatter lens will have a longer focal distance. The further the lens is located from the film (flatter lens), the larger the image becomes. Thus zoom lenses on cameras are flat while wide angle lenses are more rounded. The focal length number on a certain lens conveys the magnification ability of the lens.

The film functions like the retina of the eye in that it is light sensitive and can capture light images when exposed. However, this exposure must be brief to capture the contrasting amounts of light and a clear image. The rest of the camera functions to precisely control how much light contacts the film. The aperture is the lens opening which can open and close to let in more or less light. The temporal length of light exposure is controlled by the shutter which can be set at different speeds depending on the amount of action and level of light available. The film speed refers to the size of the light sensitive grains on the surface of the film. The larger grains absorb more light photons than the smaller grains, so film speed should be selected according to lighting conditions.

**Skill 4.1d   Explain and apply the laws of reflection and refraction**

Wave **refraction** is a change in direction of a wave due to a change in its speed. This most commonly occurs when a wave passes from one material to another, such as a light ray passing from air into water or glass. However, light is only one example of refraction; any type of wave can undergo refraction. Another example would be physical waves passing from water into oil. At the boundary of the two media, the wave velocity is altered, the direction changes, and the wavelength increases or decreases. However, the frequency remains constant.

**Snell's Law** describes how light bends, or refracts, when traveling from one medium to the next. It is expressed as

$$n_1 \sin \theta_1 = n_2 \sin \theta_2$$

where $n_i$ represents the index of refraction in medium $i$, and $\theta_i$ represents the angle the light makes with the normal in medium $i$.

Problem: The index of refraction for light traveling from air into an optical fiber is 1.44. (a) In which direction does the light bend? (b) What is the angle of refraction inside the fiber, if the angle of incidence on the end of the fiber is 22°?

Solution: (a) The light will bend toward the normal since it is traveling from a rarer region (lower $n$) to a denser region (higher $n$).

(b) Let air be medium 1 and the optical fiber be medium 2:

$$n_1 \sin\theta_1 = n_2 \sin\theta_2$$
$$(1.00)\sin 22° = (1.44)\sin\theta_2$$
$$\sin\theta_2 = \frac{1.00}{1.44}\sin 22° = (.6944)(.3746) = 0.260$$
$$\theta_2 = \sin^{-1}(0.260) = 15°$$

The angle of refraction inside the fiber is $15°$.

Light travels at different speeds in different media. The speed of light in a vacuum is represented by

$$c = 2.99792458 \times 10^8 \, m/s$$

but is usually rounded to

$$c = 3.00 \times 10^8 \, m/s.$$

Light will never travel faster than this value. The **index of refraction**, $n$, is the amount by which light slows in a given material and is defined by the formula

$$n = \frac{c}{v}$$

where $v$ represents the speed of light through the given material.

Problem: The speed of light in an unknown medium is measured to be $1.24 \times 10^8 \, m/s$. What is the index of refraction of the medium?

Solution:

$$n = \frac{c}{v}$$
$$n = \frac{3.00 \times 10^8}{1.24 \times 10^8} = 2.42$$

Referring to a standard table showing indices of refraction, we would see that this index corresponds to the index of refraction for diamond.

**Reflection** is the change in direction of a wave at an interface between two dissimilar media such that the wave returns into the medium from which it originated. The most common example of this is light waves reflecting from a mirror, but sound and water waves can also be reflected. The law of reflection states that the angle of incidence is equal to the angle of reflection.

Reflection may occur whenever a wave travels from a medium of a given refractive index to another medium with a different index. A certain fraction of the light is reflected from the interface and the remainder is refracted. However, when the wave is moving from a dense medium into one less dense, that is the refractive index of the first is greater than the second, a critical angle exists which will create a phenomenon known as **total internal reflection**. In this situation all of the wave incident at an angle greater than the critical angle is reflected. When a wave reflects off a more dense material (higher refractive index) than that from which it originated, it undergoes a 180° phase change. In contrast, a less dense, lower refractive index material will reflect light in phase. **Fiber optics** makes use of the phenomenon of total internal reflection. The light traveling through a fiber reflects off the walls at angles greater than the critical angle and thus keeps the wave confined to the narrow fiber.

### Skill 4.1e    Compare transmission, reflection, and absorption of light in matter

Light interacts with matter by **reflection, absorption** or **transmission**. In a transparent material such as a lens, most of the light is transmitted through. Opaque objects such as rocks or cars partially absorb and partially reflect light.

The image you see in a mirrored surface is the result of the reflection of the light waves off the surface. Light waves follow the "law of reflection," i.e. the angle at which the light wave approaches a flat reflecting surface is equal to the angle at which it leaves the surface. Scattering is a form of reflection where the reflection happens in multiple directions. **Rayleigh scattering** is the scattering of an electromagnetic wave by particles that are much smaller than its wavelength. The amount of scattering is inversely related to the wavelength of the wave. Thus, the greater scattering of blue light compared to red light by particles in the atmosphere results in the sky appearing blue.

Absorption is the transfer of energy from a light wave to particles of matter. In the absorption process, a material converts some of the light energy into heat. Some of the energy may be radiated at a different frequency. When light crosses the boundary between two different media, its path is bent, or refracted. For a detailed discussion of **refraction** and Snell's law see **section III.8.**

Absorption can usually be modeled as the result of the medium having a finite conductivity. Ideally, in classical electrodynamics, a perfect insulator is expected to transmit all light without any absorption. The presence of mobile charge carriers, such as free or weakly bound electrons, provides a means for absorption, where, for example, electrons acquire energy due to the presence of an electric field (and its corresponding magnetic field). The motion of the electrons may be impeded, resulting in conversion of some of the energy into heat.

**Skill 4.1f  Relate wave propagation to properties of materials (e.g., predict wave speed from density and tension)**

Mechanical waves rely on the local oscillation of each atom in a medium, but the material itself does not move; only the energy is transferred from atom to atom. Therefore the material through which the mechanical wave is traveling greatly affects the wave's propagation and speed. In particular, a material's elastic constant and density affect the speed at which a wave travels through it. Both of these properties of a medium can predict the extent to which the atoms will vibrate and pass along the energy of the wave. The general relationship between these properties and the speed of a wave in a solid is given by the following equation:

$$V = \sqrt{\frac{C_{ij}}{\rho}}$$

where $V$ is the speed of sound, $C_{ij}$ is the elastic constant, and $\rho$ is the material density. It is worth noting that the elastic constant differs depending on direction in anisotropic materials and the ij subscripts indicate that this directionality must be taken into account.

At $0°C$, the speed of sound is 331m/s in air, 1402m/s in water and 6420m/s in Aluminum. Even though water is much denser than air, it is a lot more incompressible than air and its bulk modulus is larger than that of air by a larger factor. Therefore sound travels much faster in water than in air.

In the case of a stretched string, the velocity of a transverse wave passing through it is given by

$$v = \sqrt{\frac{\tau}{\mu}}$$

where $\tau$ is the tension in the string and $\mu$ is its linear density.

**Skill 4.1g  Describe, distinguish, and solve both conceptual and numerical problems involving interference, diffraction, refraction, reflection, Doppler effect, polarization, dispersion, and scattering**

For a discussion of reflection and refraction see **Skill 4.1d**.

**Interference** occurs when two or more waves are superimposed. According to the **principle of linear superposition**, when two or more waves exist in the same place, the resultant wave is the sum of all the waves, i.e. the amplitude of the resulting wave at a point in space is the sum of the amplitudes of each of the component waves at that point. Interference is usually observed in coherent waves, well-correlated waves that have very similar frequencies or even come from the same source.

Superposition of waves may result in either constructive or destructive interference. Constructive interference occurs when the crests of the two waves meet at the same point in time. Conversely, destructive interference occurs when the crest of one wave and the trough of the other meet at the same point in time. It follows, then, that constructive interference increases amplitude and destructive interference decreases it. We can also consider interference in terms of wave phase; waves that are out of phase with one another will interfere destructively while waves that are in phase with one another will interfere constructively. In the case of two simple sine waves with identical amplitudes, for instance, amplitude will double if the waves are exactly in phase and drop to zero if the waves are exactly 180° out of phase.

A **standing wave** typically results from the interference between two waves of the same frequency traveling in opposite directions. The result is a stationary vibration pattern. Standing waves are observed in stretched strings with both ends fixed or in tubes with one or both ends closed. One of the key characteristics of standing waves is that there are points in the medium where no movement occurs. The points are called nodes and the points where motion is maximal are called antinodes. This property allows for the analysis of various typical standing waves

View an animation of how interference can create a standing wave at the following URL:

http://www.glenbrook.k12.il.us/GBSSCI/PHYS/mmedia/waves/swf.html

All wavelengths in the EM spectrum can experience interference but it is easy to comprehend instances of interference in the spectrum of visible light. One classic example of this is **Thomas Young's double-slit experiment**. In this experiment a beam of light is shone through a paper with two slits and a striated wave pattern results on the screen. The light and dark bands correspond to the areas in which the light from the two slits has constructively (bright band) and destructively (dark band) interfered. Light from any source can be used to obtain interference patterns. For example, Newton's rings can be produced with sun light. However, in general, white light is less suited for producing clear interference patterns as it is a mix of a full spectrum of colors. Sodium light is close to monochromatic and is thus more suitable for producing interference patterns. The most suitable is laser light as it is almost perfectly monochromatic.

Problem: The interference maxima (location of bright spots created by constructive interference) for double-slit interference are given by

$$\frac{n\lambda}{d} = \frac{x}{D} = \sin\theta \quad n=1,2,3...$$

where $\lambda$ is the wavelength of the light, $d$ is the distance between the two slits, $D$ is the distance between the slits and the screen on which the pattern is observed and $x$ is the location of the nth maximum. If the two slits are 0.1mm apart, the screen is 5m away from the slits, and the first maximum beyond the center one is 2.0 cm from the center of the screen, what is the wavelength of the light?

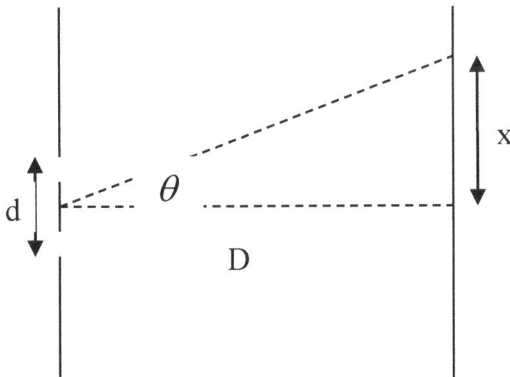

Solution: $\lambda = xd/(Dn) = 0.02 \times 0.0001/ (5 \times 1) = 400$ nanometers

**Thin-film interference** occurs when light waves reflecting off the top surface of a film interfere with the waves reflecting from the bottom surface. We see colors in soap bubbles or in oil films floating on water since the criteria for constructive or destructive interference depend on the wavelength of the light. Non-reflective coatings on materials make use of destructive thin-film interference.

**Diffraction** occurs when part of a wave front is obstructed. Diffraction and interference are essentially the same physical process. Diffraction refers to various phenomena associated with wave propagation such as the bending, spreading, and interference of waves emerging from an aperture. It occurs with any type of wave including sound waves, water waves, and electromagnetic waves such as light and radio waves.

Types of diffraction:

**1. Single-slit diffraction:** The simplest example of diffraction is single-slit diffraction in which the slit is narrow and a pattern of semi-circular ripples is formed after the wave passes through the slit.

**2. Double-slit diffraction:** These patterns are formed by the interference of light diffracting through two narrow slits.

**3. Diffraction grating:** Diffraction grating is a reflecting or transparent element whose optical properties are periodically modulated. In simple terms, diffraction gratings are fine parallel and equally spaced grooves or rulings on a material surface. When light is incident on a diffraction grating, light is reflected or transmitted in discrete directions, called diffraction orders. Because of their light dispersive properties, gratings are commonly used in monochromators and spectrophotometers. Gratings are usually designated by their groove density, expressed in grooves/millimeter. A fundamental property of gratings is that the angle of deviation of all but one of the diffracted beams depends on the wavelength of the incident light.

**4. Other forms of diffraction:**
**i) Particle diffraction:** It is the diffraction of particles such as electrons, which is used as a powerful argument for quantum theory. It is possible to observe the diffraction of particles such as neutrons or electrons and hence we are able to infer the existence of wave particle duality.

**ii) Bragg diffraction:** This is diffraction from a multiple slits, and is similar to what occurs when waves are scattered from a periodic structure such as atoms in a crystal or rulings on a diffraction grating. Bragg diffraction is used in X-ray crystallography to deduce the structure of a crystal from the angles at which the X-rays are diffracted from it.

**Dispersion** is the separation of a wave into its constituent wavelengths due to interaction with a material occurring in a wavelength-dependent manner (as in thin-film interference for instance). Dispersive prisms separate white light into these constituent colors by relying on the differences in refractive index that result from the varying frequencies of the light. Prisms rely on the fact that light changes speed as it moves from one medium to another. This then causes the light to be bent and/or reflected. The degree to which bending/reflection occurs is a function of the light's angle of incidence and the refractive indices of the media.

**Polarization** is a property of transverse waves that describes the plane perpendicular to the direction of travel in which the oscillation occurs. Note that longitudinal waves are not polarized because they can oscillate only in one direction, the direction of travel. In unpolarized light, the transverse oscillation occurs in all planes perpendicular to the direction of travel. Polarized light (created, for instance, by using polarizing filters that absorb light oscillating in other planes) oscillates in only a selected plane. An everyday example of polarization is found in polarized sunglasses which reduce glare.

Example: A polarizing filter with a horizontal axis will allow the portion of the light waves that are aligned horizontally to pass through the filter and will block the portion of the light waves that are aligned vertically. One-half of the light is being blocked or conversely, one-half of the light is being absorbed. The image being viewed is not distorted but dimmed.

Example: If two filters are used, one with a horizontal axis and one with a vertical axis, all light will be blocked.

The **Doppler effect** is the name given to the perceived change in frequency that occurs when the observer or source of a wave is moving. Specifically, the perceived frequency increases when a wave source and observer move toward each other and decreases when a source and observer move away from each other. Thus, the source and/or observer velocity must be factored in to the calculation of the perceived frequency. The mathematical statement of this effect is:

$$f' = f_0 \left( \frac{v \pm v_o}{v \pm v_s} \right)$$

where f'= observed frequency
$f_0$= emitted frequency
$v$= the speed of the waves in the medium
$v_s$= the velocity of the source (positive away from the observer)
$v_o$= the velocity of the observer (positive towards the source)

Note that any motion that changes the perceived frequency of a wave will cause the Doppler effect to occur. Thus, the wave source, the observer position, or the medium through which the wave travels could possess a velocity that would alter the observed frequency of a wave. You may view animations of stationary and moving wave sources at the following URL:

http://www.kettering.edu/~drussell/Demos/doppler/doppler.html

So, let's consider two examples involving sirens and analyze what happens when either the source or the observer moves. First, imagine a person standing on the side of a road and a police car driving by with its siren blaring. As the car approaches, the velocity of the car will mean sound waves will "hit" the observer as the car comes closer and so the pitch of the sound will be high. As it passes, the pitch will slide down and continue to lower as the car moves away from the observer. This is because the sound waves will "spread out" as the source recedes. Now consider a stationary siren on the top of fire station and a person driving by that station. The same Doppler effect will be observed: the person would hear a high frequency sound as he approached the siren and this frequency would lower as he passed and continued to drive away from the fire station.

The Doppler effect is observed with all types of electromagnetic radiation. For instance, the Doppler effect for light has been exploited by astronomers to measure the speed at which stars and galaxies are approaching. Another familiar application is the use of Doppler radar by police to detect the speed of on coming cars.

Problem: A sound source moves towards an observer at 8m/s while the observer moves towards the source at 9m/s. If the observer detects a sound of frequency 83kHz, what is the frequency of the sound emitted? The speed of sound in the medium is 343 m/s.

Solution: Using the Doppler equation, the emitted frequency $f$ is given by

$$83 = f \frac{343+9}{343-8}; \Rightarrow f = 79\,kHz$$

TEACHER CERTIFICATION STUDY GUIDE

## SUBAREA V. ELECTROMAGNETISM

## COMPETENCY 5.1 ELECTROMAGNETISM

### Skill 5.1a Describe and provide examples of electrostatic and magnetostatic phenomena

Electrostatics and magnetostatics involve the study of problems that include only stationary electric charges and currents (or magnetic dipoles). Electrostatic and magnetostatic phenomena are governed by Maxwell's equations for the case where all time derivatives are equal to zero:

$$\nabla \times \mathbf{E}(\mathbf{r},t) = \frac{\partial \mathbf{B}(\mathbf{r},t)}{\partial t} = \frac{\partial \mathbf{D}(\mathbf{r},t)}{\partial t} = 0 \qquad \nabla \times \mathbf{H}(\mathbf{r},t) = \mathbf{J}(\mathbf{r},t)$$

$$\nabla \cdot \mathbf{D}(\mathbf{r},t) = \rho(\mathbf{r},t) \qquad \nabla \cdot \mathbf{B}(\mathbf{r},t) = 0$$

In the static case, the magnetic field (**H**) and electric field (**E**) are no longer coupled; the electric field (and corresponding electric flux density, **D**, defined as ε**E**) is dependent solely on the charge density, ρ, and the magnetic field (and corresponding magnetic flux density, **B**, defined as μ**H**) is dependent solely on the current density, **J**.

Although most matter is electrically neutral on a macroscopic scale, the effects of electrostatic phenomena still can be witnessed in common, everyday experiences. Perhaps the most common example is so-called static electricity, which results from a buildup of charge on two separate objects or different regions of the same object. This excess charge, and corresponding electric potential, will repel objects with an excess charge of the same type (i.e., both positive or both negative) and attract objects of dissimilar type (i.e., positive and negative or vice versa). Thus, for example, a glass rod rubbed with a piece of silk acquires a net positive charge due to a loss of some of its negatively charged electrons. A plastic rod rubbed with wool acquires a net negative charge due to a deposit of excess electrons from the wool. These two rods, since they are of opposite charge, will attract one another.

Lightning, while not an electrostatic phenomenon, strictly speaking, results from a similar situation where an imbalance of positive and negative charge is built up in different regions of the earth or sky. This charge imbalance creates an electric potential that can be discharged as lightning.

PHYSICS

Common magnetostatic phenomena include the interaction of a compass with the Earth's magnetic field. As a result of geological factors that are not entirely understood, the Earth acts like a giant bar magnet with a north and south pole (although these are reversed from and slightly out of alignment with the geographic north and south). On a smaller scale, certain metals such as iron and some iron alloys can have or can acquire a magnetic field. The compass, itself a magnet, tends to align with the prevailing magnetic field (usually Earth's magnetic field).

Metallic magnets, for example, can be modeled using quantum mechanics, which explains the magnetic field as the result of numerous tiny current loops (or magnetic dipoles) at the atomic level. For magnetized materials, these microscopic dipoles have a net alignment in a particular direction, which determines the north and south poles of the magnet. If another magnetizable metal is brought into the magnetic field, the magnetic dipoles of the non-magnetized metal acquire a net alignment in the direction that results in an attractive force.

In addition to magnetic phenomena that result from microscopic or quantum mechanical sources, magnetic fields are also produced by currents. A current-carrying wire, for example, will deflect a compass. When formed into a loop with any number of turns, the wire then forms an electromagnet with the north and south pole being either above or below the surface of the loop. The electromagnet acts almost exactly like a bar magnet.

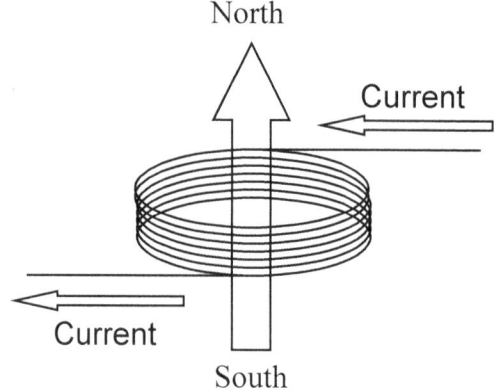

**Skill 5.1b    Predict charges or poles based on attraction/repulsion observations**

One of the most basic principles of physics is the force acting between two charged objects. This force is viewed as an exchange of photons, little particle-like ripples in an electromagnetic field. An electron is surrounded by an electric field which can be "felt" by other charged particles. One way to visualize it is that a photon leaves the electron and later bumps into or is absorbed by another charge. This intercepting charge may be the same as the charge of the electron, or the opposite charge. If the charge is the same it is repelled. If the charge is the opposite, it is attracted.

Benjamin Franklin is generally credited with giving these charges their conventional labels of positive and negative. When charged objects are combined they will attract or repel each other based on the difference or similarity of their charge. The total force of attraction or repulsion can be related mathematically based on the extent of the charge and the distance between the particles. Likewise, an object with no attraction or repulsion is said to have no charge, or to be electrically neutral.

Magnetized objects can attract and repel just like charged objects. In fact, it is the alignment of charged molecules within the magnet that give it its properties. This alignment causes every magnetized object to have a positive and negative pole. In the same way as charge particles, positive magnetic poles will repel other positive poles and attract negative magnetic poles. Negative magnetic poles repel other negative poles and are attracted to positive poles. It is not possible to create a monopole magnet. Every magnet must have a positive and negative pole. Even if a magnet is cut in half, each half of the magnet will now have two poles of its own. This is an important difference between magnetism and electricity where it is possible to have separate positive and negative charges.

By observing the attractions and repulsions of an unknown magnet with a magnet of known poles, the unknown magnet can have its poles labeled. The strength of the magnet will affect the magnitude of the force of attraction or repulsion.

**Skill 5.1c   Build a simple compass and use it to determine direction of magnetic fields, including the Earth's magnetic field**

A magnetic compass is a very simple device that consists of a magnetized needle that is allowed to turn. In fact, you can create a simple compass yourself with the following materials:

- A needle, straightened paperclip, or another piece of thin wire-like steel
- A dish to hold water such as a pie plate or petri dish with about an inch of water in it
- A small disk of buoyant material such as a cork, bottom of a Styrofoam cup, or plastic cap of a milk jug
- A magnet

The first step in creating a compass is to magnetize the needle. The easiest way to do this is with another magnet. Stroke the magnet along the needle about 20 times. Be careful to always stroke the magnet along the needle in the same direction, not back and forth along the needle.

Place the cork "float" in the middle of the dish of water. This "float" creates a nearly frictionless bearing on which the needle can turn. Center the magnetic needle on the float. It should very slowly point towards the north.

A compass like this is useful at detecting small magnetic fields, and the magnetic field of the earth. You can think of the Earth as having a giant bar magnet buried in its center from north to south. This causes the Earth to have a weak magnetic field at its surface, since the surface is so far from the magnetic center of the Earth. The weak magnetic field is the reason the compass needs to have a frictionless bearing and a lightweight needle magnet. Otherwise the force from the magnetic field would not be strong enough to turn the needle.

Of course, the Earth does not really have a bar magnet buried in its center. What it does have is a ferrous core of molten iron. Scientists think that the rotation of the Earth combined with heat convection causes the molten iron to rotate. It is believed that these rotational forces in the liquid iron lead to a weak magnetic field around the axis of spin.

The compass can detect magnetic fields from other sources as well. By placing a magnet, or several magnets around your compass, the needle will turn to point in the direction of the magnetic field lines. The north pole of your compass needle will always point in the direction of the south pole field line of the magnet you place in the vicinity. The south pole of your compass needle will always point in the direction of the field lines from the north pole of the bar magnet. It may help to use a permanent marker to label the poles of your compass needle.

By moving the compass or the magnets around on the surface of the table you can see how the magnetic field lines vary in space. You can further visualize the magnetic field lines by placing a piece of paper under the compass and magnets and drawing arrows as you move the compass around amongst the magnets. You can check your diagram by sprinkling iron filing around your magnets. The iron filings should align in the same direction as the arrows you have drawn using your magnet.

# TEACHER CERTIFICATION STUDY GUIDE

**Skill 5.1d  Analyze electric and magnetic forces, charges, and fields using Coulomb's law, the Lorentz force, and the right-hand rule**

Any point charge may experience force resulting from attraction to or repulsion from another charged object. The easiest way to begin analyzing this phenomenon and calculating this force is by considering two point charges. Let us say that the charge on the first point is $Q_1$, the charge on the second point is $Q_2$, and the distance between them is $r$. Their interaction is governed by **Coulomb's Law** which gives the formula for the force F as:

$$F = k\frac{Q_1 Q_2}{r^2}$$

where $k = 9.0 \times 10^9 \, \frac{N \cdot m^2}{C^2}$ (known as Coulomb's constant)

The charge is a scalar quantity, however, the force has direction. For two point charges, the direction of the force is along a line joining the two charges. Note that the force will be repulsive if the two charges are both positive or both negative and attractive if one charge is positive and the other negative. Thus, a negative force indicates an attractive force.

When more than one point charge is exerting force on a point charge, we simply apply Coulomb's Law multiple times and then combine the forces as we would in any statics problem. Let's examine the process in the following example problem.

Problem: Three point charges are located at the vertices of a right triangle as shown below. Charges, angles, and distances are provided (drawing not to scale). Find the force exerted on the point charge A.

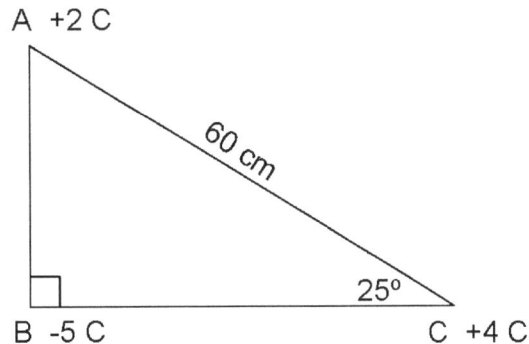

Solution: First we find the individual forces exerted on A by point B and point C. We have the information we need to find the magnitude of the force exerted on A by C.

$$F_{AC} = k\frac{Q_1 Q_2}{r^2} = 9 \times 10^9 \, \frac{N \cdot m^2}{C^2} \left(\frac{4C \times 2C}{(0.6m)^2}\right) = 2 \times 10^{11} N$$

PHYSICS 75

To determine the magnitude of the force exerted on A by B, we must first determine the distance between them.

$$\sin 25° = \frac{r_{AB}}{60cm}$$

$$r_{AB} = 60cm \times \sin 25° = 25cm$$

Now we can determine the force.

$$F_{AB} = k\frac{Q_1 Q_2}{r^2} = 9 \times 10^9 \frac{N \cdot m^2}{C^2}\left(\frac{-5C \times 2C}{(0.25m)^2}\right) = -1.4 \times 10^{12} N$$

We can see that there is an attraction in the direction of B (negative force) and repulsion in the direction of C (positive force). To find the net force, we must consider the direction of these forces (along the line connecting any two point charges). We add them together using the law of cosines.

$$F_A^2 = F_{AB}^2 + F_{AC}^2 - 2F_{AB}F_{AC}\cos 75°$$

$$F_A^2 = (-1.4 \times 10^{12} N)^2 + (2 \times 10^{11} N)^2 - 2(-1.4 \times 10^{12} N)(2 \times 10^{11} N)^2 \cos 75°$$

$$F_A = 1.5 \times 10^{12} N$$

This gives us the magnitude of the net force, now we will find its direction using the law of sines.

$$\frac{\sin \theta}{F_{AC}} = \frac{\sin 75°}{F_A}$$

$$\sin \theta = F_{AC}\frac{\sin 75°}{F_A} = 2 \times 10^{11} N \frac{\sin 75°}{1.5 \times 10^{12} N}$$

$$\theta = 7.3°$$

Thus, the net force on A is 7.3° west of south and has magnitude 1.5 × 10¹²N. Looking back at our diagram, this makes sense, because A should be attracted to B (pulled straight south) but the repulsion away from C "pushes" this force in a westward direction.

An **electric field** exists in the space surrounding a charge. Electric fields have both direction and magnitude determined by the strength and direction in which they exhibit force on a test charge. The units used to measure electric fields are newtons per coulomb (N/C). **Electric potential** is simply the **potential energy** per unit of charge. Given this definition, it is clear that electric potential must be measured in joules per coulomb and this unit is known as a volt (J/C=V).

Within an electric field there are typically differences in potential energy. This **potential difference** may be referred to as **voltage**. The difference in electrical potential between two points is the amount of work needed to move a unit charge from the first point to the second point. Stated mathematically, this is:

$$V = \frac{W}{Q}$$

where V= the potential difference
W= the work done to move the charge
Q= the charge

We know from mechanics, however, that work is simply force applied over a certain distance. We can combine this with Coulomb's law to find the work done between two charges distance r apart.

$$W = F.r = k\frac{Q_1 Q_2}{r^2}.r = k\frac{Q_1 Q_2}{r}$$

Now we can simply substitute this back into the equation above for electric potential:

$$V_2 = \frac{W}{Q_2} = \frac{k\frac{Q_1 Q_2}{r}}{Q_2} = k\frac{Q_1}{r}$$

Let's examine a sample problem involving electrical potential.

Problem: What is the electric potential at point A due to the 2 shown charges? If a charge of +2.0 C were infinitely far away, how much work would be required to bring it to point A?

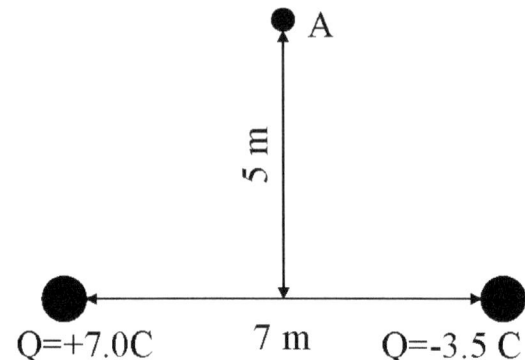

Solution: To determine the electric potential at point A, we simple find and add the potential from the two charges (this is the principle of superposition). From the diagram, we can assume that A is equidistant from each charge. Using the Pythagorean theorem, we determine this distance to be 6.1 m.

$$V = \frac{kq}{r} = k\left(\frac{7.0C}{6.1m} + \frac{-3.5C}{6.1m}\right) = 9 \times 10^9 \frac{N.m^2}{C^2}\left(0.57\frac{C}{m}\right) = 5.13 \times 10^9 V$$

Now, let's consider bringing the charged particle to point A. We assume that electric potential of these particle is initially zero because it is infinitely far away. Since now know the potential at point A, we can calculate the work necessary to bring the particle from V=0, i.e. the potential energy of the charge in the electrical field:

$$W = VQ = (5.13 \times 10^9) \times 2J = 10.26 \times 10^9 J$$

The large results for potential and work make it apparent how large the unit coulomb is. For this reason, most problems deal in microcoulombs (μC).

The magnetic force exerted on a charge moving in a magnetic field depends on the size and velocity of the charge as well as the magnitude of the magnetic field. One important fact to remember is that only the velocity of the charge in a direction perpendicular to the magnetic field will affect the force exerted. Therefore, a charge moving parallel to the magnetic field will have no force acting upon it whereas a charge will feel the greatest force when moving perpendicular to the magnetic field.

The direction of the magnetic force, or the magnetic component of the **Lorentz force** (force on a charged particle in an electrical and magnetic field), is always at a right angle to the plane formed by the velocity vector v and the magnetic field B and is given by applying the right hand rule - if the fingers of the right hand are curled in a way that seems to rotate the v vector into the B vector, the thumb points in the direction of the force. The magnitude of the force is equal to the cross product of the velocity of the charge with the magnetic field multiplied by the magnitude of the charge.

$$F=q (\mathbf{v} \times \mathbf{B}) \quad or \quad F=q v B\sin(\theta)$$

*Where θ is the angle formed between the vectors of velocity of the charge and direction of magnetic field.*

The **force on a current-carrying conductor** in a magnetic field is the sum of the forces on the moving charged particles that create the current. For a current $I$ flowing in a straight wire segment of length $l$ in a magnetic field $B$, this force is given by

$$\mathbf{F} = I\mathbf{l} \times \mathbf{B}$$

where $\mathbf{l}$ is a vector of magnitude $l$ and direction in the direction of the current.

When a current-carrying loop is placed in a magnetic field, the net force on it is zero since the forces on the different parts of the loop act in different directions and cancel each other out. There is, however, a net torque on the loop that tends to rotate it so that the area of the loop is perpendicular to the magnetic field. For a current I flowing in a loop of area A, this torque is given by

$$\tau = IA\hat{n} \times \mathbf{B}$$

where $\hat{n}$ is the unit vector perpendicular to the plane of the loop.

**Skill 5.1e    Relate electric currents to magnetic fields and describe the application of these relationships, such as in electromagnets, electric current generators, motors, and transformers**

Conductors through which electrical currents travel will produce magnetic fields: The magnetic field $dB$ induced at a distance $r$ by an element of current $Idl$ flowing through a wire element of length $dl$ is given by the **Biot-Savart** law

$$dB = \frac{\mu_0}{4\pi} \frac{Idl \times \hat{r}}{r^2}$$

where $\mu_0$ is a constant known as the permeability of free space and $\hat{r}$ is the unit vector pointing from the current element to the point where the magnetic field is calculated.

An alternate statement of this law is **Ampere's law** according to which the line integral of $B.dl$ around any closed path enclosing a steady current $I$ is given by

$$\oint_C B \cdot dl = \mu_0 I$$

The basis of this phenomenon is the same no matter what the shape of the conductor, but we will consider three common situations:

### Straight Wire
Around a current-carrying straight wire, the magnetic field lines form concentric circles around the wire. The direction of the magnetic field is given by the right-hand rule: When the thumb of the right hand points in the direction of the current, the fingers curl around the wire in the direction of the magnetic field. Note the direction of the current and magnetic field in the diagram.

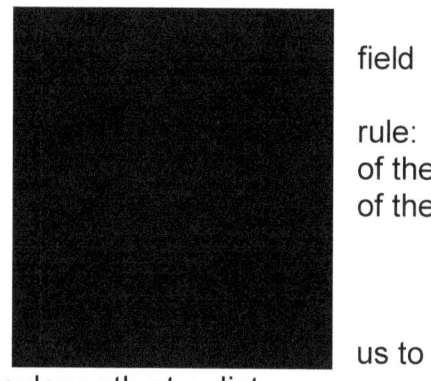

To find the magnetic field of an infinitely long (allowing us to disregarding end effects) we apply Ampere's Law to a circular path at a distance r around the wire:

$$B = \frac{\mu_0 I}{2\pi r}$$

where $\mu_0$=the permeability of free space ($4\pi \times 10^{-7}$ T·m/A)
I=current
r=distance from the wire

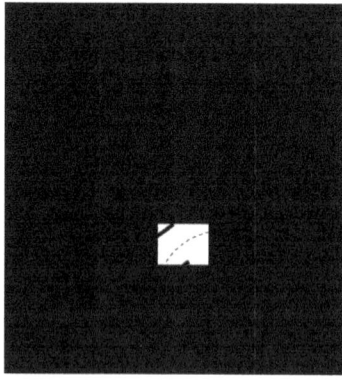

### Loops
Like the straight wire from which it's been made, a looped wire has magnetic field lines that form concentric circles with direction following the right-hand rule. However, the field are additive in the center of the loop creating a field like the one shown. The magnetic field of a loop is found similarly to that for a straight wire.

In the center of the loop, the magnetic field is:

$$B = \frac{\mu_0 I}{2r}$$

## Solenoids

A solenoid is essentially a coil of conduction wire around a central object. This means it is a series of the magnetic field is similarly a sum of the fields that form around several loops, as shown.

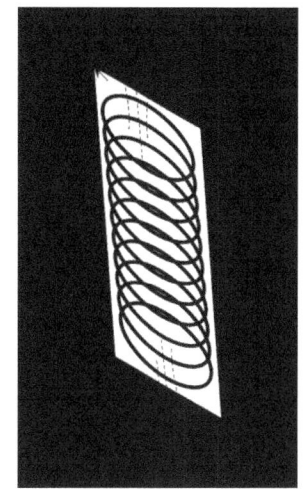

wrapped loops and would

The magnetic field of a solenoid can be found as with the following equation:

$$B = \mu_0 n I$$

In this equation, n is turn density, which is simply the number of turns divided by the length of the solenoid.

## Displacement current

While Ampere's law works perfectly for a steady current, for a situation where the current varies and a charge builds up (e.g. charging of a capacitor) it does not hold. Maxwell amended Ampere's law to include an additional term that includes the displacement current. This is not a true current but actually refers to changes in the electric field and is given by

$$I_d = \varepsilon_0 \frac{d\varphi_e}{dt}$$

where $\varphi_e$ is the flux of the electric field.

Including the displacement current, Ampere's law is given by

$$\oint \mathbf{B} \cdot d\mathbf{l} = \mu_0 I + \mu_0 \varepsilon_0 \frac{d\varphi_e}{dt}$$

The displacement current essentially indicates that changing electric flux produces a magnetic field.

When the magnetic flux through a coil is changed, a voltage is produced which is known as induced electromagnetic force. Magnetic flux is a term used to describe the number of magnetic fields lines that pass through an area and is described by the equation:

$$\Phi = B A \cos\theta$$

*Where $\Phi$ is the angle between the magnetic field B, and the normal to the plane of the coil of area A*

By changing any of these three inputs, magnetic field, area of coil, or angle between field and coil, the flux will change and an EMF can be induced. The speed at which these changes occur also affects the magnitude of the EMF, as a more rapid transition generates more EMF than a gradual one. This is described by **Faraday's law** of induction:

$$\varepsilon = -N \, \Delta \Phi / \Delta t$$

*where $\varepsilon$ is emf induced, N is the number of loops in a coil, t is time, and $\Phi$ is magnetic flux*

The negative sign signifies **Lenz's law** which states that induced emf in a coil acts to oppose any change in magnetic flux. Thus the current flows in a way that creates a magnetic field in the direction opposing the change in flux. The right hand rule for this is that if your fingers curl in the direction of the induced current, your thumb points in the direction of the magnetic field it produces through the loop. For a detailed discussion of Lenz's law see **Skill 5.1i**.

## Transformers

Electromagnetic induction is used in a transformer, a device that magnetically couples two circuits together to allow the transfer of energy between the two circuits without requiring motion. Typically, a transformer consists of a couple of coils and a magnetic core. A changing voltage applied to one coil (the primary) creates a flux in the magnetic core, which induces voltage in the other coil (the secondary). All transformers operate on this simple principle though they range in size and function from those in tiny microphones to those that connect the components of the US power grid.

One of the most important functions of transformers is that they allow us to "step-up" and "step-down" between vastly different voltages. To determine how the voltage is changed by a transformer, we employ any of the following relationships:

$$\frac{V_s}{V_p} = \frac{n_s}{n_p} = \frac{I_p}{I_s}$$

where $V_s$=secondary voltage
$V_p$=primary voltage
$n_s$=number of turns on secondary coil
$n_p$=number of turns on primary coil
$I_p$=primary current
$I_s$=secondary current

Problem: If a step-up transformer has 500 turns on its primary coil and 800 turns on its secondary coil, what will be the output (secondary) voltage be if the primary coil is supplied with 120 V?

Solution:

$$\frac{V_s}{V_p} = \frac{n_s}{n_p}$$

$$V_s = \frac{n_s}{n_p} \times V_p = \frac{800}{500} \times 120V = 192V$$

## Motors

Electric motors are found in many common appliances such as fans and washing machines. The operation of a motor is based on the principle that a magnetic field exerts a force on a current carrying conductor. This force is essentially due to the fact that the current carrying conductor itself generates a magnetic field; the basic principle that governs the behavior of an electromagnet. In a motor, this idea is used to convert **electrical energy into mechanical energy**, most commonly rotational energy. Thus the components of the simplest motors must include a strong magnet and a current-carrying coil placed in the magnetic field in such a way that the force on it causes it to rotate.

Motors may be run using DC or AC current and may be designed in a number of ways with varying levels of complexity. A very basic DC motor consists of the following components:
- A **field magnet**
- An **armature** with a coil around it that rotates between the poles of the field magnet
- A **power supply** that supplies current to the armature
- An **axle** that transfers the rotational energy of the armature to the working parts of the motor
- A set of **commutators** and **brushes** that reverse the direction of power flow every half rotation so that the armature continues to rotate

## Generators

Generators are devices that are the opposite of motors in that they convert **mechanical energy into electrical energy**. The mechanical energy can come from a variety of sources; combustion engines, blowing wind, falling water, or even a hand crank or bicycle wheel. Most generators rely upon electromagnetic induction to create an electrical current. These generators basically consist of magnets and a coil. The magnets create a magnetic field and the coil is located within this field. Mechanical energy, from whatever source, is used to spin the coil within this field. As stated by Faraday's Law, this produces a voltage.

# TEACHER CERTIFICATION STUDY GUIDE

**Skill 5.1f    Solve problems involving the relationships between electric and magnetic phenomena**

Problem: A long straight wire of radius R = 2mm carries a steady current of 30A. What is the magnetic field at the surface of the wire?

Solution: From the previous section (**Skill 5.1e**) we know that outside a current-carrying wire the magnetic field is given by

$$B = \frac{\mu_0 I}{2\pi r}$$

where
$\mu_0$=the permeability of free space ($4\pi \times 10^{-7}$ T·m/A)
I=current
r=distance from the wire

Thus the magnetic field at the surface of the wire =

$$\frac{(4\pi \times 10^{-7} T.m/A)(30A)}{(2\pi)(2 \times 10^{-3} m)} = 3 \times 10^{-3} T$$

Problem: Consider a coil lying flat on the page with a square cross section that is 10 cm by 5 cm. The coil consists of 10 loops and has a magnetic field of 0.5 T passing through it coming out of the page. Find the induced EMF when the magnetic field is changed to 0.8 T in 2 seconds.

Solution: First, let's find the initial magnetic flux $\Phi_i$.

$\Phi_i$= BA cos θ= (.5 T) (.05 m) (.1m) cos 0°= 0.0025 T m²

The final magnetic flux: $\Phi_f$ = BA cos θ= (0.8 T) (.05 m) (.1m) cos 0°= 0.004 T m²

The induced emf is calculated then by Faraday's law

ε =-N ΔΦ / Δt = - 10 (.004 T m² -.0025 T m²) / 2 s = -0.0075 volts.

To determine the direction the current flows in the coil we need to apply the right hand rule and Lenz's law. The magnetic flux is being increased out of the page, with your thumb pointing up the fingers are coiling counterclockwise. However, Lenz's law tells us the current will oppose the change in flux so the current in the coil will be flowing clockwise.

**PHYSICS**

Problem: Emf is induced in a generator by spinning a coil within a magnetic field. The emf induced in a rectangular loop of dimensions a and b with N turns rotating at frequency f in a uniform magnetic field B is given by

$$\varepsilon = 2\pi f NabB\sin(2\pi ft) = \varepsilon_0 \sin(2\pi ft).$$

Design a loop that will create an emf with $\varepsilon_0 = 150V$ when rotated at 60 rev/s in a magnetic field of 0.5T.

Solution: Using the specified equation, $150 = 2\pi \times 60 \times Nab \times 0.5$.
Therefore, we must have a loop with dimensions and number of turns such that

$$Nab = \frac{5}{2\pi} m^2.$$

Problem: Assuming we have a particle of 1 x 10$^{-6}$ kg that has a charge of -8 coulombs that is moving perpendicular to a magnetic field in a clockwise direction on a circular path with a radius of 2 m and a speed of 2000 m/s, let's determine the magnitude and direction of the magnetic field acting upon it.

Solution: We know the mass, charge, speed, and path radius of the charged particle. From **Skill 5.1d** we know that the Lorentz force on the charged particle is given by F=q v Bsin (θ) = qvB in this case since $\theta = 90^0$.

Combining the equation above with the equation for centripetal force we get

$$qvB = \frac{mv^2}{r} \quad \text{or} \quad B = \frac{mv}{qr}$$

Thus B= (1 x 10$^{-6}$ kg) (2000m/s) / (-8 C)(2 m) = 1.25 x 10$^{-4}$ Tesla

Since the particle is moving in a clockwise direction, we use the **right hand rule** and point our fingers clockwise along a circular path in the plane of the paper while pointing the thumb towards the center in the direction of the centripetal force. This requires the fingers to curl in a way that indicates that the magnetic field is pointing out of the page. However, since the particle has a negative charge we must reverse the final direction of the magnetic field into the page.

A **mass spectrometer** measures the mass to charge ratio of ions using a setup similar to the one described above. m/q is determined by measuring the path radius of particles of known velocity moving in a known magnetic field.

A **cyclotron**, a type of particle accelerator, also uses a perpendicular magnetic field to keep particles on a circular path. After each half circle, the particles are accelerated by an electric field and the path radius is increased. Thus the beam of particles moves faster and faster in a growing spiral within the confines of the cyclotron until they exit at a high speed near the outer edge. Its compactness is one of the advantages a cyclotron has over linear accelerators.

### Skill 5.1g  Define and calculate power, voltage differences, current, and resistance in simple circuits

Ohm's Law is the most important tool we posses to analyze electrical circuits. Ohm's Law states that the current passing through a conductor is directly proportional to the voltage drop and inversely proportional to the resistance of the conductor. Stated mathematically, this is:

$$V = IR$$

Problem:
The circuit diagram at right shows three resistors connected to a battery in series. A current of 1.0A flows through the circuit in the direction shown. It is known that the equivalent resistance of this circuit is 25 Ω. What is the total voltage supplied by the battery?

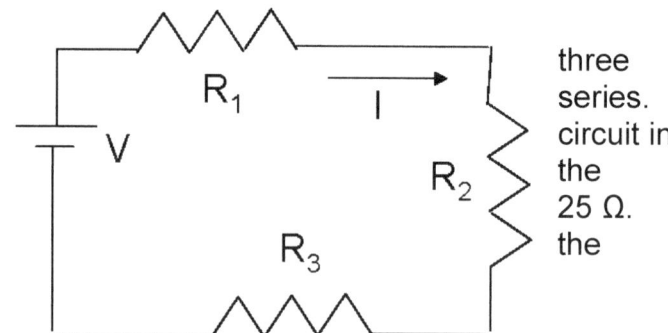

Solution:

To determine the battery's voltage, we simply apply Ohm's Law:

$$V = IR = 1.0A \times 25\Omega = 25V$$

Electrical power is a measure of energy used or available per unit time, i.e. how much work can be done by an electrical current in unit time. For descriptions of electrical potential energy, energy stored in a capacitor and electric field energy density see sections II.2 and II.4.

Electrical power has units of watts (W), i.e. Joules/second. To determine electrical power, we simply use **Joule's law**:

$$P = IV$$

where P=power
I=current
V=voltage

If we combine this with **Ohm's law** (V=IR), we generate two new equations that are useful for finding the amount of power dissipated by a resistor:

$$P = I^2 R$$

$$P = \frac{V^2}{R}$$

Problem: How much power is dissipated by a 1 kΩ resistor with a 50V voltage drop through it?

Solution: $P = \dfrac{V^2}{R} = \dfrac{(50V)^2}{1000\Omega} = 2.5W$

Alternating current (AC) is a type of electrical current with cyclically varying magnitude and direction. This is differentiated from direct current (DC), which has constant direction. AC is the type of current delivered to businesses and residences.

Though other waveforms are sometimes used, the vast majority of AC current is sinusoidal. Thus we can use wave terminology to help us describe AC current. Since AC current is a function of time, we can express it mathematically as:

$$v(t) = V_{peak} \cdot \sin(\omega t)$$

where $V_{peak}$= the peak voltage; the maximum value of the voltage

ω=angular frequency; a measure of rotation rate

t=time

The instantaneous power or energy transmission per unit time is given by $I^2_{peak} R \sin^2(\omega t)$, a value that varies over time. In order to asses the overall rate of energy transmission, however, we need some kind of average value. The **root mean square value (V**$_{rms}$**, I**$_{rms}$**)** is a specific type of average given by the following formulae:

$$V_{rms} = \frac{V_{peak}}{\sqrt{2}} \quad ; \quad I_{rms} = \frac{I_{peak}}{\sqrt{2}} \quad ; \quad I_{rms} = \frac{V_{rms}}{R}$$

V$_{rms}$ is useful because an AC current will deliver the same power as a DC current if its V$_{rms}$=V$_{DC}$, i.e. average power or average energy transmission per unit time is given by $P_{av} = V_{rms} I_{rms}$.

### Skill 5.1h  Design and interpret simple series and parallel circuits

Kirchoff's Laws are a pair of laws that apply to conservation of charge and energy in circuits and were developed by Gustav Kirchoff.

**Kirchoff's Current Law**: At any point in a circuit where charge density is constant, the sum of currents flowing toward the point must be equal to the sum of currents flowing away from that point.

**Kirchoff's Voltage Law**: The sum of the electrical potential differences around a circuit must be zero.

While these statements may seem simple, they can be very useful in analyzing DC circuits, those involving constant circuit voltages and currents.

Problem:
The circuit diagram at right shows three resistors connected to a battery in series. A current of 1.0 A is generated by the battery. The potential drop across R₁, R₂, and R₃ are 5V, 6V, and 10V. What is the total voltage supplied by the battery?

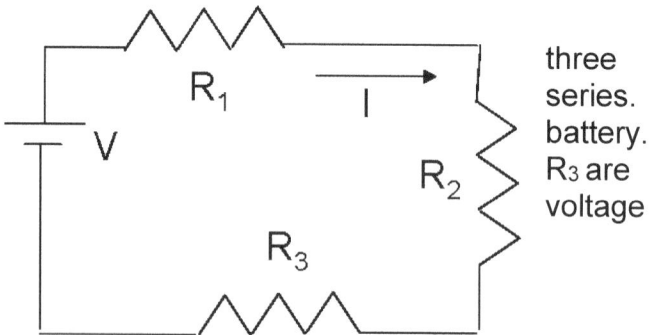

Solution:
Kirchoff's Voltage Law tells us that the total voltage supplied by the battery must be equal to the total voltage drop across the circuit. Therefore:

$$V_{battery} = V_{R_1} + V_{R_2} + V_{R_3} = 5V + 6V + 10V = 21V$$

Problem:
The circuit diagram at right shows three resistors wired in parallel with a 12V battery. The resistances of $R_1$, $R_2$, and $R_3$ are 4 Ω, 5 Ω, and 6 Ω, respectively. What is the total current?

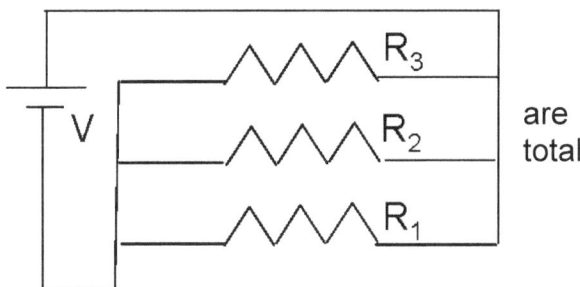

Solution:
This is a more complicated problem. Because the resistors are wired in parallel, we know that the voltage entering each resistor must be the same and equal to that supplied by the battery. We can combine this knowledge with **Ohm's Law** to determine the current across each resistor:

$$I_1 = \frac{V_1}{R_1} = \frac{12V}{4\Omega} = 3A$$

$$I_2 = \frac{V_2}{R_2} = \frac{12V}{5\Omega} = 2.4A$$

$$I_3 = \frac{V_3}{R_3} = \frac{12V}{6\Omega} = 2A$$

Finally, we use Kirchoff's Current Law to find the total current:

$$I = I_1 + I_2 + I_3 = 3A + 2.4A + 2A = 7.4A$$

Resistors and capacitors are often used together in series or parallel. Two components are in series if one end of the first element is connected to one end of the second component. The components are in parallel if both ends of one element are connected to the corresponding ends of another. A series circuit has a single path for current flow through all of its elements. A parallel circuit is one that requires more than one path for current flow in order to reach all of the circuit elements.

Below is a diagram demonstrating a simple circuit with resistors in parallel (on right) and in series (on left). Note the symbols used for a battery (noted V) and the resistors (noted R).

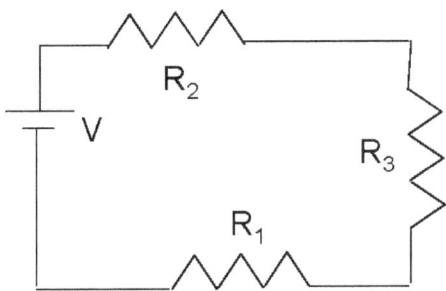 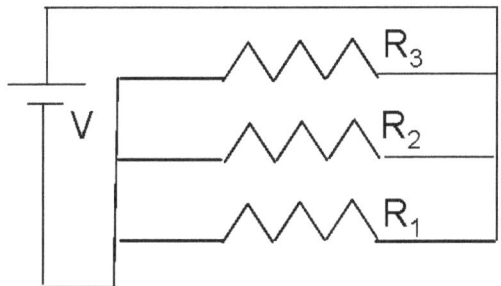

PHYSICS

Thus, when the resistors are placed in series, the current through each one will be the same. When they are placed in parallel, the voltage through each one will be the same. To understand basic circuitry, it is important to master the rules by which the equivalent resistance ($R_{eq}$) or capacitance ($C_{eq}$) can be calculated from a number of resistors or capacitors:

Resistors in parallel: $$\frac{1}{R_{eq}} = \frac{1}{R_1} + \frac{1}{R_2} + \cdots + \frac{1}{R_n}$$

Resistors in series: $$R_{eq} = R_1 + R_2 + \cdots + R_n$$

Capacitors in parallel: $$C_{eq} = C_1 + C_2 + \cdots + C_n$$

Capacitors in series: $$\frac{1}{C_{eq}} = \frac{1}{C_1} + \frac{1}{C_2} + \cdots + \frac{1}{C_n}$$

In the example problems above, we have assumed that the voltage across the terminals of a battery is equal to its emf. In reality, the terminal voltage decreases slightly as the current increases. This decrease is due to the **internal resistance** $r$ of the battery. One way to think of the internal resistance is as a small resistor in series with an ideal battery. Thus, terminal voltage drop is given by $V = \varepsilon - Ir$ where $\varepsilon$ is the emf of the battery, $r$ is the internal resistance and $I$ is the current flowing through the circuit.

**Skill 5.1i   Apply energy principles to analyze problems in electricity, magnetism, and circuit theory involving capacitors, resistors, and inductors**

**Conservation of energy in electromagnetic induction**

Heinrich Lenz was a German physicist who investigated how electromagnetic induction induces electromotive force(emf) and current. His law states: The emf induced in an electric circuit always acts in such a direction that the current it drives around the circuit opposes the change in magnetic flux which produces the emf.

Though it may not be entirely obvious initially, Lenz's law is a consequence of the conservation of energy. We can understand this by considering the physical scenario in which a permanent magnet (grey in diagram) moves through a loop of wire in the direction shown. An electric current will be induced in the wire and its direction will depend on which pole of the magnet enters the loop first. According to Lenz's law, the current will flow in the direction shown in this diagram. The direction of the current shown would be reversed if the magnet were turned so that the south pole entered first or if the magnet traveled in the direction opposite that shown by the arrow. The current is a result of the electrons in the wire being exposed to the magnetic field. As the magnet moves through the loop, an emf is induced. At the same time, however, the current in the loop produces its own magnetic field. This magnetic field will have the same direction as the permanent magnet shown in grey (i.e., directed to the right of the page).

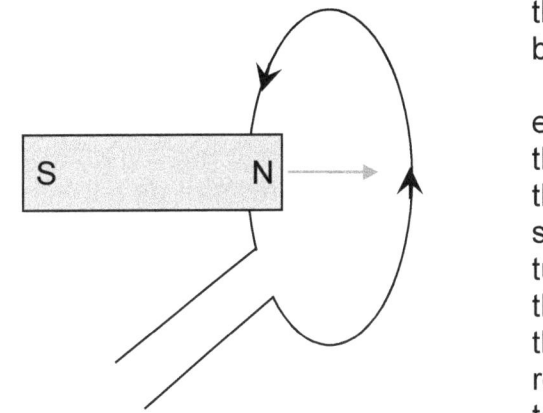

Now, suppose that Lenz's law did not hold and, instead, the magnet in the situation above induced a current in the direction opposite from that shown. That induced current would then induce a magnetic field directed toward the left of the page. This would, in turn, produce an attractive force between the permanent magnetic and the induced magnetic field. A feedback loop would emerge.

The permanent magnet would be drawn into the loop more quickly, a greater current induced, a stronger field generated, and the magnet drawn even more quickly into the loop. This would have an effect of increasing the kinetic energy of the magnet while also increasing the rate of energy dissipation of the loop. In short, energy would be created. Since this violation of the law of energy conservation cannot be correct, Lenz's law is supported.

### Conservation of energy in circuits

Within circuits, of course, energy must also be conserved. The potential energy per unit charge in an electric field is known as electrical potential. The difference of electrical potential between two points in a circuit is known as voltage. Thus, saying that voltage is conserved within a circuit is equivalent to saying that energy is conserved. This principle of conservation was stated by the German physicist Gustav Kirchhoff. It is now known as Kirchhoff's second law or Kirchhoff's voltage law: The sum of the electrical potential differences around a circuit must be zero.

Additionally, conservation of energy holds for all circuitry elements such as capacitors, resistors, or inductors. However, it is important to note that while *total* energy is conserved, *electrical* energy is not.

Resistors
Electrical potential energy (expressed as voltage) enters the resistor. The voltage drop that occurs across a resistor is actually a result of the conversion of electrical energy to thermal energy. So, electrical energy entering the resistor must equal the electrical energy exiting the resistor plus the thermal energy released. The total thermal energy W released by the resistor is the integral of the dissipated power P over time. Combining this with the equation for power dissipated by a resistor (**Skill 5.1g**):

$$W = \int_{t_0}^{t} P(t)dt = \int_{t_0}^{t} V(t)I(t)dt$$

In practice, resistors have power ratings and if these limits are exceeded, the resistor will begin to break down. In these cases, more and more electrical energy is converted to thermal energy until the resistor is totally destroyed by overheating. Note that this must be accompanied by a decrease in the electrical energy exiting the resistor. Thus, resistor break down also causes failure of the circuit.

Capacitors
Capacitors are energy storage devices. The energy stored by the capacitor must be equal to the difference in electrical energy entering and leaving the capacitor. The total energy stored by a capacitor depends on the total charge Q on the capacitor and the capacitance C of the device. It may also be expressed in terms of the capacitance and the voltage V across the capacitor.

$$E_{stored} = \int_{0}^{Q} \frac{q}{C}dq = \frac{1}{2}\frac{Q^2}{C} = \frac{1}{2}CV^2$$

Capacitors are limited in the amount of energy they can safely store. If this is exceeded, the dielectric may begin to break down. At this point, the electrical energy will either pass through the capacitor or be released as heat energy.

## Inductors

Like capacitors, inductors store energy. However, the energy is stored not as electrical energy but as magnetic energy (in a magnetic field). Thus, the electrical energy entering the inductor plus the stored magnetic energy must be equal to the electrical energy exiting the inductor. The stored energy in this case depends on the current I through the inductor and the inductance L:

$$E_{stored} = \int_0^I Lidi = \frac{1}{2}LI^2$$

It is typical that real inductors also contain some resistive elements unlike ideal inductors which are assumed to have zero resistance. Thus, as explained for resistors above, inductors also release some electrical energy as thermal energy. This will have an effect on the total energy balance for an inductor.

**Skill 5.1j  Calculate power, voltage changes, current, and resistance in multiloop circuits involving capacitors, resistors, and inductors**

While a capacitor resists a change in voltage through a circuit, an inductor resists a change in current. In a DC current circuit, a capacitor behaves like an open circuit (infinite resistance) while an inductor behaves like a short circuit (zero resistance) in the steady state following the initial transient response (where a capacitor builds up charge and an inductor builds up a magnetic field).

In an AC circuit, however, both capacitors and inductors contribute to the net **impedance** in the circuit which is a measure of opposition to the alternating current. It is similar to resistance and also has the unit ohm. However, due to the phased nature of AC, impedance is a complex number, having both real and imaginary components. The resistance is the real part of impedance while the **reactance** of capacitors and inductors constitute the imaginary part. The relationship between impedance (Z), resistance(R), and reactance (X) is given by below.

$$Z = R + Xi \quad \text{(Remember that } i=\sqrt{-1}\text{)}$$

The inductive reactance is given by $X_L = \omega L$ where $\omega$ is the angular frequency of the current and $L$ is the inductance. The capacitive reactance is given by $X_C = \frac{1}{\omega C}$ where $\omega$ is the angular frequency of the current and C is the capacitance.

Analysis of some multiloop circuits may be performed by way of simplification by combining multiple elements into a smaller number of equivalent elements. After forming a manageable equivalent circuit, the various circuit parameters may be calculated using Kirchhoff's Voltage Law and Kirchhoff's Current Law. Inductors in series or in parallel are combined in the same manner as resistors.

Inductors in parallel: $\dfrac{1}{L_{eq}} = \dfrac{1}{L_1} + \dfrac{1}{L_2} + \ldots + \dfrac{1}{L_n}$

Inductors in series: $L_{eq} = L_1 + L_2 + \ldots + L_n$

For some more complicated circuits, it may be necessary to solve a linear system of equations. The basic relationships between voltage and current for resistors, capacitors and inductors may be expressed in both the time and frequency domains, which correspond to instantaneous values and to amplitudes.

Time Domain: $\quad V_R(t) = I_R(t) R \quad\quad I_C(t) = C \dfrac{\partial V_C(t)}{\partial t} \quad\quad V_L(t) = L \dfrac{\partial I_L(t)}{\partial t}$

Frequency Domain: $V_R = I_R R \quad\quad V_C = I_C \left( \dfrac{i}{\omega C} \right) \quad\quad V_L = I_L (-i \omega L)$

In the **frequency domain**, capacitors and inductors can be treated similarly to resistors, as seen by the equations in the same form as Ohm's Law, using the more general concept of impedance (Z). Impedance is a complex number with resistance (R) as the real part and reactance (X) as the imaginary part. Impedances in series and parallel may be combined in the same manner as resistors and inductors, except that complex arithmetic must be performed.

Impedances in parallel: $\dfrac{1}{Z_{eq}} = \dfrac{1}{Z_1} + \dfrac{1}{Z_2} + \ldots + \dfrac{1}{Z_n}$

Impedances in series: $Z_{eq} = Z_1 + Z_2 + \ldots + Z_n$

Impedance in the frequency domain accounts for phase differences between the voltage and current for inductors and capacitors in the time domain through the inclusion of imaginary numbers. Use of the frequency domain forms is the most straightforward approach in cases of steady-state circuits.

Problem: Calculate the dissipated power amplitude in the following circuit operating at angular frequency ω = 2 Hz.

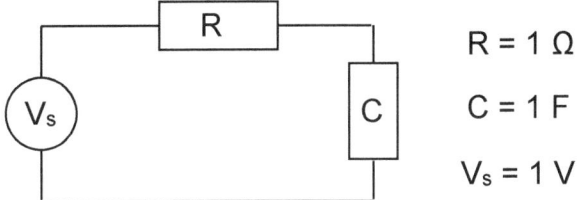

R = 1 Ω

C = 1 F

$V_s$ = 1 V

Solution: First, calculate the current through R and C.

$$Z_{eq} = R + \frac{i}{\omega C} = 1 + i0.5 \Omega$$

$$|Z_{eq}| = 1.12 \Omega$$

$$I_R = \frac{V_s}{|Z_{eq}|} = 0.89 A$$

Apply the appropriate formula to find the dissipated power.

$$P = I_R^2 R = 0.79 W$$

For **time domain** calculations, which must be used for instantaneous or transient circuit analysis, the differential equations must be used. Solution of these equations allows calculation of the current, voltage change and power dissipated for various elements at any given time. Additionally, transient analysis may be performed with this approach by imposing the appropriate initial conditions on the solutions to the differential equations. These may be derived for cases such as when a capacitor is charged and then a switch in the circuit is opened or closed, for example.

Below we will consider a simple RC circuit with a resistor and a capacitor in series connected to a DC voltage source.

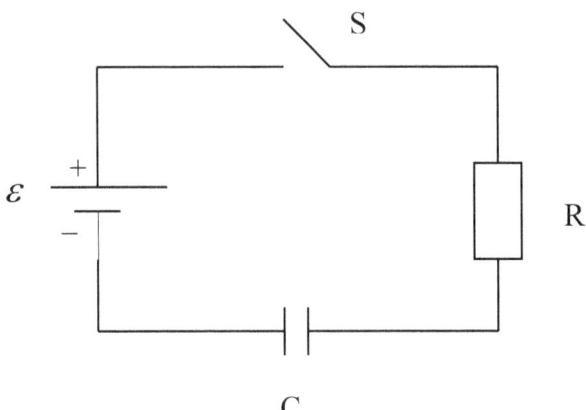

Applying Kirchhoff's first rule we get $\varepsilon = V_R + V_C = IR + \dfrac{Q}{C} = R\dfrac{dQ}{dt} + \dfrac{Q}{C}$ since the current $I$ in the circuit is equal to the rate of increase of charge on the capacitor. If the charge on the capacitor is zero when the switch is closed at time t=0, the current $I$ in the circuit starts out at the value $\varepsilon/R$ and gradually falls to zero as the capacitor charge gradually rises to its maximum value. The mathematical expressions for these two quantities are

$$Q(t) = C\varepsilon(1 - e^{-t/RC}); I(t) = \dfrac{\varepsilon}{R} e^{-t/RC}$$

The product $RC$ is known as the **time constant** of the circuit.

If the battery is now removed and the switch closed at t=0, the capacitor will slowly discharge with its charge at any point t given by

$Q(t) = Q_f e^{-t/RC}$ where $Q_f$ is the charge that the capacitor started with at t=0.

Power is dissipated only by resistors and not by ideal inductors or capacitors which are assumed to have no resistance. The power dissipated by any circuit is then the sum of the power dissipated for all the resistors in the circuit.

**Skill 5.1k  Interpret and design mixed series and parallel circuits involving capacitors, resistors, and inductors**

In most complex circuits, it is common to have elements wired such that there is a mix of parallel and series relationships. However, we can analyze these circuits by simplifying them systematically.

First, remember that:

-For resistors or inductors in series, the total resistance or inductance is the sum of the individual resistances or inductances; for resistors or inductors in parallel, the reciprocal of the total resistance or inductance is the sum of the reciprocals of the individual resistances or inductances

-For capacitors in series, the reciprocal of the total capacitance is the sum of the reciprocals of the individual capacitances; for capacitors in parallel, the total capacitance is the sum of the individual capacitances

Mixed series-parallel circuits are analyzed by defining subsets of elements that can be analyzed by the rules above. Small subsets are analyzed and then incorporated back into the larger circuit. In the following simple example, the effective resistance of a portion of the circuit is found first and the entire circuit can be analyzed.

Example:
Three resistors are connected to a battery as shown. Find an expression for the current in the circuit.

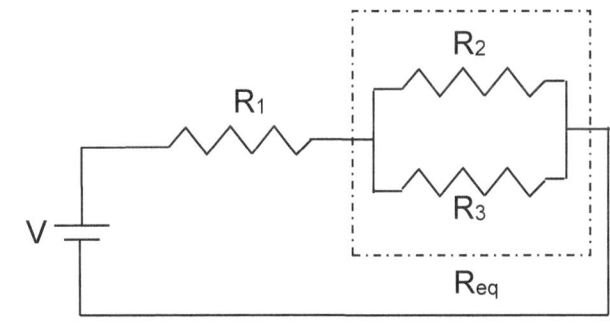

Solution:
Here we see that $R_2$ and $R_3$ are in parallel with one another and in series with $R_1$. Thus, we should begin by determining the equivalent resistance, $R_{eq}$, for $R_2$ and $R_3$ (illustrated with a dashed line). Because these resistors are in parallel:

$$\frac{1}{R_{eq}} = \frac{1}{R_2} + \frac{1}{R_3}$$

$$R_{eq} = \frac{R_2 \times R_3}{R_2 + R_3}$$

Now, we essentially have a situation in which $R_{eq}$ is in series with $R_1$, so we can find the total resistance of the circuit as:

$$R_{total} = R_1 + \frac{R_2 \times R_3}{R_2 + R_3}$$

To find the current flowing through the circuit, we simply apply Ohm's law:

$$I = \frac{V}{R_1 + \frac{R_2 \times R_3}{R_2 + R_3}}$$

Note that, because inductors are added in the same way resistors are, this problem would be very similar if the circuit involved inductors rather than resistors.

Now let's analyze a more complicated mixed parallel-series circuit, this time involving capacitors.

Example:
Find the total equivalent capacitance of this circuit.

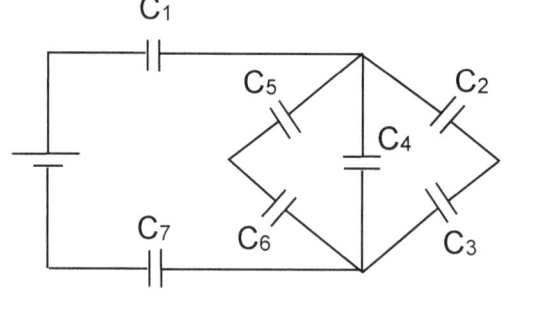

Solution:
This circuit is drawn in such a way that identifying the parallel and series relationships is difficult. The first step in simplifying it is to redraw it to elucidate those relationships.

Now we can begin to simplify the circuit in a step-wise fashion. We begin by combining $C_5$ with $C_6$ and $C_2$ with $C_3$ (these are pairs in series).

$$C_{5,6} = \left(\frac{1}{C_5} + \frac{1}{C_6}\right)^{-1} \qquad C_{2,3} = \left(\frac{1}{C_2} + \frac{1}{C_3}\right)^{-1}$$

The next steps will involve combining $C_{5,6}$ and $C_{2,3}$ with $C_4$ in parallel and the resulting equivalent capacitance in series with $C_1$ and $C_7$.

## Skill 5.1l   Explain properties of transistors, diodes, and semiconductors

Prior to the 1960s, most electronic apparatuses relied on either vacuum tubes or mechanical devices, typically relays. However, as semiconductors became increasingly available, vacuum tubes were replaced with solid-state devices. Vacuum tubes conduct electrons through a heated vacuum but semiconductors allow electrons to flow through them while still solid. Solid-state device has come to mean any circuit that does not contain the aforementioned vacuum tubes and, in short, operates with "no moving parts". The lack of these elements make solid-state devices more resistant to physical stressors such as vibration and more durable, in general, since they are less susceptible to wear. A familiar example of this are the solid-state "flash cards" that are popular for data storage. Previously hard disk players were primarily used for a similar function but their moving parts make them of limited durability and less practical to transport.

Semiconductors are extremely useful because their conductive properties can be controlled. This is done by "doping" or introducing impurities. The impurity or dopant is used to introduce extra electrons or extra free orbital space that can be filled with electrons. This allows much freer movement of electrons and, therefore, flow of current through the material. Semiconductors doped to contain extra electrons are known as N-type while those doped to contain extra "holes" are known as P-type. Typically, either type of semiconductor can be made from the same base material. For instance, silicon can be doped with boron to create a P-type semiconductor or with phosphorus to create an N-type semiconductor. Two of the most common and important semiconductor devices today are diodes and transistors.

Diodes: Diodes restrict the direction of current (electron) flow to a given direction. Somewhat analagous to a check valve, they allow the electrical current to flow in one direction but not in the other. Thus diodes are found in almost all circuits where single direction current flow is required. While early diodes were made from vacuum tubes, today most are made from semiconductors. This is often done by designing a diode with P-type semiconduting material on one side and N-type on the other. The current flows into the P-type side and on to the N-type side but cannot flow in the opposite direction. Alternatively, the diode can be made from a conducting metal and a semiconductor and function in a similar fashion.

Transistors: Just like the vaccum tubes they replaced, transistors control current flow. They serve a variety of functions in circuits and can act as amplifiers, switches, voltage regulators, signal modulators, or oscillators. They are perhaps the most important building block of modern circuitry and electronics. As in solid-state diodes, the properties of semiconductors are exploited in transistors to control the flow of current. However, where the diode is analagous to a check valve, a transistor functions more like a tap on a sink and is able to control the rate of current flow or eliminate it all together.Today most transistors are either bipolar junction transistors (BJT) or field effect transistors (FET). Both accomplish control of current flow but it is done by applying current in the BJTs and voltage in the FETs.

# TEACHER CERTIFICATION STUDY GUIDE

| SUBAREA VI. | QUANTUM MECHANICS AND THE STANDARD MODEL OF PARTICLES |
|---|---|

## COMPETENCY 6.1 QUANTUM MECHANICS AND THE STANDARD MODEL OF PARTICLES

**Skill 6.1a** Distinguish the four fundamental forces of nature, describe their ranges, and identify their force carriers

See **Skill 1.1m**.

**Skill 6.1b** Evaluate the assumptions and relevance of the Bohr model of the atom

In the West, the Greek philosophers Democritus and Leucippus first suggested the concept of the atom. They believed that all atoms were made of the same material but that varied sizes and shapes of atoms resulted in the varied properties of different materials. By the 19th century, John Dalton had advanced a theory stating that each element possesses atoms of a unique type. These atoms were also thought to be the smallest pieces of matter which could not be split or destroyed.

Atomic structure began to be better understood when, in 1897, JJ Thompson discovered the electron while working with cathode ray tubes. Thompson realized the negatively charged electrons were subatomic particles and formulated the "plum pudding model" of the atom to explain how the atom could still have a neutral charge overall. In this model, the negatively charged electrons were randomly present and free to move within a soup or cloud of positive charge.

Ernest Rutherford disproved this model with the discovery of the nucleus in 1909. Rutherford proposed a new "planetary" model of the atom in which electrons orbited around a positively charged nucleus like planets around the sun. Over the next 20 years, protons and neutrons (subnuclear particles) were discovered while additional experiments showed the inadequacy of the planetary model.

PHYSICS

As quantum theory was developed and popularized (primarily by Max Planck and Albert Einstein), chemists and physicists began to consider how it might apply to atomic structure. Niels Bohr put forward a model of the atom in which electrons could only orbit the nucleus in circular orbitals with specific distances from the nucleus, energy levels, and angular momentums. In this model, electrons could only make instantaneous "quantum leaps" between the fixed energy levels of the various orbitals. They emit or absorb radiation only during these transitions between stationary states. The Bohr model of the atom was altered slightly by Arnold Sommerfeld in 1916 to reflect the fact that the orbitals were elliptical instead of round.

Though the Bohr model is still thought to be largely correct, it was discovered that electrons do not truly occupy neat, cleanly defined orbitals. Rather, they exist as more of an "electron cloud." The work of Louis de Broglie, Erwin Schrödinger, and Werner Heisenberg showed that an electron can actually be located at any distance from the nucleus. However, we can find the *probability* that the electrons exists at given energy levels (i.e., in particular orbitals) and those probabilities will show that the electrons are most frequently organized within the orbitals originally described in the Bohr model. The Bohr model is applicable particularly for a simple atom such as the hydrogen atom for which the Bohr model very accurately predicts the wavelengths of the spectral lines.

TEACHER CERTIFICATION STUDY GUIDE

### PART II. SKILLS AND ABILITIES APPLICABLE TO THE CONTENT DOMAINS IN SCIENCE

**SUBAREA 1.0**                        **INVESTIGATION AND EXPERIMENTATION**

**COMPETENCY 1.1 QUESTION FORMULATION**

**Skill 1.1a.**    **Formulate and evaluate a viable hypothesis**

The first step in scientific inquiry is posing a question to be answered. Next, one forms a hypothesis, and then conducts an experiment to test the hypothesis. Comparison between the predicted and observed results is the next step. Conclusions are then formed based on the analysis and it is determined whether the hypothesis is correct or incorrect. If incorrect, the next step is to form a new hypothesis and the process is repeated.

Let's use the following everyday situation as an example. Through the course of making breakfast, you bring three eggs from the refrigerator over to the stove. Your hands are full and you accidentally drop an egg on the floor, which immediately shatters all over the tile floor. As you clean up the mess you wonder if you had carried the eggs in their cardboard container, would they have broken if dropped? Similarly, if dropped would they have broken on a softer surface, for example linoleum?

Once the question is formulated take an educated guess about the answer to the problem or question. For our scientist above, a plausible hypothesis might be that even if dropped, the egg would not have broken if it had been enclosed in its protective cardboard box.

**Skill 1.1b.**    **Recognize the value and role of observation prior to question formulation**

The scientist conducting our imaginary egg experiment made observations prior to the experiment. He knows that eggshells are fragile, and that their interior is liquid. He also noted that his floor was made of tile, a hard surface, and that the broken egg had not been protected. His observations, however general they may have seemed, led him to create a viable question and an educated guess (hypothesis) about what he expected. While scientists often have laboratories set up to study a specific thing, it is likely that along the way they will find an unexpected result. It is always important to be open-minded and to look at all of the information. An open-minded approach to science provides room for more questioning, and, hence, more learning.

**Skill 1.1c.   Recognize the iterative nature of questioning**

The question stage of scientific inquiry involves repetition. By repeating the experiment you can discover whether or not you have reproducibility.
If results are reproducible, the hypothesis is valid. If the results are not reproducible, one has more questions to ask.

**Skill 1.1d.   Given an experimental design, identify possible hypotheses that it may test**

An experiment is proposed and performed with the sole objective of testing a hypothesis. You discover the aforementioned scientist conducting an experiment with the following characteristics. He has two rows each set up with four stations. The first row has a piece of tile as the base at each station. The second row has a piece of linoleum as the base at each station. The scientist has eight eggs and is prepared to drop one over each station. What is he testing? He is trying to answer whether or not the egg is more likely to break when dropped over one material as opposed to the other. His hypothesis might have been: The egg will be less likely to break when dropped on linoleum.

# TEACHER CERTIFICATION STUDY GUIDE

## COMPETENCY 1.2 PLANNING A SCIENTIFIC INVESTIGATION (INCLUDING EXPERIMENTAL DESIGN)

### Skill 1.2a. Given a hypothesis, formulate an investigation or experimental design to test that hypothesis

Suppose our junior scientist wants to look at his initial question, "if you had carried the eggs in their cardboard container, would they have broken if dropped?" A sensible hypothesis to this question would be that an egg would be less likely to break if it was dropped in its cardboard container, than if it were unprotected. Because reproducibility is important, we need to set up multiple identical stations, or use the same station for repeatedly conducting the same experiment. Either way it is key that everything is identical. If the scientist wants to study the break rate for one egg in it's container, then it needs to be just one egg dropped each time in an identical way. The investigator should systematically walk to each station and drop an egg over each station and record the results. The first four times, the egg should be dropped without enclosing it in a cardboard carton. This is the control. It is a recreation of what happened accidentally in the kitchen and one would expect the results to be the same- an egg dropped onto tile will break. The next four times, the egg should be dropped nestled within its original, store manufactured, cardboard container. One would expect that the egg would not break, or would break less often under these conditions.

### Skill 1.2b. Evaluate an experimental design for its suitability to test a given hypothesis

When designing an experiment, one needs to clearly define what one is testing. One also needs to consider the question asked. The more limited the question, the easier it is to set up an experiment to answer it.

Ideally, if an egg were dropped, the egg would be safest when dropped in a protective carton over a soft surface. However, one should not measure multiple variables at once. Studying multiple variables at once makes the results difficult to analyze. How would the investigator discern which variable was responsible for the result? When evaluating experimental design, make sure to look at the number of variables, how clearly they were defined, and how accurately they were measured. Also, was the experiment applicable? Did it make sense and address the hypothesis?

PHYSICS

**Skill 1.2c.  Distinguish between variable and controlled parameters**

The procedure used to obtain data is important to the outcome.  Experiments consist of **controls** and **variables**.  A control is the experiment run under normal conditions.  The variable includes a factor that is changed.  In biology, the variable may be light, temperature, pH, time, etc.  The differences in tested variables may be used to make a prediction or form a hypothesis.  Only one variable should be tested at a time.  One would not alter both the temperature and pH of the experimental subject.

An **independent variable** is one that is changed or manipulated by the researcher. This could be the amount of light given to a plant or the temperature at which bacteria is grown. The **dependent variable** is that which is influenced by the independent variable.

## COMPETENCY 1.3 OBSERVATION AND DATA COLLECTION

**Skill 1.3a.** Identify changes in natural phenomena over time without manipulating the phenomena (e.g. a tree limb, a grove of trees, a stream, a hill slope)

Scientists identify changes in natural phenomena over time using basic tools of measurement and observation. Scientists measure growth of plants by measuring plant dimensions at different time intervals, changes in plant and animal populations by counting, and changes in environmental conditions by observation. The following are four examples of natural phenomena, and the observation techniques used to measure change in each case.

To identify change in a tree limb, we measure the dimensions (length, circumference) of the limb at different time intervals. In addition, we can study the types and amount of organisms growing on the limb by observing a small sample and applying the observations to make estimations about the entire limb. Finally, we can watch for the presence of disease or bacterial infection by observing the color and consistency of the limb and any changes over time.

To identify change in a grove of trees, we employ similar techniques as used in the observation of a tree limb. First, we measure the size of the trees at different time intervals.

If the grove contains many trees, we may measure only a representative sample of trees and apply the results to make conjectures about the grove population. Finally, we closely monitor the trees for changes that may indicate disease or infection.

To identify change in a stream, we measure and observe characteristics of both the stream itself and the organisms living in it. First, we measure the width and depth of the stream at different time intervals to monitor erosion. Second, we observe the water level at different time intervals to monitor the effect of weather patterns. Finally, using sampling techniques, we observe and measure the types and number of organisms present in the stream and how these characteristics change over time.

To identify change on a hill slope, we measure the angle and dimensions of the slope at different time intervals to monitor the effects of erosion by wind and rain. In addition, we use sampling techniques to make generalizations about the organisms living on the slope. Finally, we can monitor how the types and amounts of vegetation on the slope change in relation to the change in the angle of the slope (i.e. determine which types of plants have the ability to grow in certain conditions).

**Skill 1.3b.  Analyze the locations, sequences, and time intervals that are characteristic of natural phenomena (e.g. locations of planets over time, succession of species in an ecosystem)**

One of the main goals of science is the study and explanation of natural phenomena. When studying natural phenomena, scientists describe the characteristic locations, sequences, and time intervals. Examples of natural phenomena studied by scientists include the locations of planets over time and the succession of species in an ecosystem.

The eight planets of the solar system (Pluto was formerly included as a planet but has been removed as of summer 2006) orbit the sun in a specific sequence. The time it takes to complete an orbit of the Sun is different for each planet. In addition, we can determine the location of each planet in relation to the Sun and to each other using mathematical models and charts.

Mercury orbits closest to the sun, followed by Venus, Earth, Mars, Jupiter, Saturn, Uranus, and Neptune. Neptune is farthest from the Sun for 20 of every 248 years. Planets will never collide because one is always higher than the other, even when their orbits do intersect.

The amount of time a planet takes to complete one orbit of the Sun increases as the distance from the Sun increases. This value, called the sidereal period, ranges from 0.241 years for Mercury to 248.1 years.

The synodic period measures the amount of time it takes for a planet to return to the same point in the sky as observed from Earth. Mercury has the shortest synodic period of 116 days while Mars has the longest of 780 days. The synodic periods of Jupiter, Saturn, Uranus, and Neptune are similar, slightly less than 400 days for each.

Succession of species is the change in the type and number of plants, animals, and microorganisms that occurs periodically in all ecosystems. The two types of succession are primary and secondary. Primary succession describes the creation and subsequent development of a new, unoccupied habitat (e.g. a lava flow). Secondary succession describes the disruption of an existing community (e.g. fire, human tampering, flood) and the response of the community to the disruption. Succession is usually a very long process. New communities often take hundreds or thousands of years to reach a fully developed state (climax community). And, while succession in climax communities is minimal, environmental disruption can easily restart the succession process.

In general, simple organisms (e.g. bacteria, small plants) dominate new communities and prepare the environment for the development of larger, more complex species. For example, the dominant vegetation of an empty field will progress sequentially from grasses to small shrubs to soft wood trees to hard wood trees. We can observe and measure succession in two ways. First, we can measure the changes in a single community over time. Second, we can observe and compare similar communities at different stages of development. We are limited in the amount of data we can gather using the first method because of the slow nature of the succession process. The techniques used to observe succession include fossil observation, geological study, and environmental sampling.

**Skill 1.3c. Select and use appropriate tools and technology (e.g. computer-linked probes, spreadsheets, graphing calculators) to perform tests, collect data, analyze relationships, and display data**

Scientists use a variety of tools and technologies to perform tests, collect and display data, and analyze relationships. Examples of commonly used tools include computer-linked probes, spreadsheets, and graphing calculators.

Scientists use computer-linked probes to measure various environmental factors including temperature, dissolved oxygen, pH, ionic concentration, and pressure. The advantage of computer-linked probes, as compared to more traditional observational tools, is that the probes automatically gather data and present it in an accessible format. This property of computer-linked probes eliminates the need for constant human observation and manipulation.

Scientists use spreadsheets to organize, analyze, and display data. For example, conservation ecologists use spreadsheets to model population growth and development, apply sampling techniques, and create statistical distributions to analyze relationships. Spreadsheet use simplifies data collection and manipulation and allows the presentation of data in a logical and understandable format.

Graphing calculators are another technology with many applications to science. For example, biologists use algebraic functions to analyze growth, development and other natural processes. Graphing calculators can manipulate algebraic data and create graphs for analysis and observation. In addition, biologists use the matrix function of graphing calculators to model problems in genetics. The use of graphing calculators simplifies the creation of graphical displays including histograms, scatter plots, and line graphs. Scientists can also transfer data and displays to computers for further analysis. Finally, scientists connect computer-linked probes, used to collect data, to graphing calculators to ease the collection, transmission, and analysis of data.

## Skill 1.3d. Evaluate the precision, accuracy, and reproducibility of data

Accuracy is the degree of conformity of a measured, calculated quantity to its actual (true) value. Precision also called reproducibility or repeatability and is the degree to which further measurements or calculations will show the same or similar results.

Accuracy is the degree of veracity while precision is the degree of reproducibility. The best analogy to explain accuracy and precision is the target comparison. Repeated measurements are compared to arrows that are fired at a target. Accuracy describes the closeness of arrows to the bull's eye at the target center. Arrows that strike closer to the bull's eye are considered more accurate.

## Skill 1.3e. Identify and analyze possible reasons for inconsistent results, such as sources of error or uncontrolled conditions

Reproducibility is highly important when considering science. If results are not reproducible, they are usually not given much credit, regardless of the hypothesis. For this reason, we pay close attention to minimizing sources of error. Examples of common sources of error might be contamination or an improperly mixed buffer. In addition, one should remember that scientists are humans, and human error is always a possibility.

All experimental uncertainty is due to either random errors or systematic errors. Random errors are statistical fluctuations in the measured data due to the precision limitations of the measurement device.

Random errors usually result from the experimenter's inability to take the same measurement in exactly the same way to get exactly the same number. Systematic errors, by contrast, are reproducible inaccuracies that are consistently in the same direction. Systematic errors are often due to a problem that persists throughout the entire experiment. Systematic and random errors refer to problems associated with making measurements. Mistakes made in the calculations or in reading the instrument are not considered in error analysis.

## TEACHER CERTIFICATION STUDY GUIDE

**Skill 1.3f.  Identify and communicate sources of unavoidable experimental error**

Unavoidable experimental error is the random error inherent in scientific experiments regardless of the methods used.  One source of unavoidable error is measurement and the use of measurement devices.  Using measurement devices is an imprecise process because it is often impossible to accurately read measurements.  For example, when using a ruler to measure the length of an object, if the length falls between markings on the ruler, we must estimate the true value.  Another source of unavoidable error is the randomness of population sampling and the behavior of any random variable.  For example, when sampling a population we cannot guarantee that our sample is completely representative of the larger population.  In addition, because we cannot constantly monitor the behavior of a random variable, any observations necessarily contain some level of unavoidable error.

**Skill 1.3g.  Recognize the issues of statistical variability and explain the need for controlled tests**

Statistical variability is the deviation of an individual in a population from the mean of the population.  Variability is inherent in biology because living things are innately unique.  For example, the individual weights of humans vary greatly from the mean weight of the population.  Thus, when conducting experiments involving the study of living things, we must control for innate variability.  Control groups are identical to the experimental group in every way with the exception of the variable being studied.  Comparing the experimental group to the control group allows us to determine the effects of the manipulated variable in relation to statistical variability.

**Skill 1.3h.  Know and evaluate the safety issues when designing an experiment and implement appropriate solutions to safety problems**

All science labs should contain the following items of **safety equipment**.  Those marked with an asterisk are requirements by state laws.

* fire blanket which is visible and accessible
*Ground Fault Circuit Interrupters (GCFI) within two feet of water supplies
*signs designating room exits
*emergency shower providing a continuous flow of water
*emergency eye wash station which can be activated by the foot or forearm
*eye protection for every student and a means of sanitizing equipment
*emergency exhaust fans providing ventilation to the outside of the building
*master cut-off switches for gas, electric and compressed air.  Switches must have permanently attached handles.  Cut-off switches must be clearly labeled.
*an ABC fire extinguisher
*storage cabinets for flammable materials
-chemical spill control kit
-fume hood with a motor which is spark proof
-protective laboratory aprons made of flame retardant material

PHYSICS

-signs which will alert to potential hazardous conditions
-containers for broken glassware, flammables, corrosives, and waste. Containers should be labeled.

Students should wear safety goggles when performing dissections, heating, or while using acids and bases. Hair should always be tied back and objects should never be placed in the mouth. Food should not be consumed while in the laboratory. Hands should always be washed before and after laboratory experiments. In case of an accident, eye washes and showers should be used for eye contamination or a chemical spill that covers the student's body. Small chemical spills should only be contained and cleaned by the teacher.

Kitty litter or a chemical spill kit should be used to clean spills. For large spills, the school administration and the local fire department should be notified. Biological spills should also be handled only by the teacher. Contamination with biological waste can be cleaned by using bleach when appropriate.
Accidents and injuries should always be reported to the school administration and local health facilities. The severity of the accident or injury will determine the course of action to pursue.

It is the responsibility of the teacher to provide a safe environment for their students. Proper supervision greatly reduces the risk of injury and a teacher should never leave a class for any reason without providing alternate supervision. After an accident, two factors are considered; **foreseeability** and **negligence**. Foreseeability is the anticipation that an event may occur under certain circumstances. Negligence is the failure to exercise ordinary or reasonable care. Safety procedures should be a part of the science curriculum and a well managed classroom is important to avoid potential lawsuits.

**Skill 1.3i.** **Appropriately employ a variety of print and electronic resources (e.g. the World Wide Web) to collect information and evidence as part of a research project**

Scientists use print and electronic resources to collect information and evidence. Gathering information from scientific literature is a necessary element in successful research project design. Scientific journals, a major source of scientific information, provide starting points for experimental design and points of comparison in the interpretation of experimental results. Examples of important scientific journals are *Science*, *Nature*, and *Cell*. Scientists use the World Wide Web to search and access scientific journal articles through databases such as PubMed, JSTOR, and Google Scholar. In addition, the World Wide Web is a rich source of basic background information useful in the design and implementation of research projects. Examples of relevant online resources include scientific encyclopedias, general science websites, and research laboratory homepages.

**Skill 1.3j.** **Assess the accuracy validity and reliability of information gathered from a variety of sources**

Because people often attempt to use scientific evidence in support of political or personal agendas, the ability to evaluate the credibility of scientific claims is a necessary skill in today's society. In evaluating scientific claims made in the media, public debates, and advertising, one should follow several guidelines.

First, scientific, peer-reviewed journals are the most accepted source for information on scientific experiments and studies. One should carefully scrutinize any claim that does not reference peer-reviewed literature.

Second, the media and those with an agenda to advance (advertisers, debaters, etc.) often overemphasize the certainty and importance of experimental results. One should question any scientific claim that sounds fantastical or overly certain.

Finally, knowledge of experimental design and the scientific method is important in evaluating the credibility of studies. For example, one should look for the inclusion of control groups and the presence of data to support the given conclusions.

## COMPETENCY 1.4 DATA ANALYSIS/GRAPHING

**Skill 1.4a.** Construct appropriate graphs from data and develop qualitative and quantitative statements about relationships between variables

**Graphing** is an important skill to visually display collected data for analysis. The two types of graphs most commonly used are the **line graph** and the **bar graph** (histogram).

Line graphs are set up to show two variables represented by one point on the graph. The X-axis is the horizontal axis and represents the dependent variable. Dependent variables are those that would be present independently of the experiment. A common example of a dependent variable is time. Time proceeds regardless of anything else going on. The Y-axis is the vertical axis and represents the independent variable. Independent variables are manipulated by the experiment, such as the amount of light, or the height of a plant. Graphs should be calibrated at equal intervals. If one space represents one day, the next space may not represent ten days. A "best fit" line is drawn to join the points and may not include all the points in the data. Axes must always be labeled. A good title will describe both the dependent and the independent variable. Bar graphs are set up similarly in regards to axes, but points are not plotted. Instead, the dependent variable is set up as a bar where the X-axis intersects with the Y-axis. Each bar is a separate item of data and is not joined by a continuous line.
When drawing conclusions from graphs, one can make quantitative or qualitative statements. Quantitative is derived from quantity (numerical, precise) and qualitative (impressive) is derived from quality. For example, stating that the median is 12 would be a quantitative assessment.

The type of graphic representation used to display observations depends on the data that is collected. **Line graphs** are used to compare different sets of related data or to predict data that has not yet been measured. An example of a line graph would be comparing the rate of activity of different enzymes at varying temperatures. A **bar graph** or **histogram** is used to compare different items and make comparisons based on this data. An example of a bar graph would be comparing the ages of children in a classroom. A **pie chart** is useful when organizing data as part of a whole. A good use for a pie chart would be displaying the percent of time students spend on various after school activities.

**Skill 1.4b. Recognize the slope of the linear graph as the constant in the relationship y=kx and apply this principle in interpreting graphs constructed from data**

Analyzing graphs is a useful method for determining the mathematical relationship between the dependent and independent variables of an experiment. The usefulness of the method lies in the fact that the variables on the axes of a straight-line graph are represented by the expression, y = m*x + b, where m=the slope of the line, b=the y intercept of the line. This equation works only if the data fit a straight-line graph. Thus, once the data set has been collected, and modified, and plotted to achieve a straight-line graph, the mathematical equation can be derived.

**Skill 1.4c. Apply simple mathematical relationships to determine a missing quantity in an algebraic expression, given the two remaining terms (e.g., speed = distance/time, density = mass/volume, force = pressure x area, volume = area x height)**

Science and mathematics are related. Science data is strongest when accurate, and is therefore described in terms of units. To acquire proper units, one must apply math skills. Some common examples include speed, density, force, and volume. Let us look at density –

D = m/v
Where
D = density g/cm
m = mass in grams
v = volume in cm

One would substitute known quantities for the alphabetical symbols. It is absolutely important to write the appropriate units e.g., g (gram), cm (centimeter) etc. This is fundamental algebra.

The second example is the formula for calculating momentum of an object.

M = mass (kg) times velocity (meters/second)
M = mv
The units of momentum are kg (m/s)

**Skill 1.4d.  Determine whether a relationship on a given graph is linear or non-linear and determine the appropriateness of extrapolating the data**

The individual data points on the graph of a linear relationship cluster around a line of best fit. In other words, a relationship is linear if we can sketch a straight line that roughly fits the data points. Consider the following examples of linear and non-linear relationships.

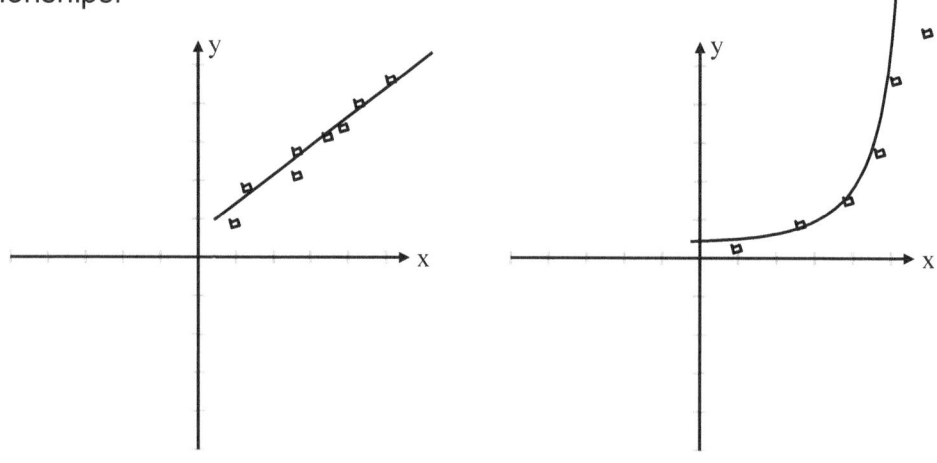

Linear Relationship  Non- Linear Relationship

Note that the non- linear relationship, an exponential relationship in this case, appears linear in parts of the curve. In addition, contrast the preceding graphs to the graph of a data set that shows no relationship between variables.

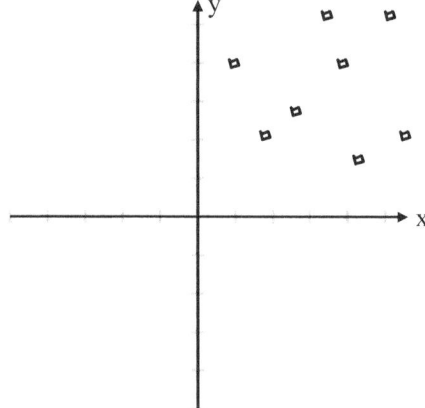

Extrapolation is the process of estimating data points outside a known set of data points. When extrapolating data of a linear relationship, we extend the line of best fit beyond the known values. The extension of the line represents the estimated data points. Extrapolating data is only appropriate if we are relatively certain that the relationship is indeed linear. For example, the death rate of an emerging disease may increase rapidly at first and level off as time goes on. Thus, extrapolating the death rate as if it were linear would yield inappropriately high values at later times. Similarly, extrapolating certain data in a strictly linear fashion, with no restrictions, may yield obviously inappropriate results. For instance, if the number of plant species in a forest were decreasing with time in a linear fashion, extrapolating the data set to infinity would eventually yield a negative number of species, which is clearly unreasonable.

**Skill 1.4e.  Solve scientific problems by using quadratic equations and simple trigonometric, exponential, and logarithmic functions**

Scientists use mathematical tools and equations to model and solve scientific problems. Solving scientific problems often involves the use of quadratic, trigonometric, exponential, and logarithmic functions.

Quadratic equations take the standard form $ax^2 + bx + c = 0$. The most appropriate method of solving quadratic equations in scientific problems is the use of the quadratic formula. The quadratic formula produces the solutions of a standard form quadratic equation.

$$x = \frac{-b \pm \sqrt{b^2 - 4ac}}{2a} \quad \text{\{Quadratic Formula\}}$$

One common application of quadratic equations is the description of biochemical reaction equilibriums. Consider the following problem.

Example:

80.0 g of ethanoic acid (MW = 60g) reacts with 85.0 g of ethanol (MW = 46g) until equilibrium. The equilibrium constant is 4.00. Determine the amounts of ethyl acetate and water produced at equilibrium.

$$CH_3COOH + CH_3CH_2OH = CH_3CO_2C_2H_5 + H_2O$$

The equilibrium constant, K, describes equilibrium of the reaction, relating the concentrations of products to reactants.

$$K = \frac{[CH_3CO_2C_2H_5][H_2O]}{[CH_3CO_2H][CH_3CH_2OH]} = 4.00$$

The equilibrium values of reactants and products are listed in the following table.

|  | $CH_3COOH$ | $CH_3CH_2OH$ | $CH_3CO_2C_2H_5$ | $H_2O$ |
|---|---|---|---|---|
| Initial | 80/60 = 1.33 mol | 85/46 = 1.85 mol | 0 | 0 |
| Equilibrium | 1.33 – x | 1.85 – x | x | x |

Thus, $K = \dfrac{[x][x]}{[1.33-x][1.85-x]} = \dfrac{x^2}{2.46-3.18x+x^2} = 4.00$.

Rearrange the equation to produce a standard form quadratic equation.

$$\dfrac{x^2}{2.46-3.18x+x^2} = 4.00$$
$$x^2 = 4.00(2.46-3.18x+x^2) = 9.84-12.72x+4x^2$$
$$0 = 3x^2 - 12.72x + 9.84$$

Use the quadratic formula to solve for x.

$$x = \dfrac{-(-12.72) \pm \sqrt{(-12.72)^2 - 4(3)(9.84)}}{2(3)} = 3.22 \text{ or } 1.02$$

3.22 is not an appropriate answer, because we started with only 3.18 moles of reactants. Thus, the amount of each product produced at equilibrium is 1.02 moles.

Scientists use trigonometric functions to define angles and lengths. For example, field biologists can use trigonometric functions to estimate distances and directions. The basic trigonometric functions are sine, cosine, and tangent.
Consider the following triangle describing these relationships.

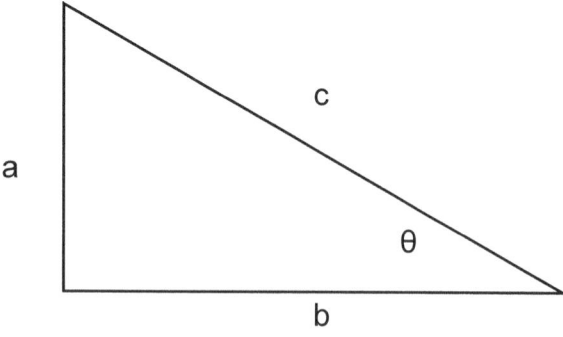

$$\sin \theta = \dfrac{a}{c}, \cos \theta = \dfrac{b}{c}, \tan \theta = \dfrac{a}{b}$$

Exponential functions are useful in modeling many scientific phenomena. For example, scientists use exponential functions to describe bacterial growth and radioactive decay. The general form of exponential equations is f(x) = $Ca^x$ (C is a constant). Consider the following problem involving bacterial growth.

Example:

Determine the number of bacteria present in a culture inoculated with a single bacterium after 24 hours if the bacterial population doubles every 2 hours. Use $N(t) = N_0 e^{kt}$ as a model of bacterial growth where N(t) is the size of the population at time $t$, $N_0$ is the initial population size, and k is the growth constant.

We must first determine the growth constant, k. At t = 2, the size of the population doubles from 1 to 2. Thus, we substitute and solve for k.

$$2 = 1(e^{2k})$$

$$\ln 2 = \ln e^{2k} \quad \text{Take the natural log of each side.}$$

$$\ln 2 = 2k(\ln e) = 2k \quad \ln e = 1$$

$$k = \frac{\ln 2}{2} \quad \text{Solve for k.}$$

The population size at t = 24 is

$$N(24) = e^{(\frac{\ln 2}{2})24} = e^{12 \ln 2} = 4096.$$

Finally, logarithmic functions have many applications to science and biology. One simple example of a logarithmic application is the pH scale. Scientists define pH as follows.

pH = - $\log_{10}$ [H⁺], where [H⁺] is the concentration of hydrogen ions

Thus, we can determine the pH of a solution with a [H⁺] value of 0.0005 mol/L by using the logarithmic formula.

pH = - $\log_{10}$ [0.0005] = 3.3

## COMPETENCY 1.5 DRAWING CONCLUSIONS AND COMMUNICATING EXPLANATIONS

The state of California needs to ensure that its licensed teachers are capable of the list below. These items are not items that can be explained in essay format; rather they are an accumulation of your years of learning. You will be able to find correlations with these items in other areas of this manual.

Skill 1.5a. Draw appropriate and logical conclusions from data

Skill 1.5b. Communicate the logical connection among hypotheses, science concepts, tests conducted, data collected, and conclusions drawn from the scientific evidence

Skill 1.5c. Communicate the steps and results of an investigation in written reports and oral presentations

Skill 1.5d. Recognize whether evidence is consistent with a proposed explanation

Skill 1.5e. Construct appropriate visual representations of scientific phenomenon and processes (e.g., motion of Earth's plates, cell structure)

Skill 1.5f. Read topographic and geologic maps for evidence provided on the maps and construct and interpret a simple scale map

# TEACHER CERTIFICATION STUDY GUIDE

## DOMAIN II.   NATURE OF SCIENCE

### COMPETENCY 2.1 SCIENTIFIC INQUIRY

**Skill 2.1a.**   Distinguish among the terms hypothesis, theory, and prediction as used in scientific investigations

Science may be defined as a body of knowledge that is systematically derived from study, observations, and experimentation. Its goal is to identify and establish principles and theories that may be applied to solve problems. Pseudoscience, on the other hand, is a belief that is not warranted. There is no scientific methodology or application. Some of the more classic examples of pseudoscience include witchcraft, alien encounters or any topic that is explained by hearsay.

Scientific theory and experimentation must be repeatable. It is also possible to be disproved and is capable of change. Science depends on communication, agreement, and disagreement among scientists. It is composed of theories, laws, and hypotheses.

**Theory -** the formation of principles or relationships which have been verified and accepted.

**Law -** an explanation of events that occur with uniformity under the same conditions (laws of nature, law of gravitation).

**Hypothesis -** an unproved theory or educated guess followed by research to best explain a phenomenon. A theory is a proven hypothesis.

Science is limited by the available technology. An example of this would be the relationship of the discovery of the cell and the invention of the microscope. As our technology improves, more hypotheses will become theories and possibly laws. Science is also limited by the data that is able to be collected. Data may be interpreted differently on different occasions. Science limitations cause explanations to be changeable as new technologies emerge.

The first step in scientific inquiry is posing a question to be answered. Next, a hypothesis is formed to provide a plausible explanation. An experiment is then proposed and performed to test this hypothesis. A comparison between the predicted and observed results is the next step. Conclusions are then formed and it is determined whether the hypothesis is correct or incorrect. If incorrect, the next step is to form a new hypothesis and the process is repeated.

### Skill 2.1b. Evaluate the usefulness, limitations, and interdisciplinary and cumulative nature of scientific evidence as it relates to the development of models and theories as representations of reality

All evidence can be manipulated by the presenter for their own purposes. This is why we stress that one must carefully evaluate resources. For instance, when reading a scientific article: Is it published in a well known journal, does it use controls, does it make sense, is the experiment clearly explained, are the results reproducible? One must also recognize the limitations of research. An experiment is more clearly analyzed if it only has one variable. Would the research still be true if another variable, for example, heat, time, or substrate were changed? One must consider the conditions under which the research was conducted. Were the most advanced technological machines used, or would there be a more applicable way to study the issue? For example, no one realized there was more to know about microscopic life until microscopy became more advanced. We now use scanning electron microscopes (SEM's), making light microscopes somewhat obsolete, and opening our eyes to a whole new level of thoroughness. As technology changes, so too does our knowledge and our awareness of reality. Galileo was a major scientist of his time (often referred to as the father of science) and used mathematics to properly describe scientific events. For all of his great efforts, though, as our machines have grown in power, we have had to rethink some of his theories. His improvements on the telescope enabled him to locate and accurately name many planets, stars, and systems. He was unable, however, to correctly ascertain the orbits of planets and the genesis of tides. Sir Isaac Newton expounded upon previous works, including Galileo's, when creating his laws of physics. Thus, tides were finally explained accurately, through an accumulation of knowledge.

### Skill 2.1c. Recognize that when observations do not agree with an accepted scientific theory, either the observations are mistaken or fraudulent, or the accepted theory is erroneous or incorrect

Sir Isaac Newton must have sensed that Galileo's tide theory didn't make sense - it didn't hold up to his observations. He had the opportunity, like present day scientists, to review his observations for error, or find a better explanation. One must note, though, that better in this case must be scientifically accurate in order to be impressive to peers specializing in science.

### Skill 2.1d. Understand that reproducibility of data is critical to the scientific endeavor

In order to have your theory accepted, it must be accurate and clearly derived. This means that another scientist could recreate your experiment from your notes, find similar data, and draw the same conclusions. In this way the validity of science is substantiated.

### Skill 2.1e. Recognize that science is a self- correcting process that eventually identifies misconceptions and experimental biases

The scientific process encourages periodic reassessment. The conclusion step allows one to examine the hypothesis as it relates to the experimental data. At this point, one can find positive correlations or discord. When results are unexpected, one should revisit all possible sources of error. If an error is not found to explain the results, one can reconsider the hypothesis and also think about other possibilities. This is why experimentation often results in further experimentation.

### Skill 2.1f. Recognize that an inquiring mind is at the heart of the scientific method and that doing science involves thinking critically about the evidence presented, the usefulness of models, and the limitations of theories

Science is not merely about creating; it is also about assessment and solutions. Science can be thought of as a loop. One questions something, and creates an experiment to study it. One can learn from this evidence, and then ask more questions. In depth learning involves looking at the experimental data from all angles and continuing to seek knowledge. Learning in depth does not occur by looking at something superficially or by taking someone else's data as 'proof.' Go one step further: analyze the evidence as if you were searching for a problem- maybe there won't be one, but you will be more likely to find it if there is!

**Skill 2.1g.** **Recognize that theories are judged by how well they explain observations and predict results and that when they represent new ideas that are counter to mainstream ideas they often encounter vigorous criticism**

If a theory explains a phenomenon well, it is worth considering, even if it turns out to be incorrect later on. The problem with this is two fold. First, a person can use a theory to push their own beliefs. This is the case with people seeing what they want to see, and then forming theories based around their opinions. An example would be if a scientist expected certain results, and then found ways to skew the results to match his theory. A theory based upon opinions will soon be seen as transparent and will be dismissed because it has no pertinent data to support it. Even if a theory is developed well, it still may not be readily accepted. A new theory is almost always difficult to introduce to an established community. To have a theory hold up to scrutiny, the author must have accurate data. Second, the author must continue to publicize the information. Just because a theory is not commonplace, does not mean it is incorrect. Novel ideas often become cornerstones in understanding, but it doesn't happen overnight. If the experiment has reproducible results and strong mathematics, people will eventually be swayed.

**Skill 2.1h.** **Recognize that when observations, data, or experimental results do not agree, the unexpected results are not necessarily mistakes; to discard the unusual in order to reach the expected is to guarantee that nothing but what is expected will ever be seen**

Often, results other than what were expected are from an error. However, this is not always the case. Consider a scientist who has double checked his work multiple times and can find no errors. He cannot explain what has happened except to assume that his theory was wrong. Maybe there is a fundamental scientific phenomenon that has yet to be explained and he couldn't possibly have known. Discoveries can occur in this way. If the scientist were to give up, he and society would lose the opportunity to learn something new. If the scientist opens his mind to the discovery, there are limitless possibilities for learning.

**Skill 2.1i.** **Know why curiosity, honesty, openness, and skepticism are so highly regarded in science and how they are incorporated into the way science is carried out**

Curiosity fuels research. It prompts the questions that turn into scientific inquiry. Honesty is paramount to the scientific way. To put the research out there, and be true in your report of the findings, is to help mankind and cooperate in scientific endeavors. While antonyms, openness and skepticism are both necessary in the field of research. One should be humble. One should be open to others' ideas, and open to their own unexpected findings, but be critical in evaluation of the work as it was conducted. It is key to incorporate all of these traits and to conduct yourself in a respectable manner.

## Competency 2.2 Scientific Ethics

To understand scientific ethics, we need to have a clear understanding of ethics. Ethics is defined as a system of public, general rules for guiding human conduct. The rules are general because they are supposed to all people at all times and they are public because they are not secret codes or practices.

Philosophers have given a number of moral theories to justify moral rules, which range from utilitarianism (a theory of ethics that prescribes the quantitative maximization of good consequences for a population. It is a form of consequentialism. This theory was proposed by Mozi, a Chinese philosopher who lived during BC 471-381), Kantianism (a theory proposed by Immanuel Kant, a German philosopher who lived during 1724-1804, which ascribes intrinsic value to rational beings and is the philosophical foundation of contemporary human rights) to social contract theory (a view of the ancient Greeks which states that the person's moral and or political obligations are dependent upon a contract or agreement between them to form society).

The following are some of the guiding principles of scientific ethics:

1. Scientific Honesty: not to fabricate or misinterpret data for personal gain
2. Caution: to avoid errors and sloppiness in all scientific experimentation
3. Credit: to give credit where credit is due and not to copy
4. Responsibility: only to report reliable information to the public and not to mislead in the name of science
5. Freedom: freedom to criticize old ideas, question new research and freedom to research

**Skill 2.2a.   Understand that honesty is at the core of scientific ethics; first and foremost is the honest and accurate reporting of procedures used and data collected**

Scientists are expected to show good conduct in their scientific pursuits. Conduct here refers to all aspects of scientific activity including experimentation, testing, education, data evaluation, data analysis, data storing, peer review, government funding, the staff, etc.

# TEACHER CERTIFICATION STUDY GUIDE

**Skill 2.2b.** **Know that all scientists are obligated to evaluate the safety of an investigation and ensure the safety of those performing the experiment**

As a teacher, the safety of your classroom is your responsibility. One should make every effort to ensure students' safety. You will need to be aware of all potential safety concerns. Advance preparation will prepare you to take the necessary precautions related to the specific experiment. You should use the applicable MSDS and check pertinent regulations (at your place of employment as well as on the state/national levels). It will be necessary to take foreseeability and negligence into consideration. It is the responsibility of the scientist to make sure that all organisms associated with the project are kept safe. This refers to both people and animals.

**Skill 2.2c.** **Know the procedures for respectful treatment of all living organisms in experimentation and other investigations**

No dissections may be performed on living mammalian vertebrates or birds. Lower order life and invertebrates may be used. Biological experiments may be done with all animals except mammalian vertebrates or birds. No physiological harm may result to the animal. All animals housed and cared for in the school must be handled in a safe and humane manner. Animals are not to remain on school premises during extended vacations unless adequate care is provided. Any instructor who intentionally refuses to comply with the laws may be suspended or dismissed.

Pathogenic organisms must never be used for experimentation. Students should adhere to the following rules at all times when working with microorganisms to avoid accidental contamination:

1. Treat all microorganisms as if they were pathogenic.
2. Maintain sterile conditions at all times

**Dissection and alternatives to dissection**
Animals which were not obtained from recognized sources should not be used. Decaying animals or those of unknown origin may harbor pathogens and/or parasites. Specimens should be rinsed before handling. Latex gloves are desirable. If not available, students with sores or scratches should be excused from the activity. Formaldehyde is likely carcinogenic and should be avoided or disposed of according to district regulations.

Students objecting to dissections for moral reasons should be given an alternative assignment. Interactive dissections are available online or from software companies for those students who object to performing dissections. There should be no penalty for those students who refuse to physically perform a dissection.

## COMPETENCY 2.3 HISTORICAL PERSPECTIVES

**Skill 2.3a.  Discuss the cumulative nature of scientific evidence as it relates to the development of models and theories**

Science is an ongoing process. There was a time when microscopes, telescopes, calculators, and computers did not exist. Their current availability has led to many discoveries. We have had the opportunity to investigate why people become sick, and the mechanisms responsible for their illnesses. We have also broadened our knowledge of physical science- the laws that govern the universe. With each new breakthrough we either build upon current knowledge, or if the new piece doesn't work with previous thoughts, we reevaluate the validity of all of the information, past and present. For this reason, models and theories are continuously evolving.

# TEACHER CERTIFICATION STUDY GUIDE

**Skill 2.3b.** Recognize that as knowledge in science evolves, when observations do not support an accepted scientific theory, the observations are reconsidered to determine if they are mistaken or fraudulent, or if the accepted theory is erroneous or incomplete (e.g., an erroneous theory is the Piltdown Man fossil; an incomplete theory is Newton's laws of gravity)

When one realizes that their results do not match those previously established, the new results must be reconsidered. At this point, one of four possibilities exist. One should look closely at the new results. The first place for disagreement is the new observations- they may be mistaken. Was there an error in data collection or analysis? Repeating the experiment may yield results that more closely agree with the previous theory. If the results of the follow up experiment are the same, an observer may wonder if the new data is fraudulent (second possibility). Take for example the scientist who fabricates data, but repeatedly insists on its integrity, even though it contradicts previous studies (remember that having a current study contradict a previous one would be acceptable, providing the results were true and reproducible). Another possibility would be a problem with the previously accepted theory. An erroneous theory is one which was created with misinformation. An example of an erroneous theory would be the Piltdown Man fossil. The Piltdown Man fossil consisted of fragments of a skull and jaw bone collected in the early 1900's from a gravel pit at Piltdown, a village in England. The claim was asserted that this discovery was the fossilized remains of an unknown early form of man. In 1953 it was exposed as a forgery, and properly evaluated as the lower jaw bone of an ape combined with the skull of a fully developed, modern man. There is still some debate as to who created the forgery, but it provided quite a stir in the scientific community. The problem with an erroneous theory is that it can be believable, and then future assumptions may be based on its inaccuracy. When theories become entrenched this way it is difficult sometimes to go back and locate the error. This can be seen when studying phylogenies. If Piltdown Man was assumed to come from ancestors, and to have generations below him, the accusation of his being fraudulent sheds new light on the phylogenic tree as it was proposed. A final source for dispute would be that the original theory was incomplete, such as was true with Newton's laws of gravity. Galileo had created an erroneous theory to describe the motion of planets. It was discredited when Sir Isaac Newton established his famous laws of gravity. Newton's concept of gravity held until the beginning of the 20th century, when Einstein proposed his general theory of relativity. The key to Einstein's version is that inertia occurs when objects are in free- fall instead of when they are at rest. The theory of general relativity has been well accepted because of how its predictions have been repeatedly confirmed.

**Skill 2.3c.** Recognize and provide specific examples that scientific advances sometimes result in profound paradigm shifts in scientific theories

PHYSICS

A paradigm shift is a change in the underlying assumptions that define a particular scientific theory. Scientific advances, such as increased technology allowing different or more reliable data collection, sometimes result in paradigm shifts in scientific theories.

One classic example of a scientific paradigm shift is the transition from a geocentric (Earth- centered) to heliocentric (Sun- centered) model of the universe. Invention and development of the telescope allowed for greater observation of the planets and the Sun. The theory that the Sun is the center of the universe around which the planets, including the Earth, rotate gained acceptance largely because of the advances in observational technology.

Another example of a paradigm shift is the acceptance of plate tectonics as the explanation for large- scale movements in the Earth's crust. Advances in seismic imaging and observation techniques allowed for the collection of sufficient data to establish plate tectonics as a legitimate geological theory.

**Skill 2.3d. Discuss the need for clear and understandable communication of scientific endeavors so that they may be reproduced and why reproduction of these endeavors is important**

Clear and understandable communication is essential for continuity and progress in science. When scientists complete scientific endeavors, such as research experiments, it is important that they carefully record their methods and results. Such precise communication and record keeping allows other scientists to reproduce the experiments in the future.

Reproduction of scientific endeavors is important because it simplifies the verification process. Because scientific experiments are subject to many sources of error, verification of results is essential. Scientists must verify results from scientific endeavors in order to justify the use of the acquired data in developing theories and future experiments.

In addition, clear communication of scientific endeavors allows scientists to learn from the work of others. Such sharing of information speeds the process of scientific research and development.

# TEACHER CERTIFICATION STUDY GUIDE

## SUBAREA III.  SCIENCE AND SOCIETY

### COMPETENCY 3.1 SCIENCE LITERACY

**Skill 3.1a.  Recognize that science attempts to make sense of how the natural and the designed world function**

Human beings reside at the top of the food web for many reasons including physical dexterity and size, but largely because of brain power. We are thinkers, designed to be curious (as are our friends, the primates). Science is our attempt to understand the world around us, and to live within it. Science is not always accurate, and often theories are inadequate, or believed to be true only to be disproven later. Please remember that science is a man made endeavor, and you and your students should treat it as such.

**Skill 3.1b.  Demonstrate the ability to apply critical and independent thinking to weigh alternative explanations of events**

In section 1.3j we demonstrated the importance of assessing the validity of information. One should consider the suggestions given in 1.3j when weighing evidence. Additional information on this subject may be found in Scientific Inquiry: Section 2.1 a- k.

**Skill 3.1c.  Apply evidence, numbers, patterns, and logical arguments to solve problems**

Two of the most important aspects of science are data and honesty. In the scientific realm, numbers are stronger than words, so be sure to back up your comments with accurate data and examples. By using the scientific method, you will be more likely to catch mistakes, correct biases, and obtain accurate results. When assessing experimental data utilize the proper tools and mathematical concepts discussed in this guide. For an in depth review of the scientific method please see Subarea 1: Investigation and Experimentation.

**Skill 3.1d.  Understand that, although much has been learned about the objects, events and phenomena in nature, there are many unanswered questions, i.e., science is a work in progress**

The combination of science, mathematics and technology forms the scientific endeavor and makes science a success. It is impossible to study science on its own without the support of other disciplines like mathematics, technology, geology, physics and other disciplines as well. Science is an ongoing process involving multiple fields and individuals. Technology also plays a role in scientific discoveries- we are limited by technology. We are constantly creating new devices for experimentation, and with each one comes new revelations.

PHYSICS

As such, science is constantly developing. The nature of science mainly consists of three important things:

### The scientific world view
This includes some very important issues such as – it is possible to understand this highly organized world and its complexities with the help of the latest technology. Scientific ideas are subject to change. After repeated experiments, a theory is established, but this theory could be changed or supported in future. Only laws that occur naturally do not change.

Scientific knowledge may not be discarded but is modified – e.g., Albert Einstein didn't discard the Newtonian principles but modified them in his theory of relativity. Also, science can't answer all our questions. We can't find answers to questions related to our beliefs, moral values and norms.

### Scientific inquiry
Scientific inquiry starts with a simple question. This simple question leads to information gathering, an educated guess otherwise known as hypothesis. To prove the hypothesis, an experiment has to be conducted, which yields data and the conclusion. All experiments must be repeated at least twice to get reliable results. Thus scientific inquiry leads to new knowledge or verifying established theories.

Science requires proof or evidence. Science is dependent on accuracy, not bias or prejudice. In science, there is no place for preconceived ideas or premeditated results. By using their senses and modern technology, scientists will be able to get reliable information.

Science is a combination of logic and imagination. A scientist needs to think and imagine and be able to reason.

Science explains, reasons and predicts. These three are interwoven and are inseparable. While reasoning is absolutely important for science, there should be no bias or prejudice.

Science is not authoritarian, because history has shown that scientific authority has sometimes been proven wrong. Nobody can determine or make decisions for others on any issue.

### Scientific enterprise
Science is a complex activity involving various people and places. A scientist may work alone or in a laboratory, classroom or for that matter anywhere. Mostly science is a group activity requiring lot of social skills, such as cooperation, communication of results or findings, consultations, discussions etc.

Science demands a high degree of communication to governments, funding authorities and to the public.

## Skill 3.1e. Know that the ability of science and technology to resolve societal problems depends on the scientific literacy of a society

The most common definitions of science literacy are: scientific awareness and scientific ways of knowing. In simple terms, scientific literacy is a combination of concepts, history, and philosophy that help us to understand the scientific issues of our time. The aim is to have a society which is aware of scientific developments.

The benefits to any society of being scientifically literate are –

1. To understand current issues
2. To appreciate the role of natural laws in individuals' lives
3. To have an idea of scientific advances

We are living in an age of scientific discoveries and technology. On TV and in the newspapers, we are constantly fed news related to science and technology. Scientific and technological issues are dominating our lives. We need to be scientifically literate to understand these issues. Understanding these debates has become as important as reading and writing. In order to appreciate the world around us and to be able to make informed personal decisions, we need to be scientifically literate.

It is the responsibility of the scientific community and educators to help the public to cope with the fast paced changes that are taking place now in the fields of science and technology.

Scientific literacy is based on the understanding of the most general principles and a broad knowledge of science. A society that is scientifically aware possesses facts and vocabulary sufficient to understand the context of the daily news. If one can understand articles about genetic engineering, the ozone hole, and greenhouse effect as well as sports, politics, arts, or the theater, then one is scientifically literate.

Scientific literacy is different from technological literacy and many times people are not clear about this. A survey indicated that less than 7% of adults, 22% of college graduates and 26% of those with graduate degrees are scientifically literate. These numbers are not encouraging. In order to rectify this problem, more emphasis has been placed on science education in K-12 and at the college level.

# TEACHER CERTIFICATION STUDY GUIDE

## COMPETENCY 3.2 DIVERSITY

**Skill 3.2a.** **Identify examples of women and men of various social and ethnic backgrounds with diverse interests, talents, qualities and motivations who are, or who have been, engaged in activities of science and related fields**

Curiosity is the heart of science. Maybe this is why so many diverse people are drawn to it. In the area of zoology one of the most recognized scientists is Jane Goodall. Miss Goodall is known for her research with chimpanzees in Africa. Jane has spent many years abroad conducting long term studies of chimp interactions, and returns from Africa to lecture and provide information about Africa, the chimpanzees, and her institute located in Tanzania.

In the area of chemistry we recognize Dorothy Crowfoot Hodgkin. She studied at Oxford and won the Nobel Prize of Chemistry in 1964 for recognizing the shape of the vitamin B 12.

Have you ever heard of Florence Nightingale? She was a true person living in the 1800's and she shaped the nursing profession. Florence was born into wealth and shocked her family by choosing to study health reforms for the poor in lieu of attending the expected social events. Florence studied nursing in Paris and became involved in the Crimean war. The British lacked supplies and the secretary of war asked for Florence's assistance. She earned her nickname walking the floors at night checking on patients and writing letters to British officials demanding supplies.

In 1903 the Nobel Prize in Physics was jointly awarded to three individuals: Marie Curie, Pierre Curie, and Becquerel. Marie was the first woman ever to receive this prestigious award. In addition, she received the Nobel Prize in chemistry in 1911, making her the only person to receive two Nobel awards in science. Ironically, her cause of death in 1934 was of overexposure to radioactivity, the research for which she was so respected.

Neil Armstrong is an American icon. He will always be symbolically linked to our aeronautics program. This astronaut and naval aviator is known for being the first human to set foot on the Moon.

Sir Alexander Fleming was a pharmacologist from Scotland who isolated the antibiotic penicillin from a fungus in 1928. Fleming also noted that bacteria developed resistance whenever too little penicillin was used or when it was used for too short a period, a key problem we still face today.

# COMPETENCY 3.3 SCIENCE, TECHNOLOGY, AND SOCIETY

## Skill 3.3 a. Identify and evaluate the impact of scientific advances on society

Society as a whole impacts biological research. The pressure from the majority of society has led to bans and restrictions on human cloning research. Human cloning has been restricted in the United States and many other countries. The U.S. legislature has banned the use of federal funds for the development of human cloning techniques. Some individual states have banned human cloning regardless of where the funds originate.

The demand for genetically modified crops by society and industry has steadily increased over the years. Genetic engineering in the agricultural field has led to improved crops for human use and consumption. Crops are genetically modified for increased growth and insect resistance because of the demand for larger and greater quantities of produce.

With advances in biotechnology come those in society who oppose it. Ethical questions come into play when discussing animal and human research. Does it need to be done? What are the effects on humans and animals? There are no right or wrong answers to these questions. There are governmental agencies in place to regulate the use of humans and animals for research.

Science and technology are often referred to as a "double- edged sword". Although advances in medicine have greatly improved the quality and length of life, certain moral and ethical controversies have arisen. Unforeseen environmental problems may result from technological advances. Advances in science have led to an improved economy through biotechnology as applied to agriculture, yet it has put our health care system at risk and has caused the cost of medical care to skyrocket. Society depends on science, yet is necessary that the public be scientifically literate and informed in order to prevent potentially unethical procedures from occurring. Especially vulnerable are the areas of genetic research and fertility. It is important for science teachers to stay abreast of current research and to involve students in critical thinking and ethics whenever possible.

**Skill 3.3 b.  Recognize that scientific advances may challenge individuals to reevaluate their personal beliefs**

It is easy to say one is for or against something. Biotechnological advances are reaching new heights. This is both exciting and, to some, it creates anxiety. We are stretching our boundaries and rethinking old standards. Things we never thought possible, such as the human genome project, now seem ordinary, and cloning, once in the realm of science fiction, is now available. These revelations force us to rethink our stance on issues.

It is normal to reevaluate one's beliefs. Reevaluation requires truly thinking about a topic, which in turn allows for recommitment to a topic or, possibly, a new, well thought out, position.

# TEACHER CERTIFICATION STUDY GUIDE

## COMPETENCY 3.4 SAFETY

### Skill 3.4a. Choose appropriate safety equipment for a given activity (e.g., goggles, apron, vented hood)

It is the responsibility of the teacher to provide a safe environment for their students. Proper supervision greatly reduces the risk of injury and a teacher should never leave a class for any reason without providing alternate supervision. After an accident, two factors are considered; **foreseeability** and **negligence**. Foreseeability is the anticipation that an event may occur under certain circumstances. Negligence is the failure to exercise ordinary or reasonable care. Safety procedures should be a part of the science curriculum and a well managed classroom is important to avoid potential lawsuits. Students should wear safety goggles when performing dissections, heating, or while using acids and bases. Hair should always be tied back and objects should never be placed in the mouth. Food should not be consumed while in the laboratory. Hands should always be washed before and after laboratory experiments. In case of an accident, eye washes and showers should be used for eye contamination or a chemical spill that covers the student's body. Small chemical spills should only be contained and cleaned by the teacher. Kitty litter or a chemical spill kit should be used to clean spill. For large spills, the school administration and the local fire department should be notified. Biological spills should also be handled only by the teacher. Contamination with biological waste can be cleaned by using bleach when appropriate.
Accidents and injuries should always be reported to the school administration and local health facilities. The severity of the accident or injury will determine the course of action to pursue.

### Skill 3.4b. Discuss the safe use, storage, and disposal of commonly used chemicals and biological specimens

All laboratory solutions should be prepared as directed in the lab manual. Care should be taken to avoid contamination. All glassware should be rinsed thoroughly with distilled water before using and cleaned well after use. All solutions should be made with distilled water as tap water contains dissolved particles that may affect the results of an experiment. Unused solutions should be disposed of according to local disposal procedures.

The "Right to Know Law" covers science teachers who work with potentially hazardous chemicals. Briefly, the law states that employees must be informed of potentially toxic chemicals. An inventory must be made available if requested.
The inventory must contain information about the hazards and properties of the chemicals. This inventory is to be checked against the "Substance List". Training must be provided on the safe handling and interpretation of the Material Safety Data Sheet.

The following chemicals are potential carcinogens and not allowed in school facilities: Acrylonitriel, Arsenic compounds, Asbestos, Bensidine, Benzene, Cadmium compounds, Chloroform, Chromium compounds, Ethylene oxide, Ortho- toluidine, Nickel powder, and Mercury.

Chemicals should not be stored on bench tops or heat sources. They should be stored in groups based on their reactivity with one another and in protective storage cabinets. All containers within the lab must be labeled. Suspect and known carcinogens must be labeled as such and segregated within trays to contain leaks and spills.

Chemical waste should be disposed of in properly labeled containers. Waste should be separated based on their reactivity with other chemicals.

Biological material should never be stored near food or water used for human consumption. All biological material should be appropriately labeled. All blood and body fluids should be put in a well- contained container with a secure lid to prevent leaking. All biological waste should be disposed of in biological hazardous waste bags.

Material safety data sheets are available for every chemical and biological substance. These are available directly from the company of acquisition or the internet. The manuals for equipment used in the lab should be read and understood before using them.

### Skill 3.4c. Assess the safety conditions needed to maintain a science laboratory (e.g., eye wash, shower, fire extinguisher)

All science labs should contain the following items of **safety equipment**. Those marked with an asterisk are requirements by state laws.

\* fire blanket which is visible and accessible
\*Ground Fault Circuit Interrupters (GCFI) within two feet of water supplies
\*signs designating room exits
\*emergency shower providing a continuous flow of water
\*emergency eye wash station which can be activated by the foot or forearm
\*eye protection for every student and a means of sanitizing equipment
\*emergency exhaust fans providing ventilation to the outside of the building
\*master cut-off switches for gas, electric and compressed air.  Switches must have permanently attached handles.  Cut-off switches must be clearly labeled.
\*an ABC fire extinguisher
\*storage cabinets for flammable materials
-chemical spill control kit
-fume hood with a motor which is spark proof
-protective laboratory aprons made of flame retardant material
-signs which will alert potential hazardous conditions
-containers for broken glassware, flammables, corrosives, and waste
Containers should be labeled.

# TEACHER CERTIFICATION STUDY GUIDE

**Skill 3.4d. Read and decode MSDS/OSHA (Material Safety Data Sheet/Occupational Safety and Health Administration) labels on laboratory supplies and equipment**

In addition to the safety laws set forth by the government regarding equipment necessary to the lab, OSHA (Occupational Safety and Health Administration) has helped to make environments safer by instituting signs that are bilingual. These signs use pictures rather than/in addition to words and feature eye-catching colors. Some of the best known examples are exit, restrooms, and handicap accessible.

Of particular importance to laboratories are diamond safety signs, prohibitive signs, and triangle danger signs. Each sign encloses a descriptive picture.

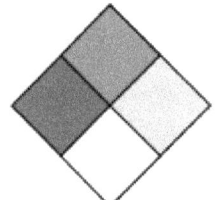    

As a teacher, you should utilize a MSDS (Material Safety Data Sheet) whenever you are preparing an experiment. It is designed to provide people with the proper procedures for handling or working with a particular substance. MSDS's include information such as physical data (melting point, boiling point, etc.), toxicity, health effects, first aid, reactivity, storage, disposal, protective gear, and spill/leak procedures. These are particularly important if a spill or other accident occurs. You should review a few, available commonly online, and understand the listing procedures.

**Skill 3.4e.  Discuss key issues in the disposal of hazardous materials in either the laboratory or the local community**

Hazardous materials should never be disposed of in regular trash. Hazardous materials include many cleansers, paints, batteries, oil, and biohazardous products. Labels which caution one to wear gloves, to never place an item near another item (e.g., fire, electrical outlet), or to always use an item in a well ventilated area, should be taken as signals that the item is hazardous. Disposal of waste down the sink or in regular trash receptacles means that it will eventually enter the water/sewer system or ground, where it could cause contamination. Liquid remains/spills should be solidified using cat litter and then disposed of carefully. Sharps bins are used for the disposal of sharp objects and glass. Red biohazard bags/containers are used for the disposal of biohazard refuse.

**Skill 3.4f.  Be familiar with standard safety procedures such as those outlined in the Science Safety Handbook for California Schools (1999)**

In addition to the standard safety precautions covered in this section, the state of California has published a document entitled *Science Safety Handbook for California Schools*. This handbook can be purchased or printed at http://www.cde.ca.gov/pd/ca/sc/documents/scisafebk.pdf#search=%22CA%20science%20safety%20book%20for%20CA%20schools%22.

# TEACHER CERTIFICATION STUDY GUIDE

## Sample Test

*DIRECTIONS: Read each item and select the best response.*

1. A skateboarder accelerates down a ramp, with constant acceleration of two meters per second squared, from rest. The distance in meters, covered after four seconds, is: *(Rigorous) (Skill 1.1a)*

   A. 10

   B. 16

   C. 23

   D. 37

2. The magnitude of a force is: *(Easy) (Skill 1.1b)*

   A. Directly proportional to mass and inversely to acceleration

   B. Inversely proportional to mass and directly to acceleration

   C. Directly proportional to both mass and acceleration

   D. Inversely proportional to both mass and acceleration

3. If a force of magnitude *F* gives a mass *M* an acceleration *A*, then a force 3*F* would give a mass 3*M* an acceleration: *(Average Rigor) (Skill 1.1b)*

   A. *A*

   B. 12*A*

   C. *A*/2

   D. 6*A*

4. A classroom demonstration shows a needle floating in a tray of water. This demonstrates the property of: *(Easy) (Skill 1.1c)*

   A. Specific Heat

   B. Surface Tension

   C. Oil-Water Interference

   D. Archimedes' Principle

PHYSICS

5. Given a vase full of water, with holes punched at various heights. The water squirts out of the holes, achieving different distances before hitting the ground. Which of the following accurately describes the situation?
*(Average Rigor) (Skill 1.1c)*

   A. Water from higher holes goes farther, due to Pascal's Principle.

   B. Water from higher holes goes farther, due to Bernoulli's Principle.

   C. Water from lower holes goes farther, due to Pascal's Principle.

   D. Water from lower holes goes farther, due to Bernoulli's Principle.

6. When acceleration is plotted versus time, the area under the graph represents:
*(Average Rigor) (Skill 1.1f)*

   A. Time

   B. Distance

   C. Velocity

   D. Acceleration

7. What is an equivalent expression in rectangular coordinates for the spherical unit vector $\hat{r}$ (assume θ is measured from the positive z axis and φ is measured from the positive x axis)?
*(Rigorous) (Skill 1.1g)*

   A. $\hat{x}$ sinθ cosφ + $\hat{y}$ sinθ sinφ + $\hat{z}$ cosθ

   B. $\hat{x}$ cosθ cosφ + $\hat{y}$ cosθ sinφ + $\hat{z}$ cosθ

   C. −$\hat{x}$ sinθ cosφ − $\hat{y}$ sinθ sinφ + $\hat{z}$ cosθ

   D. $\hat{x}$ sinθ sinφ + $\hat{y}$ sinθ cosφ + $\hat{z}$ sinθ

8. A 100 g mass revolving around a fixed point, on the end of a 0.5 meter string, circles once every 0.25 seconds. What is the magnitude of the centripetal acceleration?
*(Average Rigor) (Skill 1.1h)*

   A. 1.23 m/s$^2$

   B. 31.6 m/s$^2$

   C. 100 m/s$^2$

   D. 316 m/s$^2$

9. A satellite is in a circular orbit above the earth. Which statement is false?
*(Average Rigor) (Skill 1.1h)*

A. An external force causes the satellite to maintain orbit.

B. The satellite's inertia causes it to maintain orbit.

C. The satellite is accelerating toward the earth.

D. The satellite's velocity and acceleration are not in the same direction.

10. A force is given by the vector 5 N x + 3 N y (where x and y are the unit vectors for the x- and y- axes, respectively). This force is applied to move a 10 kg object 5 m, in the x direction. How much work was done?
*(Rigorous) (Skill 1.1h and 1.1i)*

A. 250 J

B. 400 J

C. 40 J

D. 25 J

11. An inclined plane is tilted by gradually increasing the angle of elevation $\theta$, until the block will slide down at a constant velocity. The coefficient of friction, $\mu_k$, is given by:
*(Rigorous) (Skill 1.1b and 1.1j)*

A. $\cos \theta$

B. $\sin \theta$

C. cosecant $\theta$

D. tangent $\theta$

12. A wave generator is used to create a succession of waves. The rate of wave generation is one every 0.33 seconds. The period of these waves is:
*(Average Rigor) (Skill 1.1k)*

A. 2.0 seconds

B. 1.0 seconds

C. 0.33 seconds

D. 3.0 seconds

13. Which statement best describes the relationship of simple harmonic motion to a simple pendulum of length L, mass m and displacement of arc length s?
*(Average Rigor) (Skill 1.1k)*

    A. A simple pendulum cannot be modeled using simple harmonic motion

    B. A simple pendulum may be modeled using the same expression as Hooke's law for displacement s, but with a spring constant equal to the tension on the string

    C. A simple pendulum may be modeled using the same expression as Hooke's law for displacement s, but with a spring constant equal to m g/L

    D. A simple pendulum typically does not undergo simple harmonic motion

14. A uniform pole weighing 100 grams, that is one meter in length, is supported by a pivot at 40 centimeters from the left end. In order to maintain static position, a 200 gram mass must be placed _____ centimeters from the left end.
*(Rigorous) (Skill 1.1i 1.1j, and 1.1l)*

    A. 10

    B. 45

    C. 35

    D. 50

15. An office building entry ramp uses the principle of which simple machine?
*(Easy) (Skill 1.1n)*

    A. Lever

    B. Pulley

    C. Wedge

    D. Inclined Plane

16. A projectile with a mass of 1.0 kg has a muzzle velocity of 1500.0 m/s when it is fired from a cannon with a mass of 500.0 kg. If the cannon slides on a frictionless track, it will recoil with a velocity of ____ m/s.
*(Rigorous) (Skill 2.1a)*

   A. 2.4

   B. 3.0

   C. 3.5

   D. 1500

17. What is the maximum displacement from equilibrium of a 1 kg mass that is attached to a spring with constant k = 100 kg/s$^2$ if the mass has a velocity of 3 m/s at the equilibrium point?
*(Rigorous) (Skill 2.1a)*

   A. 0.1 m

   B. 0.3 m

   C. 3 m

   D. 10 m

18. A car (mass $m_1$) is driving at velocity v, when it smashes into an unmoving car (mass $m_2$), locking bumpers. Both cars move together at the same velocity. The common velocity will be given by:
*(Rigorous) (Skill 2.1b)*

   A. $m_1v/m_2$

   B. $m_2v/m_1$

   C. $m_1v/(m_1 + m_2)$

   D. $(m_1 + m_2)v/m_1$

19. The kinetic energy of an object is _____ proportional to its _____.
*(Average Rigor) (Skill 2.1c)*

   A. Inversely…inertia

   B. Inversely…velocity

   C. Directly…mass

   D. Directly…time

20. An object traveling through air loses part of its energy of motion due to friction. Which statement best describes what has happened to this energy?
(Easy) (Skill 2.1e)

   A. The energy is destroyed

   B. The energy is converted to static charge

   C. The energy is radiated as electromagnetic waves

   D. The energy is lost to heating of the air

21. A long copper bar has a temperature of 60°C at one end and 0°C at the other. The bar reaches thermal equilibrium (barring outside influences) by the process of heat:
(Average Rigor) (Skill 3.1a)

   A. Fusion

   B. Convection

   C. Conduction

   D. Microwaving

22. The number of calories required to raise the temperature of 40 grams of water at 30°C to steam at 100°C is:
(Rigorous) (Skill 3.1a)

   A. 7500

   B. 23,000

   C. 24,400

   D. 30,500

23. A cooking thermometer in an oven works because the metals it is composed of have different:
(Average Rigor) (Skill 3.1b)

   A. Melting points

   B. Heat convection

   C. Magnetic fields

   D. Coefficients of expansion

24. In an experiment where a brass cylinder is transferred from boiling water into a beaker of cold water with a thermometer in it, we are measuring:
(Average Rigor) (Skill 3.1b)

   A. Fluid viscosity

   B. Heat of fission

   C. Specific heat

   D. Nonspecific heat

25. Which of the following is not an assumption upon which the kinetic-molecular theory of gases is based?
*(Rigorous) (Skill 3.1c)*

    A. Quantum mechanical effects may be neglected

    B. The particles of a gas may be treated statistically

    C. The particles of the gas are treated as very small masses

    D. Collisions between gas particles and container walls are inelastic

26. If the internal energy of a system remains constant, how much work is done by the system if 1 kJ of heat energy is added?
*(Average Rigor) (Skill 3.1c and 3.1e)*

    A. 0 kJ

    B. -1 kJ

    C. 1 kJ

    D. 3.14 KJ

27. Which best describes the correct name of the intersection point of the curves on a phase diagram, such as is shown below, and what is its significance?
*(Average Rigor) (Skill 3.1d)*

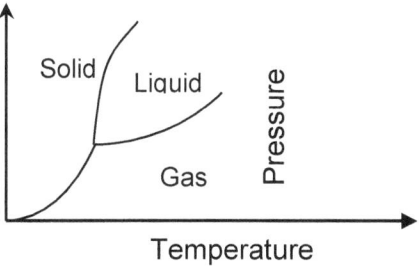

   A. Triple point; the point at which solid, liquid and gas phases coexist or are indistinguishable

   B. Plasma point; the point at which the material exists as a plasma

   C. Phase point; the point at which the material cannot be said to have a phase

   D. Solid-liquid-gas point; the point at which the material is partially solid, partially liquid and partially gas

28. Use the information on heats below to solve this problem. An ice block at 0° Celsius is dropped into 100 g of liquid water at 18° Celsius. When thermal equilibrium is achieved, only liquid water at 0° Celsius is left. What was the mass, in grams, of the original block of ice?

Given:
Heat of fusion of ice = 80 cal/g
Heat of vaporization of ice = 540 cal/g
Specific Heat of ice = 0.50 cal/g°C
Specific Heat of water = 1 cal/g°C
*(Rigorous) (Skill 3.1e)*

A. 2.0

B. 5.0

C. 10.0

D. 22.5

29. Solids expand when heated because:
*(Average Rigor) (Skill 3.1f)*

A. Molecular motion causes expansion

B. PV = nRT

C. Magnetic forces stretch the chemical bonds

D. All material is effectively fluid

30. The wave phenomenon of polarization applies only to:
*(Average Rigor) (Skill 4.1a)*

A. Longitudinal waves

B. Transverse waves

C. Sound

D. Light

31. A quantum of light energy is called a:
*(Easy) (Skill 4.1b)*

A. Dalton

B. Photon

C. Curie

D. Heat Packet

32. A monochromatic ray of light passes from air to a thick slab of glass (n=1.41) at an angle of 45° from the normal. At what angle does it leave the air/glass interface?
*(Rigorous) (Skill 4.1d)*

A. 45°

B. 30°

C. 15°

D. 55°

33. Rainbows are created by:
   *(Easy) (Skill 4.1e)*

   A. Reflection, dispersion, and recombination

   B. Reflection, resistance, and expansion

   C. Reflection, compression, and specific heat

   D. Reflection, refraction, and dispersion

34. The following statements about sound waves are true except:
   *(Average Rigor) (Skill 4.1f)*

   A. Sound travels faster in liquids than in gases.

   B. Sound waves travel through a vacuum.

   C. Sound travels faster through solids than liquids.

   D. Ultrasound can be reflected by the human body.

35. A stationary sound source produces a wave of frequency $F$. An observer at position A is moving toward the horn, while an observer at position B is moving away from the horn. Which of the following is true?
   *(Rigorous) (Skill 4.1g)*

   A. $F_A < F < F_B$

   B. $F_B < F < F_A$

   C. $F < F_A < F_B$

   D. $F_B < F_A < F$

36. If an object is 20 cm from a convex lens whose focal length is 10 cm, the image is:
   *(Rigorous) (Skill 4.1g)*

   A. Virtual and upright

   B. Real and inverted

   C. Larger than the object

   D. Smaller than the object

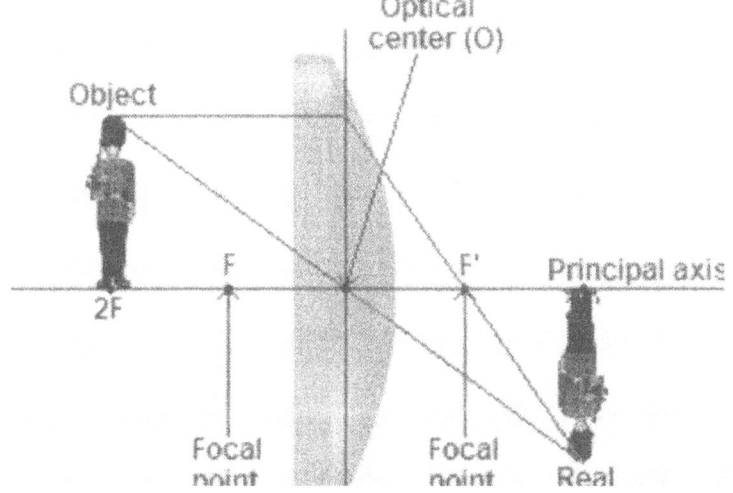

37. Static electricity generation occurs by:
 (Easy) (Skill 5.1a)

 A. Telepathy

 B. Friction

 C. Removal of heat

 D. Evaporation

38. Which of the following statements may be taken as a legitimate inference based upon the Maxwell equation that states $\nabla \cdot \mathbf{B} = 0$?
 (Average Rigor) (Skill 5.1b)

 A. The electric and magnetic fields are decoupled

 B. The electric and magnetic fields are mediated by the W boson

 C. There are no photons

 D. There are no magnetic monopoles

39. What effect might an applied external magnetic field have on the magnetic domains of a ferromagnetic material?
 (Rigorous) (Skill 5.1b)

 A. The domains that are not aligned with the external field increase in size, but those that are aligned decrease in size

 B. The domains that are not aligned with the external field decrease in size, but those that are aligned increase in size

 C. The domains align perpendicular to the external field

 D. There is no effect on the magnetic domains

40. What is the electric flux density (or electric displacement) through each face of a cube, of side length 2 meters, that contains a central point charge of 2 Coulombs?
 (Rigorous) (Skill 5.1d)

 A. 0.50 Coulomb/m$^2$

 B. 0.33 Coulomb/m$^2$

 C. 0.13 Coulomb/m$^2$

 D. 0.33 Tesla

41. What is the effect of running current in the same direction along two parallel wires, as shown below?
*(Rigorous) (Skill 5.1e)*

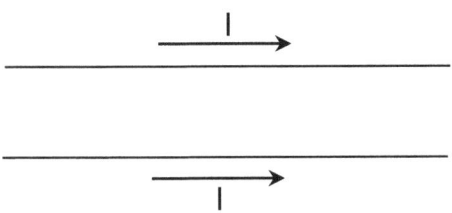

A. There is no effect

B. The wires attract one another

C. The wires repel one another

D. A torque is applied to both wires

42. What is the direction of the magnetic field at the center of the loop of current (I) shown below (i.e., at point A)?
*(Easy) (Skill 5.1f)*

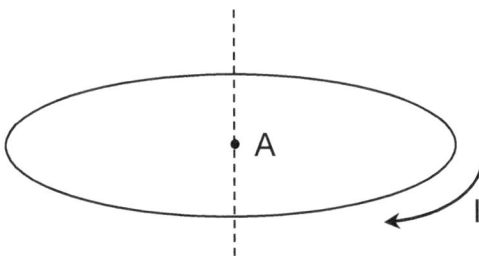

A. Down, along the axis (dotted line)

B. Up, along the axis (dotted line)

C. The magnetic field is oriented in a radial direction

D. There is no magnetic field at point A

43. A 10 ohm resistor and a 50 ohm resistor are connected in parallel. If the current in the 10 ohm resistor is 5 amperes, the current (in amperes) running through the 50 ohm resistor is:
*(Rigorous) (Skill 5.1g and 5.1h)*

A. 1

B. 50

C. 25

D. 60

44. The greatest number of 100 watt lamps that can be connected in parallel with a 120 volt system without blowing a 5 amp fuse is:
*(Rigorous) (Skill 5.1h)*

A. 24

B. 12

C. 6

D. 1

45. The current induced in a coil is defined by which of the following laws?
*(Easy) (Skill 5.1i)*

A. Lenz's Law

B. Burke's Law

C. The Law of Spontaneous Combustion

D. Snell's Law

46. How much power is dissipated through the following resistive circuit?
*(Average Rigor) (Skill 5.1j and 5.1k)*

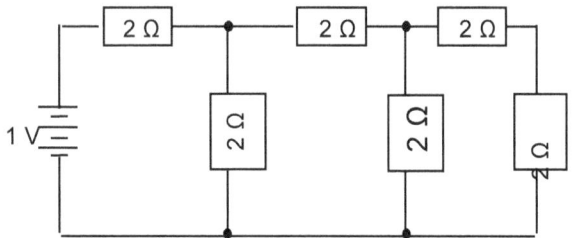

A. 0 W

B. 0.22 W

C. 0.31 W

D. 0.49 W

47. A semi-conductor allows current to flow:
*(Easy) (Skill 5.1l)*

A. Never

B. Always

C. As long as it stays below a maximum temperature

D. When a minimum voltage is applied

48. All of the following use semi-conductor technology, except a(n):
*(Average Rigor) (Skill 5.1l)*

A. Transistor

B. Diode

C. Capacitor

D. Operational Amplifier

49. What best describes an appropriate view of scale in scientific investigation?
*(Rigorous) (Skill 6.1a)*

A. Scale is irrelevant: the same fundamental principles apply at all scale levels

B. Scale has no bearing on experimentation, although it may have a part in some theories

C. Scale has only a practical effect: it may make certain experiments more or less difficult due to limitations on equipment, but it has no fundamental or theoretical impact

D. Scale is an important consideration both experimentally and theoretically: certain phenomena may have negligible effect at one scale, but may have an overwhelming effect at another scale

**50.** Bohr's theory of the atom was the first to quantize:
*(Average Rigor) (Skill 6.1b)*

    A. Work

    B. Angular Momentum

    C. Torque

    D. Duality

## Additional questions Pertaining to the Nature of Science

51. Which statement best describes a valid approach to testing a scientific hypothesis? *(Easy) (Skill 1.1a)*

   A. Use computer simulations to verify the hypothesis

   B. Perform a mathematical analysis of the hypothesis

   C. Design experiments to test the hypothesis

   D. All of the above

52. Which of the following aspects of the use of computers for collecting experimental data is not a concern for the scientist? *(Rigorous) (Skill 1.3c)*

   A. The relative speeds of the processor, peripheral, memory storage unit and any other components included in data acquisition equipment

   B. The financial cost of the equipment, utilities and maintenance

   C. Numerical error due to a lack of infinite precision in digital equipment

   D. The order of complexity of data analysis algorithms

53. Which of the following best describes the relationship of precision and accuracy in scientific measurements? *(Easy) (Skill 1.3d)*

   A. Accuracy is how well a particular measurement agrees with the value of the actual parameter being measured; precision is how well a particular measurement agrees with the average of other measurements taken for the same value

   B. Precision is how well a particular measurement agrees with the value of the actual parameter being measured; accuracy is how well a particular measurement agrees with the average of other measurements taken for the same value

   C. Accuracy is the same as precision

   D. Accuracy is a measure of numerical error; precision is a measure of human error

54. Which statement best describes a rationale for the use of statistical analysis in characterizing the numerical results of a scientific experiment or investigation? *(Average Rigor) (Skill 1.3g)*

    A. Experimental results need to be adjusted, through the use of statistics, to conform to theoretical predictions and computer models

    B. Since experiments are prone to a number of errors and uncertainties, statistical analysis provides a method for characterizing experimental measurements by accounting for or quantifying these undesirable effects

    C. Experiments are not able to provide any useful information, and statistical analysis is needed to impose a theoretical framework on the results

    D. Statistical analysis is needed to relate experimental measurements to computer-simulated values

55. Which of the following devices would be best suited for an experiment designed to measure alpha particle emissions from a sample? *(Average Rigor) (Skill 1.3i)*

    A. Photomultiplier tube

    B. Thermocouple

    C. Geiger-Müller tube

    D. Transistor

56. Which of the following is not a key purpose for the use of open communication about and peer-review of the results of scientific investigations? *(Average Rigor) (Skill 1.3j and 1.5c)*

    A. Testing, by other scientists, of the results of an investigation for the purpose of refuting any evidence contrary to an established theory

    B. Testing, by other scientists, of the results of an investigation for the purpose of finding or eliminating any errors in reasoning or measurement

    C. Maintaining an open, public process to better promote honesty and integrity in science

    D. Provide a forum to help promote progress through mutual sharing and review of the results of investigations

57. Which statement best characterizes the relationship of mathematics and experimentation in physics?
*(Easy) (Skill 1.4a)*

    A. Experimentation has no bearing on the mathematical models that are developed for physical phenomena

    B. Mathematics is a tool that assists in the development of models for various physical phenomena as they are studied experimentally, with observations of the phenomena being a test of the validity of the mathematical model

    C. Mathematics is used to test the validity of experimental apparatus for physical measurements

    D. Mathematics is an abstract field with no relationship to concrete experimentation

58. Which of the following mathematical tools would not typically be used for the analysis of an electromagnetic phenomenon?
*(Rigorous) (Skills 1.4c and 1.4e)*

    A. Trigonometry

    B. Vector calculus

    C. Group theory

    D. Numerical methods

59. For a problem that involves parameters that vary in rate with direction and location, which of the following mathematical tools would most likely be of greatest value?
*(Rigorous) (Skill 1.4e)*

    A. Trigonometry

    B. Numerical analysis

    C. Group theory

    D. Vector calculus

60. Which description best describes the role of a scientific model of a physical phenomenon?
*(Average Rigor) (Skill 2.1a)*

    A. An explanation that provides a reasonably accurate approximation of the phenomenon

    B. A theoretical explanation that describes exactly what is taking place

    C. A purely mathematical formulation of the phenomenon

    D. A predictive tool that has no interest in what is actually occurring

61. If a particular experimental observation contradicts a theory, what is the most appropriate approach that a physicist should take?
(Average Rigor) (Skill 2.1c)

A. Immediately reject the theory and begin developing a new theory that better fits the observed results

B. Report the experimental result in the literature without further ado

C. Repeat the observations and check the experimental apparatus for any potential faulty components or human error, and then compare the results once more with the theory

D. Immediately reject the observation as in error due to its conflict with theory

62. Which situation calls might best be described as involving an ethical dilemma for a scientist?
(Rigorous) (Skill 2.2b)

A. Submission to a peer-review journal of a paper that refutes an established theory

B. Synthesis of a new radioactive isotope of an element

C. Use of a computer for modeling a newly-constructed nuclear reactor

D. Use of a pen-and-paper approach to a difficult problem

63. Which of the following theories can be best described as the result of a scientific revolution in physics in the early decades of the twentieth century?
(Easy) (Skill 2.3c)

A. String theory

B. Classical electrodynamics

C. Quantum theory

D. Galilean relativity

# TEACHER CERTIFICATION STUDY GUIDE

64. Which of the following theories may be said to have had the largest technological impact on human culture?
*(Average Rigor) (Skill 3.3a)*

   A. The Standard Model

   B. General relativity

   C. Quantum mechanics

   D. String theory

65. Which of the following experiments presents the most likely cause for concern about laboratory safety?
*(Average Rigor) (Skill 3.4a)*

   A. Computer simulation of a nuclear reactor

   B. Vibration measurement with a laser

   C. Measurement of fluorescent light intensity with a battery-powered photodiode circuit

   D. Ambient indoor ionizing radiation measurement with a Geiger counter.

## Free Response Questions

1. A 2 meter square loop of wire, connected to a resistive load, is arranged near a power line carrying 100 Amperes of current at 60 Hertz, as shown below. Assuming that the load is negligible in size, calculate the voltage amplitude across the load.

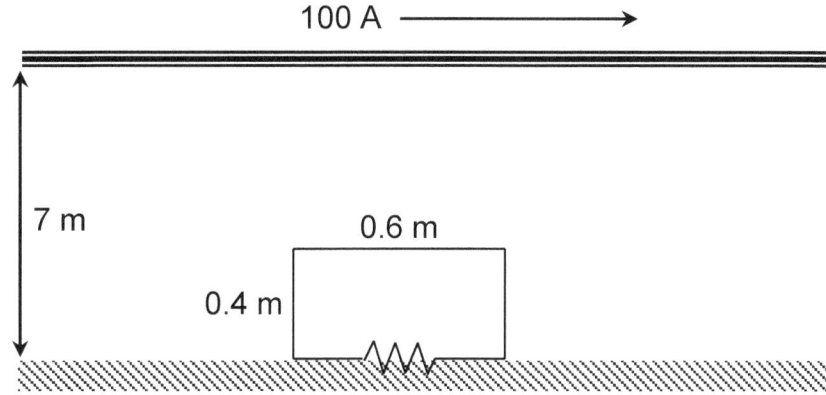

2. A 2,000 kg space vessel is designed to be accelerated away from the Sun using radiation pressure exerted on a sail of area 100 m² that has 95% reflectivity. (Assume that the sail absorbs the rest of the photons.) If the photon flux is assumed to be uniform over the space of interest, and if it has nominal average values of about 3.8x10²¹ photons m⁻² s⁻¹ and 5.5x10¹⁴ Hz frequency, what is the acceleration of the space vessel?

3. A 4 kg sphere, having a radius of 0.25 m and a uniform density, is rotating at f = 3 Hertz. If this sphere is dropped into a 2 liter, thermally isolated container of water at 25° Celsius, what is the final temperature of the water when the sphere (and water) stops rotating?

## Answer Key

| | | | | | |
|---|---|---|---|---|---|
| 1. | B | 25. | D | 49. | D |
| 2. | C | 26. | C | 50. | B |
| 3. | A | 27. | A | 51. | D |
| 4. | B | 28. | D | 52. | D |
| 5. | D | 29. | A | 53. | A |
| 6. | C | 30. | B | 54. | B |
| 7. | A | 31. | B | 55. | C |
| 8. | D | 32. | B | 56. | A |
| 9. | B | 33. | D | 57. | B |
| 10. | D | 34. | B | 58. | C |
| 11. | D | 35. | B | 59. | D |
| 12. | C | 36. | B | 60. | A |
| 13. | C | 37. | B | 61. | C |
| 14. | C | 38. | D | 62. | B |
| 15. | D | 39. | B | 63. | C |
| 16. | B | 40. | B | 64. | C |
| 17. | B | 41. | B | 65. | B |
| 18. | C | 42. | A | | |
| 19. | C | 43. | A | | |
| 20. | D | 44. | C | | |
| 21. | C | 45. | A | | |
| 22. | C | 46. | C | | |
| 23. | D | 47. | D | | |
| 24. | C | 48. | C | | |

## Rigor Analysis Table

| Easy | 21% | 2, 4, 15, 20, 31, 33, 37, 42, 45, 47, 51, 53, 57, 63 |
|---|---|---|
| Average Rigor | 40% | 3, 5, 6, 8, 9, 12, 13, 19, 21, 23, 24, 26, 27, 29, 30, 34, 38, 46, 50, 54, 55, 56, 60, 61, 64, 65 |
| Rigorous | 39% | 1, 7, 10, 11, 14, 16, 17, 18, 22, 25, 28, 32, 35, 36, 39, 40, 41, 43, 44, 48, 49, 52, 58, 59, 62 |

TEACHER CERTIFICATION STUDY GUIDE

## Rationales with Sample Questions

1. **A skateboarder accelerates down a ramp, with constant acceleration of two meters per second squared, from rest. The distance in meters, covered after four seconds, is:**
   *(Rigorous) (Skill 1.1a)*

   A. 10

   B. 16

   C. 23

   D. 37

**Answer: B**

To answer this question, recall the equation relating constant acceleration to distance and time:

$x = \frac{1}{2} a t^2 + v_0 t + x_0$ where x is position; a is acceleration; t is time; $v_0$ and $x_0$ are initial velocity and position (both zero in this case)

thus, to solve for x:

$x = \frac{1}{2} (2 \text{ m/s}^2) (4^2 \text{s}^2) + 0 + 0$

$x = 16 \text{ m}$

This is consistent only with answer (B).

# TEACHER CERTIFICATION STUDY GUIDE

2. **The magnitude of a force is:**
   *(Easy) (Skill 1.1b)*

   A. Directly proportional to mass and inversely to acceleration

   B. Inversely proportional to mass and directly to acceleration

   C. Directly proportional to both mass and acceleration

   D. Inversely proportional to both mass and acceleration

**Answer: C**

To solve this problem, recall Newton's 2$^{nd}$ Law, i.e. net force is equal to mass times acceleration. Therefore, the only possible answer is (C).

3. **If a force of magnitude *F* gives a mass *M* an acceleration *A*, then a force 3*F* would give a mass 3*M* an acceleration:**
   *(Average Rigor) (Skill 1.1b)*

   A. *A*

   B. 12*A*

   C. *A*/2

   D. 6*A*

**Answer: A**

To solve this problem, apply Newton's Second Law, which is also implied by the first part of the problem:

*Force = (Mass)(Acceleration)*

*F = MA*

Then apply the same law to the second case, and isolate the unknown:

3*F* = 3*M* x

x = (3*F*)/(3*M*)

x = *F*/*M*

x = *A* (by substituting from our first equation)

Only answer (A) matches these calculations.

PHYSICS

# TEACHER CERTIFICATION STUDY GUIDE

4. **A classroom demonstration shows a needle floating in a tray of water. This demonstrates the property of:**
   *(Easy) (Skill 1.1c)*

   A. Specific Heat

   B. Surface Tension

   C. Oil-Water Interference

   D. Archimedes' Principle

**Answer: B**

To answer this question, note that the only information given is that the needle (a small object) floats on the water. This occurs because although the needle is denser than the water, the surface tension of the water causes sufficient resistance to support the small needle. Thus the answer can only be (B). Answer (A) is unrelated to objects floating, and while answers (C) and (D) could be related to water experiments, they are not correct in this case. There is no oil in the experiment, and Archimedes' Principle allows the equivalence of displaced volumes, which is not relevant here.

5. Given a vase full of water, with holes punched at various heights. The water squirts out of the holes, achieving different distances before hitting the ground. Which of the following accurately describes the situation?
*(Average Rigor) (Skill 1.1c)*

    A. Water from higher holes goes farther, due to Pascal's Principle.

    B. Water from higher holes goes farther, due to Bernoulli's Principle.

    C. Water from lower holes goes farther, due to Pascal's Principle.

    D. Water from lower holes goes farther, due to Bernoulli's Principle.

**Answer: D**

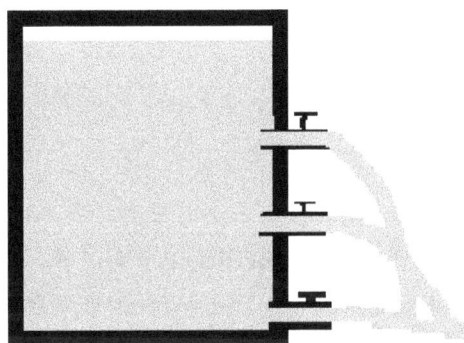

To answer this question, consider the pressure on the water in the vase. The deeper the water, the higher the pressure. Thus, when a hole is punched, the water stream will achieve higher velocity as it equalizes to atmospheric pressure. The lower streams will therefore travel farther before hitting the ground. This eliminates answers (A) and (B). Then recall that Pascal's Principle provides for immediate pressure changes throughout a fluid, while Bernoulli's Principle translates pressure, velocity, and height energy into each other. In this case, the pressure energy is being transformed into velocity energy, and Bernoulli's Principle applies. Therefore, the only appropriate answer is (D).

6. **When acceleration is plotted versus time, the area under the graph represents:**
   *(Average Rigor) (Skill 1.1f)*

   A. Time

   B. Distance

   C. Velocity

   D. Acceleration

**Answer: C**

The area under a graph will have units equal to the product of the units of the two axes. (To visualize this, picture a graphed rectangle with its area equal to length times width.)

Therefore, multiply units of acceleration by units of time:

(length/time$^2$)(time)

This equals length/time, i.e. units of velocity.

7. **What is an equivalent expression in rectangular coordinates for the spherical unit vector $\hat{r}$ (assume θ is measured from the positive z axis and φ is measured from the positive x axis)?**
   *(Rigorous) (Skill 1.1g)*

   A. $\hat{x}$ sinθ cosφ + $\hat{y}$ sinθ sinφ + $\hat{z}$ cosθ

   B. $\hat{x}$ cosθ cosφ + $\hat{y}$ cosθ sinφ + $\hat{z}$ cosθ

   C. −$\hat{x}$ sinθ cosφ − $\hat{y}$ sinθ sinφ + $\hat{z}$ cosθ

   D. $\hat{x}$ sinθ sinφ + $\hat{y}$ sinθ cosφ + $\hat{z}$ sinθ

**Answer: A**

The answer to this question may be recalled from memory of vector algebra, or it can be derived using pencil and paper. The best approach for derivation is to draw an arbitrary unit vector $\hat{r}$ in rectangular coordinates, noting the angles θ and φ, and determine the contribution of each rectangular unit vector. The sum is the result in answer A.

# TEACHER CERTIFICATION STUDY GUIDE

8. **A 100 g mass revolving around a fixed point, on the end of a 0.5 meter string, circles once every 0.25 seconds. What is the magnitude of the centripetal acceleration?**
   *(Average Rigor) (Skill 1.1h)*

   A. 1.23 m/s$^2$

   B. 31.6 m/s$^2$

   C. 100 m/s$^2$

   D. 316 m/s$^2$

   **Answer: D**

   The centripetal acceleration is equal to the product of the radius and the square of the angular frequency ω. In this case, ω is equal to 25.1 Hz. Squaring this value and multiplying by 0.5 m yields the result in answer D.

9. **A satellite is in a circular orbit above the earth. Which statement is false?**
   *(Average Rigor) (Skill 1.1h)*

   A. An external force causes the satellite to maintain orbit.

   B. The satellite's inertia causes it to maintain orbit.

   C. The satellite is accelerating toward the earth.

   D. The satellite's velocity and acceleration are not in the same direction.

   **Answer: B**

   To answer this question, recall that in circular motion, an object's inertia tends to keep it moving straight (tangent to the orbit), so a centripetal force (leading to centripetal acceleration) must be applied. In this case, the centripetal force is gravity due to the earth, which keeps the object in motion. Thus, (A), (C), and (D) are true, and (B) is the only false statement.

10. A force is given by the vector 5 N x + 3 N y (where x and y are the unit vectors for the x- and y- axes, respectively). This force is applied to move a 10 kg object 5 m, in the x direction. How much work was done? *(Rigorous) (Skill 1.1h and 1.1i)*

    A. 250 J

    B. 400 J

    C. 40 J

    D. 25 J

**Answer: D**

To find out how much work was done, note that work counts only the force in the direction of motion. Therefore, the only part of the vector that we use is the 5 N in the x-direction. Note, too, that the mass of the object is not relevant in this problem. We use the work equation:

Work = (Force in direction of motion) (Distance moved)

Work = (5 N) (5 m)

Work = 25 J

This is consistent only with answer (D).

11. An inclined plane is tilted by gradually increasing the angle of elevation θ, until the block will slide down at a constant velocity. The coefficient of friction, $\mu_k$, is given by:
   (Rigorous) (Skill 1.1b and 1.1j)

   A. cos θ

   B. sin θ

   C. cosecant θ

   D. tangent θ

**Answer: D**

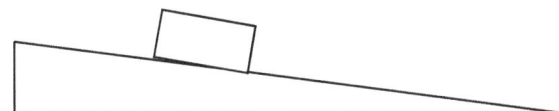

When the block moves, its force upstream (due to friction) must equal its force downstream (due to gravity).

The friction force is given by

$F_f = \mu_k N$

where $\mu_k$ is the friction coefficient and N is the normal force.

Using similar triangles, the gravity force is given by

$F_g$ = mg sin θ

and the normal force is given by

N = mg cos θ

When the block moves at constant velocity, it must have zero net force, so set equal the force of gravity and the force due to friction:

$F_f = F_g$

$\mu_k$ mg cos θ = mg sin θ

$\mu_k$ = tan θ

Answer (D) is the only appropriate choice in this case.

12. A wave generator is used to create a succession of waves. The rate of wave generation is one every 0.33 seconds. The period of these waves is:
*(Average Rigor) (Skill 1.1k)*

   A. 2.0 seconds

   B. 1.0 seconds

   C. 0.33 seconds

   D. 3.0 seconds

**Answer: C**

The definition of a period is the length of time between wave crests. Therefore, when waves are generated one per 0.33 seconds, that same time (0.33 seconds) is the period. This is consistent only with answer (C). Do not be trapped into calculating the number of waves per second, which might lead you to choose answer (D).

# TEACHER CERTIFICATION STUDY GUIDE

13. Which statement best describes the relationship of simple harmonic motion to a simple pendulum of length L, mass m and displacement of arc length s?
    *(Average Rigor) (Skill 1.1k)*

    A. A simple pendulum cannot be modeled using simple harmonic motion

    B. A simple pendulum may be modeled using the same expression as Hooke's law for displacement s, but with a spring constant equal to the tension on the string

    C. A simple pendulum may be modeled using the same expression as Hooke's law for displacement s, but with a spring constant equal to m g/L

    D. A simple pendulum typically does not undergo simple harmonic motion

    **Answer: C**

The force on a simple pendulum may be expressed approximately (when displacement s is small) according to the following equation:

$$F \approx -\frac{mg}{L}s$$

This expression has the same form as Hooke's law (F = -kx). Thus, answer C is the most correct response. Another approach to the question is to eliminate answers A and D as obviously incorrect, and then to eliminate answer B as not having appropriate units for the spring constant.

**14.** A uniform pole weighing 100 grams, that is one meter in length, is supported by a pivot at 40 centimeters from the left end. In order to maintain static position, a 200 gram mass must be placed _____ centimeters from the left end.
*(Rigorous) (Skill 1.1i 1.1j, and 1.1l)*

    A. 10

    B. 45

    C. 35

    D. 50

**Answer: C**

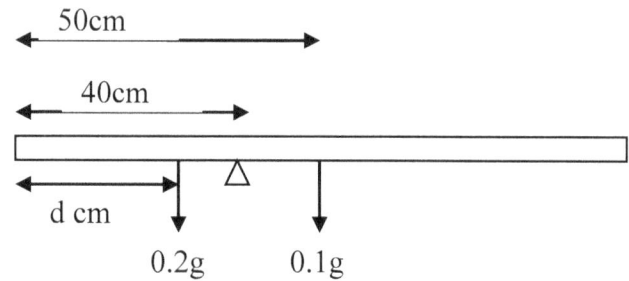

Since the pole is uniform, we can assume that its weight 0.1g acts at the center, i.e. 50 cm from the left end. In order to keep the pole balanced on the pivot, the 200 gram mass must be placed such that the torque on the pole due to the mass is equal and opposite to the torque due to the pole's weight. Thus, if the 200 gram mass is placed d cm from the left end of the pole,

$(40 - d) \times 0.2g = 10 \times 0.1g$;  $40 - d = 5$;  $d = 35$ cm

15. An office building entry ramp uses the principle of which simple machine?
    *(Easy) (Skill 1.1n)*

    A. Lever

    B. Pulley

    C. Wedge

    D. Inclined Plane

**Answer: D**

To answer this question, recall the definitions of the various simple machines. A ramp, which trades a longer traversed distance for a shallower slope, is an example of an Inclined Plane, consistent with answer (D). Levers and Pulleys act to change size and/or direction of an input force, which is not relevant here. Wedges apply the same force over a smaller area, increasing pressure—again, not relevant in this case.

# TEACHER CERTIFICATION STUDY GUIDE

16. A projectile with a mass of 1.0 kg has a muzzle velocity of 1500.0 m/s when it is fired from a cannon with a mass of 500.0 kg. If the cannon slides on a frictionless track, it will recoil with a velocity of _____ m/s. (Rigorous) (Skill 2.1a)

    A. 2.4

    B. 3.0

    C. 3.5

    D. 1500

**Answer: B**

To solve this problem, apply Conservation of Momentum to the cannon-projectile system. The system is initially at rest, with total momentum of 0 kg m/s. Since the cannon slides on a frictionless track, we can assume that the net momentum stays the same for the system. Therefore, the momentum forward (of the projectile) must equal the momentum backward (of the cannon). Thus:

$p_{projectile} = p_{cannon}$
$m_{projectile} \, v_{projectile} = m_{cannon} \, v_{cannon}$
$(1.0 \text{ kg})(1500.0 \text{ m/s}) = (500.0 \text{ kg})(x)$
$x = 3.0$ m/s
Only answer (B) matches these calculations.

17. What is the maximum displacement from equilibrium of a 1 kg mass that is attached to a spring with constant k = 100 kg/s² if the mass has a velocity of 3 m/s at the equilibrium point?
*(Rigorous) (Skill 2.1a)*

    A. 0.1 m

    B. 0.3 m

    C. 3 m

    D. 10 m

**Answer: B**

This problem may be solved using simple differential equation analysis. Alternatively, it may be noted that since harmonic motion involves sinusoidal functions, one may simply assume that the mass has a displacement $x(t) = A \sin \omega t$. Thus, at time t = 0, the mass is at the equilibrium point (x = 0). The spring constant may be used with the known mass to determine the frequency of oscillation according to the equation $k = m\omega^2$. The result is $\omega$ = 10 radians/sec. Differentiating x(t) with respect to time and setting the result equal to 3 m/s at time t = 0 allows for the determination of A, which is 0.3 m. This is the maximum displacement of the mass.

Alternatively, recalling the expression for the potential energy of a spring, we can use conservation of energy and set the total energy at the equilibrium point (entirely kinetic) equal to the total energy at the point of maximum displacement (entirely potential): $1/2 mv^2 = 1/2 kA^2$.

# TEACHER CERTIFICATION STUDY GUIDE

18. A car (mass $m_1$) is driving at velocity $v$, when it smashes into an unmoving car (mass $m_2$), locking bumpers. Both cars move together at the same velocity. The common velocity will be given by:
    *(Rigorous) (Skill 2.1b)*

    A. $m_1v/m_2$

    B. $m_2v/m_1$

    C. $m_1v/(m_1 + m_2)$

    D. $(m_1 + m_2)v/m_1$

**Answer: C**

In this problem, there is an inelastic collision, so the best method is to assume that momentum is conserved. (Recall that momentum is equal to the product of mass and velocity.)

Therefore, apply Conservation of Momentum to the two-car system:

*Momentum at Start = Momentum at End*

*(Mom. of Car 1) + (Mom. of Car 2) = (Mom. of 2 Cars Coupled)*

$m_1v + 0 = (m_1 + m_2)x$

$x = m_1v/(m_1 + m_2)$

Only answer (C) matches these calculations.

Watch out for the other answers, because errors in algebra could lead to a match with incorrect answer (D), and assumption of an elastic collision could lead to a match with incorrect answer (A).

19. The kinetic energy of an object is _____ proportional to its _____.
(Average Rigor) (Skill 2.1c)

    A. Inversely...inertia

    B. Inversely...velocity

    C. Directly...mass

    D. Directly...time

**Answer: C**

To answer this question, recall that kinetic energy is equal to one-half of the product of an object's mass and the square of its velocity:

KE = ½ m v²

Therefore, kinetic energy is directly proportional to mass, and the answer is (C). Note that although kinetic energy is associated with both velocity and momentum (a measure of inertia), it is not *inversely* proportional to either one.

20. An object traveling through air loses part of its energy of motion due to friction. Which statement best describes what has happened to this energy?
(Easy) (Skill 2.1e)

    A. The energy is destroyed

    B. The energy is converted to static charge

    C. The energy is radiated as electromagnetic waves

    D. The energy is lost to heating of the air

**Answer: D**

Since energy must be conserved, the energy of motion of the object is converted, in part, to energy of motion of the molecules in the air (and, to some extent, in the object). This additional motion is equivalent to an increase in heat. Thus, friction is a loss of energy of motion through heating.

21. A long copper bar has a temperature of 60°C at one end and 0°C at the other. The bar reaches thermal equilibrium (barring outside influences) by the process of heat:
*(Average Rigor) (Skill 3.1a)*

    A. Fusion

    B. Convection

    C. Conduction

    D. Microwaving

**Answer: C**

To answer this question, recall the different methods of heat transfer. (Note that since the bar is warm at one end and cold at the other, heat must transfer through the bar from warm to cold, until temperature is equalized.) "Convection" is the heat transfer via fluid currents. "Conduction" is the heat transfer via connected solid material. "Fusion" and "Microwaving" are not methods of heat transfer. Therefore the only appropriate answer is (C).

# TEACHER CERTIFICATION STUDY GUIDE

**22.** **The number of calories required to raise the temperature of 40 grams of water at 30°C to steam at 100°C is:**
*(Rigorous) (Skill 3.1a)*

    A. 7500

    B. 23,000

    C. 24,400

    D. 30,500

**Answer: C**

To answer this question, apply the equations for heat transfer due to temperature and phase changes:

$Q = mC\Delta T + mL$

where Q is heat; m is mass; C is specific heat; $\Delta T$ is temperature change; L is heat of phase change.

In this problem, we are trying to find Q, and we are given:

m = 40 g

C = 1 cal/g°C for water (this should be memorized)

$\Delta T$ = 70 °C

L = 540 cal/g for liquid to gas change in water (this should be memorized)

thus Q = (40 g)(1 cal/g°C)(70 °C) + (40 g)(540 cal/g)

Q = 24,400 cal

This is consistent only with answer (C).

PHYSICS

23. **A cooking thermometer in an oven works because the metals it is composed of have different:**
*(Average Rigor) (Skill 3.1b)*

    A. Melting points

    B. Heat convection

    C. Magnetic fields

    D. Coefficients of expansion

**Answer: D**

A thermometer of the type that can withstand oven temperatures works by having more than one metal strip. These strips expand at different rates with temperature increases, causing the dial to register the new temperature. This is consistent only with answer (D). If you did not know how an oven thermometer works, you could still omit the incorrect answers: It is unlikely that the metals in a thermometer would melt in the oven to display the temperature; the magnetic fields would not be useful information in this context; heat convection applies in fluids, not solids.

24. **In an experiment where a brass cylinder is transferred from boiling water into a beaker of cold water with a thermometer in it, we are measuring:**
*(Average Rigor) (Skill 3.1b)*

    A. Fluid viscosity

    B. Heat of fission

    C. Specific heat

    D. Nonspecific heat

**Answer: C**

In this question, we consider an experiment to measure temperature change of water (with the thermometer) as the cylinder cools and the water warms. This information can be used to calculate heat changes, and therefore specific heat. Therefore, (C) is the correct answer. Even if you were unable to deduce that specific heat is being measured, you could eliminate the other answer choices: viscosity cannot be measured with a thermometer; fission takes place at much higher temperatures than this experiment, and under quite different conditions; there is no such thing as "nonspecific heat".

# TEACHER CERTIFICATION STUDY GUIDE

25. **Which of the following is not an assumption upon which the kinetic-molecular theory of gases is based?**
    *(Rigorous) (Skill 3.1c)*

    A. Quantum mechanical effects may be neglected

    B. The particles of a gas may be treated statistically

    C. The particles of the gas are treated as very small masses

    D. Collisions between gas particles and container walls are inelastic

    **Answer: D**

    Since the kinetic-molecular theory is classical in nature, quantum mechanical effects are indeed ignored, and answer A is incorrect. The theory also treats gases as a statistical collection of point-like particles with finite masses. As a result, answers B and C may also be eliminated. Thus, answer D is correct: collisions between gas particles and container walls are treated as elastic in the kinetic-molecular theory.

26. **If the internal energy of a system remains constant, how much work is done by the system if 1 kJ of heat energy is added?**
    *(Average Rigor) (Skill 3.1c and 3.1e)*

    A. 0 kJ

    B. -1 kJ

    C. 1 kJ

    D. 3.14 kJ

    **Answer: C**

    According to the first law of thermodynamics, if the internal energy of a system remains constant, then any heat energy added to the system must be balanced by the system performing work on its surroundings. In the case of an ideal gas, the gas would necessarily expand when heated, assuming a constant internal energy was somehow maintained. Applying conservation of energy, answer C is found to be correct.

27. Which best describes the correct name of the intersection point of the curves on a phase diagram, such as is shown below, and what is its significance?
(Average Rigor) (Skill 3.1d)

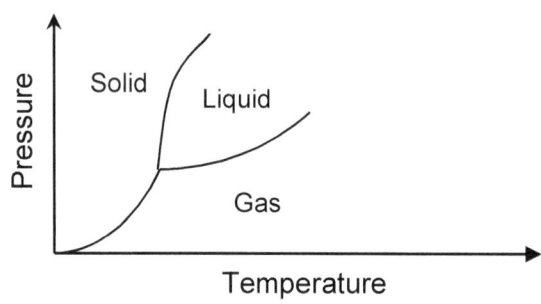

A. Triple point; the point at which solid, liquid and gas phases coexist or are indistinguishable

B. Plasma point; the point at which the material exists as a plasma

C. Phase point; the point at which the material cannot be said to have a phase

D. Solid-liquid-gas point; the point at which the material is partially solid, partially liquid and partially gas

**Answer: A**

The phase diagram above contains a triple point, which is a temperature and pressure at which the material can exist at any one of the phases and also be in thermal equilibrium. Thus, even if the specific name cannot be recalled, the description of the significance of the triple point should be sufficient to ascertain that answer A is correct. The other answers may be eliminated.

28. Use the information on heats below to solve this problem. An ice block at 0° Celsius is dropped into 100 g of liquid water at 18° Celsius. When thermal equilibrium is achieved, only liquid water at 0° Celsius is left. What was the mass, in grams, of the original block of ice?

   Given:  Heat of fusion of ice = 80 cal/g
   Heat of vaporization of ice = 540 cal/g
   Specific Heat of ice = 0.50 cal/g°C
   Specific Heat of water = 1 cal/g°C

*(Rigorous) (Skill 3.1e)*

   A. 2.0

   B. 5.0

   C. 10.0

   D. 22.5

**Answer: D**

To solve this problem, apply Conservation of Energy to the ice-water system. Any gain of heat to the melting ice must be balanced by loss of heat in the liquid water. Use the two equations relating temperature, mass, and energy:

Q = m C ΔT (for heat loss/gain from change in temperature)

Q = m L (for heat loss/gain from phase change)

where Q is heat change; m is mass; C is specific heat; ΔT is change in temperature; L is heat of phase change (in this case, melting, also known as "fusion").

Then

$Q_{\text{ice to water}} = Q_{\text{water to ice}}$

(Note that the ice only melts; it stays at 0° Celsius—otherwise, we would have to include a term for warming the ice as well. Also the information on the heat of vaporization for water is irrelevant to this problem.)

m L = m C ΔT

x (80 cal/g) = 100g 1cal/g°C 18°C

x (80 cal/g) = 1800 cal

x = 22.5 g

Only answer (D) matches this result.

PHYSICS

### 29. Solids expand when heated because:
*(Average Rigor) (Skill 3.1f)*

    A. Molecular motion causes expansion

    B. PV = nRT

    C. Magnetic forces stretch the chemical bonds

    D. All material is effectively fluid

**Answer: A**

When any material is heated, the heat energy becomes energy of motion for the material's molecules. This increased motion causes the material to expand (or sometimes to change phase). Therefore, the answer is (A). Answer (B) is the ideal gas law, which gives a relationship between temperature, pressure, and volume for gases. Answer (C) is a red herring (misleading answer that is untrue). Answer (D) may or may not be true, but it is not the best answer to this question.

### 30. The wave phenomenon of polarization applies only to:
*(Average Rigor) (Skill 4.1a)*

    A. Longitudinal waves

    B. Transverse waves

    C. Sound

    D. Light

**Answer: B**

To answer this question, recall that polarization is when waves are screened so that they come out aligned in a certain direction. (To illustrate this, take two pairs of polarizing sunglasses, and note the light differences when rotating one lens over another. When the lenses are polarizing perpendicularly, no light gets through.) This applies only to transverse waves, which have wave parts to align. Light can be polarized, but it is not the only wave that can be. Thus, the correct answer is (B).

# TEACHER CERTIFICATION STUDY GUIDE

**31.** A quantum of light energy is called a:
*(Easy) (Skill 4.1b)*

  A. Dalton

  B. Photon

  C. Curie

  D. Heat Packet

**Answer: B**

The smallest "packet" (quantum) of light energy is a photon. "Heat Packet" does not have any relevant meaning, and while "Dalton" and "Curie" have other meanings, they are not connected to light. Therefore, only (B) is a correct answer.

**32.** A monochromatic ray of light passes from air to a thick slab of glass (n=1.41) at an angle of 45° from the normal. At what angle does it leave the air/glass interface?
*(Rigorous) (Skill 4.1d)*

  A. 45°

  B. 30°

  C. 15°

  D. 55°

**Answer: B**

To solve this problem use Snell's Law:
$n_1 \sin\theta_1 = n_2 \sin\theta_2$ (where $n_1$ and $n_2$ are the indexes of refraction and $\theta_1$ and $\theta_2$ are the angles of incidence and refraction).

Then, since the index of refraction for air is 1.0, we deduce:
$1 \sin 45° = 1.41 \sin x$
$x = \sin^{-1}((1/1.41) \sin 45°)$
$x = 30°$

This is consistent only with answer (B). Also, note that you could eliminate answers (A) and (D) in any case, because the refracted light will have to bend at a smaller angle when entering glass.

PHYSICS

33. Rainbows are created by:
    (Easy) (Skill 4.1e)

    A. Reflection, dispersion, and recombination

    B. Reflection, resistance, and expansion

    C. Reflection, compression, and specific heat

    D. Reflection, refraction, and dispersion

**Answer: D**

To answer this question, recall that rainbows are formed by light that goes through water droplets and is dispersed into its colors. This is consistent with both answers (A) and (D). Then note that refraction is important in bending the differently colored light waves, while recombination is not a relevant concept here. Therefore, the answer is (D).

34. The following statements about sound waves are true *except:*
    (Average Rigor) (Skill 4.1f)

    A. Sound travels faster in liquids than in gases.

    B. Sound waves travel through a vacuum.

    C. Sound travels faster through solids than liquids.

    D. Ultrasound can be reflected by the human body.

**Answer: B**

Sound waves require a medium to travel. The sound wave agitates the material, and this occurs fastest in solids, then liquids, then gases. Ultrasound waves are reflected by parts of the body, and this is useful in medical imaging. Therefore, the only correct answer is (B).

# TEACHER CERTIFICATION STUDY GUIDE

35. A stationary sound source produces a wave of frequency $F$. An observer at position A is moving toward the horn, while an observer at position B is moving away from the horn. Which of the following is true?
(Rigorous) (Skill 4.1g)

   A. $F_A < F < F_B$

   B. $F_B < F < F_A$

   C. $F < F_A < F_B$

   D. $F_B < F_A < F$

**Answer: B**

To answer this question, recall the Doppler Effect. As a moving observer approaches a sound source, s/he intercepts wave fronts sooner than if s/he were standing still. Therefore, the wave fronts seem to be coming more frequently. Similarly, as an observer moves away from a sound source, the wave fronts take longer to reach him/her. Therefore, the wave fronts seem to be coming less frequently. Because of this effect, the frequency at B will seem lower than the original frequency, and the frequency at A will seem higher than the original frequency. The only answer consistent with this is (B). Note also, that even if you weren't sure of which frequency should be greater/smaller, you could still reason that A and B should have opposite effects, and be able to eliminate answer choices (C) and (D).

36. If an object is 20 cm from a convex lens whose focal length is 10 cm, the image is:
   (Rigorous) (Skill 4.1g)

   A. Virtual and upright

   B. Real and inverted

   C. Larger than the object

   D. Smaller than the object

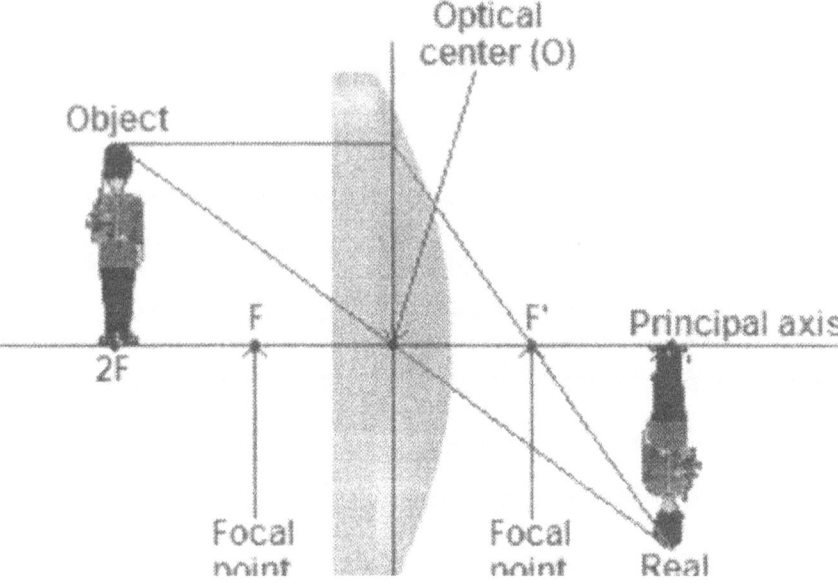

**Answer: B**

To solve this problem, draw a lens diagram with the lens, focal length, and image size.

The ray from the top of the object straight to the lens is focused through the far focus point; the ray from the top of the object through the near focus goes straight through the lens; the ray from the top of the object through the center of the lens continues. These three meet to form the "top" of the image, which is therefore real and inverted. This is consistent only with answer (B).

37. Static electricity generation occurs by:
    (Easy) (Skill 5.1a)

    A. Telepathy

    B. Friction

    C. Removal of heat

    D. Evaporation

**Answer: B**

Static electricity occurs because of friction and electric charge build-up. There is no such thing as telepathy, and neither removal of heat nor evaporation are causes of static electricity. Therefore, the only possible answer is (B).

38. Which of the following statements may be taken as a legitimate inference based upon the Maxwell equation that states $\nabla \cdot \mathbf{B} = 0$?
    (Average Rigor) (Skill 5.1b)

    A. The electric and magnetic fields are decoupled

    B. The electric and magnetic fields are mediated by the W boson

    C. There are no photons

    D. There are no magnetic monopoles

**Answer: D**

Since the divergence of the magnetic flux density is always zero, there cannot be any magnetic monopoles (charges), given this Maxwell equation. If Gauss's law is applied to magnetic flux in the same manner as it is to electric flux, then the total magnetic "charge" contained within any closed surface must always be zero. This is another way of viewing the problem. Thus, answer D is correct. This answer may also be chosen by elimination of the other statements, which are untenable.

39. What effect might an applied external magnetic field have on the magnetic domains of a ferromagnetic material?
(Rigorous) (Skill 5.1b)

    A. The domains that are not aligned with the external field increase in size, but those that are aligned decrease in size

    B. The domains that are not aligned with the external field decrease in size, but those that are aligned increase in size

    C. The domains align perpendicular to the external field

    D. There is no effect on the magnetic domains

**Answer: B**

Recall that ferromagnetic domains are portions of a magnetic material that have a local magnetic moment. The material may have an overall lack of a magnetic moment due to random alignment of its domains. In the presence of an applied field, the domains may align with the field to some extent, or the boundaries of the domains may shift to give greater weight to those domains that are aligned with the field, at the expense of those domains that are not aligned with the field. As a result, of the possibilities above, B is the best answer.

40. What is the electric flux density (or electric displacement) through each face of a cube, of side length 2 meters, that contains a central point charge of 2 Coulombs?
(Rigorous) (Skill 5.1d)

    A. 0.50 Coulomb/$m^2$

    B. 0.33 Coulomb/$m^2$

    C. 0.13 Coulomb/$m^2$

    D. 0.33 Tesla

**Answer: B**

Since the point charge is located at the center of the cube, a symmetric situation exists. Furthermore, since electric flux density has the same value regardless of the shape or size of the surface that encloses the charge, the size of the cube is irrelevant. The amount of flux, therefore, is the same through each face of the cube. Simply divide the charge by the number of cube faces (six) to obtain the result in answer B.

41. **What is the effect of running current in the same direction along two parallel wires, as shown below?**
    *(Rigorous) (Skill 5.1e)*

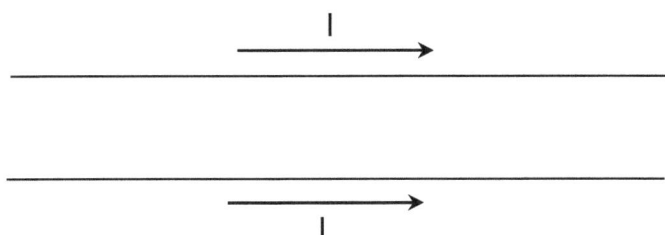

   A. There is no effect

   B. The wires attract one another

   C. The wires repel one another

   D. A torque is applied to both wires

**Answer: B**

Since the direction of the force on a current element is proportional to the cross product of the direction of the current element and the magnetic field, there is either an attractive or repulsive force between the two wires shown above. Using the right hand rule, it can be found that the magnetic field on the top wire due to the bottom wire is directed out of the plane of the page. Performing the cross product shows that the force on the upper wire is directed toward the lower wire. A similar argument can be used for the lower wire. Thus, the correct answer is B: an attractive force is exerted on the wires.

42. What is the direction of the magnetic field at the center of the loop of current (I) shown below (i.e., at point A)?
(Easy) (Skill 5.1f)

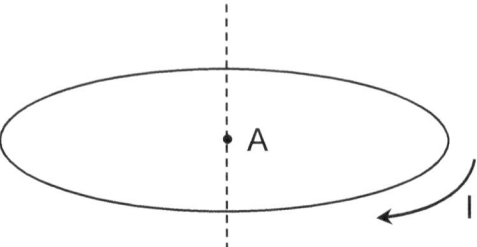

A. Down, along the axis (dotted line)

B. Up, along the axis (dotted line)

C. The magnetic field is oriented in a radial direction

D. There is no magnetic field at point A

**Answer: A**

The magnetic field may be found by applying the right-hand rule. The magnetic field curls around the wire in the direction of the curled fingers when the thumb is pointed in the direction of the current. Since there is a degree of symmetry, with point A lying in the center of the loop, the contributions of all the current elements on the loop must yield a field that is either directed up or down at the axis. Use of the right-hand rule indicates that the field is directed down. Thus, answer A is correct.

# TEACHER CERTIFICATION STUDY GUIDE

**43.** A 10 ohm resistor and a 50 ohm resistor are connected in parallel. If the current in the 10 ohm resistor is 5 amperes, the current (in amperes) running through the 50 ohm resistor is:
*(Rigorous) (Skill 5.1g and 5.1h)*

    A. 1

    B. 50

    C. 25

    D. 60

**Answer: A**

To answer this question, use Ohm's Law, which relates voltage to current and resistance:

$$V = IR$$

where V is voltage; I is current; R is resistance.

We also use the fact that in a parallel circuit, the voltage is the same across the branches.

Because we are given that in one branch, the current is 5 amperes and the resistance is 10 ohms, we deduce that the voltage in this circuit is their product, 50 volts (from $V = IR$).

We then use $V = IR$ again, this time to find I in the second branch. Because V is 50 volts, and R is 50 ohm, we calculate that I has to be 1 ampere.

This is consistent only with answer (A).

PHYSICS

# TEACHER CERTIFICATION STUDY GUIDE

44. **The greatest number of 100 watt lamps that can be connected in parallel with a 120 volt system without blowing a 5 amp fuse is:**
*(Rigorous) (Skill 5.1h)*

   A. 24

   B. 12

   C. 6

   D. 1

**Answer: C**

To solve fuse problems, you must add together all the drawn current in the parallel branches, and make sure that it is less than the fuse's amp measure. Because we know that electrical power is equal to the product of current and voltage, we can deduce that:

I = P/V (I = current (amperes); P = power (watts); V = voltage (volts))

Therefore, for each lamp, the current is 100/120 amperes, or 5/6 ampere. The highest possible number of lamps is thus six, because six lamps at 5/6 ampere each adds to 5 amperes; more will blow the fuse.

This is consistent only with answer (C).

45. **The current induced in a coil is defined by which of the following laws?**
*(Easy) (Skill 5.1i)*

   A. Lenz's Law

   B. Burke's Law

   C. The Law of Spontaneous Combustion

   D. Snell's Law

**Answer: A**

Lenz's Law states that an induced electromagnetic force always gives rise to a current whose magnetic field opposes the original flux change. There is no relevant "Snell's Law," "Burke's Law," or "Law of Spontaneous Combustion" in electromagnetism. (In fact, only Snell's Law is a real law of these three, and it refers to refracted light.) Therefore, the only appropriate answer is (A).

46. How much power is dissipated through the following resistive circuit? *(Average Rigor) (Skill 5.1j and 5.1k)*

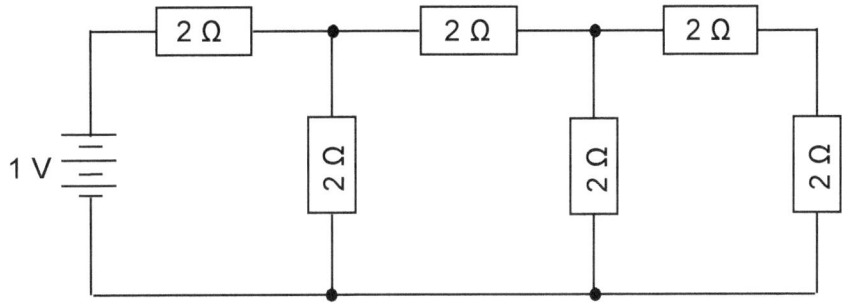

   A. 0 W

   B. 0.22 W

   C. 0.31 W

   D. 0.49 W

**Answer: C**

Use the rules of series and parallel resistors to quickly form an equivalent circuit with a single voltage source and a single resistor. In this case, the equivalent resistance is 3.25 Ω. The power dissipated by the circuit is the square of the voltage divided by the resistance. The final answer is C.

47. A semi-conductor allows current to flow: *(Easy) (Skill 5.1l)*

   A. Never

   B. Always

   C. As long as it stays below a maximum temperature

   D. When a minimum voltage is applied

**Answer: D**

To answer this question, recall that semiconductors do not conduct as well as conductors (eliminating answer (B)), but they conduct better than insulators (eliminating answer (A)). Semiconductors can conduct better when the temperature is higher (eliminating answer (C)), and their electrons move most readily under a potential difference. Thus the answer can only be (D).

48. All of the following use semi-conductor technology, except a(n):
    *(Average Rigor) (Skill 5.1I)*

    A. Transistor

    B. Diode

    C. Capacitor

    D. Operational Amplifier

**Answer: C**

Semi-conductor technology is used in transistors and operational amplifiers, and diodes are the basic unit of semi-conductors. Therefore the only possible answer is (C), and indeed a capacitor does not require semi-conductor technology.

49. What best describes an appropriate view of scale in scientific investigation?
    *(Rigorous) (Skill 6.1a)*

    A. Scale is irrelevant: the same fundamental principles apply at all scale levels

    B. Scale has no bearing on experimentation, although it may have a part in some theories

    C. Scale has only a practical effect: it may make certain experiments more or less difficult due to limitations on equipment, but it has no fundamental or theoretical impact

    D. Scale is an important consideration both experimentally and theoretically: certain phenomena may have negligible effect at one scale, but may have an overwhelming effect at another scale

**Answer: D**

Although A is, in a sense, correct, in that the same principles do apply at all scales, their relative effect at various scales can vary drastically. Gravitational and quantum effects each may dominate at different scale levels, for example. As a result, both B and C are incorrect, since scale is a factor both theoretically and experimentally.

**50. Bohr's theory of the atom was the first to quantize:**
   *(Average Rigor) (Skill 6.1b)*

   A. Work

   B. Angular Momentum

   C. Torque

   D. Duality

**Answer: B**

Bohr was the first to quantize the angular momentum of electrons, as he combined Rutherford's planet-style model with his knowledge of emerging quantum theory. Recall that he derived a "quantum condition" for the single electron, requiring electrons to exist at specific energy levels.

# TEACHER CERTIFICATION STUDY GUIDE

## Additional questions Pertaining to the Nature of Science

51. **Which statement best describes a valid approach to testing a scientific hypothesis?**
*(Easy) (Skill 1.1a)*

   A. Use computer simulations to verify the hypothesis

   B. Perform a mathematical analysis of the hypothesis

   C. Design experiments to test the hypothesis

   D. All of the above

**Answer: D**

Each of the answers A, B and C can have a crucial part in testing a scientific hypothesis. Although experiments may hold more weight than mathematical or computer-based analysis, these latter two methods of analysis can be critical, especially when experimental design is highly time consuming or financially costly.

52. **Which of the following aspects of the use of computers for collecting experimental data is not a concern for the scientist?**
*(Rigorous) (Skill 1.3c)*

   A. The relative speeds of the processor, peripheral, memory storage unit and any other components included in data acquisition equipment

   B. The financial cost of the equipment, utilities and maintenance

   C. Numerical error due to a lack of infinite precision in digital equipment

   D. The order of complexity of data analysis algorithms

**Answer: D**

Although answer D might be a concern for later, when actual analysis of the data is undertaken, the collection of data typically does not suffer from this problem. The use of computers does, however, pose problems when, for example, a peripheral collects data at a rate faster than the computer can process it (A), or if the cost of running the equipment or of purchasing the equipment is prohibitive (B). Numerical error is always a concern with any digital data acquisition system, since the data that is collected is never exact.

53. Which of the following best describes the relationship of precision and accuracy in scientific measurements?
    *(Easy) (Skill 1.3d)*

    A. Accuracy is how well a particular measurement agrees with the value of the actual parameter being measured; precision is how well a particular measurement agrees with the average of other measurements taken for the same value

    B. Precision is how well a particular measurement agrees with the value of the actual parameter being measured; accuracy is how well a particular measurement agrees with the average of other measurements taken for the same value

    C. Accuracy is the same as precision

    D. Accuracy is a measure of numerical error; precision is a measure of human error

**Answer: A**

The accuracy of a measurement is how close the measurement is to the "true" value of the parameter being measured. Precision is how closely a group of measurements is to the mean value of all the measurements. By analogy, accuracy is how close a measurement is to the center of the bulls-eye, and precision is how tight a group is formed by multiple measurements, regardless of accuracy. Thus, measurements may be very precise and not very accurate, or they may be accurate but not overly precise, or they may be both or neither.

54. Which statement best describes a rationale for the use of statistical analysis in characterizing the numerical results of a scientific experiment or investigation?
*(Average Rigor) (Skill 1.3g)*

- A. Experimental results need to be adjusted, through the use of statistics, to conform to theoretical predictions and computer models

- B. Since experiments are prone to a number of errors and uncertainties, statistical analysis provides a method for characterizing experimental measurements by accounting for or quantifying these undesirable effects

- C. Experiments are not able to provide any useful information, and statistical analysis is needed to impose a theoretical framework on the results

- D. Statistical analysis is needed to relate experimental measurements to computer-simulated values

**Answer: B**

One of the main reasons for the use of statistical analysis is that various types of noise, errors and uncertainties can easily enter into experimental results. Among other things, statistics can help alleviate these difficulties by quantifying an average measurement value and a variance or standard deviation of the set of measurements. This helps determine the accuracy and precision of a set of experimental results. Answers A, C and D do not accurately describe ideal scientific experiments or the use of statistics.

55. Which of the following devices would be best suited for an experiment designed to measure alpha particle emissions from a sample?
*(Average Rigor) (Skill 1.3i)*

    A. Photomultiplier tube

    B. Thermocouple

    C. Geiger-Müller tube

    D. Transistor

**Answer: C**

The Geiger-Müller tube is the main component of the so-called Geiger counter, which is designed specifically for detecting ionizing radiation emissions, including alpha particles. The photomultiplier tube is better suited to measurement of electromagnetic radiation closer to the visible range (A), and the thermocouple is better suited to measurement of temperature (B). Transistors may be involved in instrumentation, but they are not sensors.

56. Which of the following is not a key purpose for the use of open communication about and peer-review of the results of scientific investigations?
*(Average Rigor) (Skill 1.3j and 1.5c)*

    A. Testing, by other scientists, of the results of an investigation for the purpose of refuting any evidence contrary to an established theory

    B. Testing, by other scientists, of the results of an investigation for the purpose of finding or eliminating any errors in reasoning or measurement

    C. Maintaining an open, public process to better promote honesty and integrity in science

    D. Provide a forum to help promote progress through mutual sharing and review of the results of investigations

**Answer: A**

Answers B, C and D all are important rationales for the use of open communication and peer-review in science. Answer A, however, would suggest that the purpose of these processes is to simply maintain the status quo; the history of science, however, suggests that this cannot and should not be the case.

# TEACHER CERTIFICATION STUDY GUIDE

**57.** **Which statement best characterizes the relationship of mathematics and experimentation in physics?**
*(Easy) (Skill 1.4a)*

A. Experimentation has no bearing on the mathematical models that are developed for physical phenomena

B. Mathematics is a tool that assists in the development of models for various physical phenomena as they are studied experimentally, with observations of the phenomena being a test of the validity of the mathematical model

C. Mathematics is used to test the validity of experimental apparatus for physical measurements

D. Mathematics is an abstract field with no relationship to concrete experimentation

**Answer: B**

Mathematics is used extensively in the study of physics for creating models of various phenomena. Since mathematics is abstract and not necessarily tied to physical reality, it must be tempered by experimental results. Although a particular theory may be mathematically elegant, it may have no explanatory power due to its inability to account for certain aspects of physical reality, or due to its inclusion of gratuitous aspects that seem to have no physical analog. Thus, experimentation is foundational, with mathematics being a tool for organizing and providing a greater context for observational results.

58. Which of the following mathematical tools would not typically be used for the analysis of an electromagnetic phenomenon?
(Rigorous) (Skills 1.4c and 1.4e)

   A. Trigonometry

   B. Vector calculus

   C. Group theory

   D. Numerical methods

**Answer: C**

Trigonometry and vector calculus are both key tools for solving problems in electromagnetics. These are, primarily, analytical methods, although they play a part in numerical analysis as well. Numerical methods are helpful for many problems that are otherwise intractable analytically. Group theory, although it may have some applications in certain highly specific areas, is generally not used in the study of electromagnetics.

59. For a problem that involves parameters that vary in rate with direction and location, which of the following mathematical tools would most likely be of greatest value?
(Rigorous) (Skill 1.4e)

   A. Trigonometry

   B. Numerical analysis

   C. Group theory

   D. Vector calculus

**Answer: D**

Each of the above answers might have some value for individual problems, but, generally speaking, those problems that deal with quantities that have direction and magnitude (vectors), and that deal with rates, would most likely be amenable to analysis using vector calculus (D).

60. **Which description best describes the role of a scientific model of a physical phenomenon?**
    *(Average Rigor) (Skill 2.1a)*

    A. An explanation that provides a reasonably accurate approximation of the phenomenon

    B. A theoretical explanation that describes exactly what is taking place

    C. A purely mathematical formulation of the phenomenon

    D. A predictive tool that has no interest in what is actually occurring

**Answer: A**

A scientific model seeks to provide the most fundamental and accurate description possible for physical phenomena, but, given the fact that natural science takes an *a posteriori* approach, models are always tentative and must be treated with some amount of skepticism. As a result, A is a better answer than B. Answers C and D overly emphasize one or another aspect of a model, rather than a synthesis of a number of aspects (such as a mathematical and predictive aspect).

61. **If a particular experimental observation contradicts a theory, what is the most appropriate approach that a physicist should take?**
    *(Average Rigor) (Skill 2.1c)*

    A. Immediately reject the theory and begin developing a new theory that better fits the observed results

    B. Report the experimental result in the literature without further ado

    C. Repeat the observations and check the experimental apparatus for any potential faulty components or human error, and then compare the results once more with the theory

    D. Immediately reject the observation as in error due to its conflict with theory

**Answer: C**

When experimental results contradict a reigning physical theory, as they do from time to time, it is almost never appropriate to immediately reject the theory (A) *or* the observational results (D). Also, since this is the case, reporting the result in the literature, without further analysis to provide an adequate explanation of the discrepancy, is unwise and unwarranted. Further testing is appropriate to determine whether the experiment is repeatable and whether any equipment or human errors have occurred. Only after further testing may the physicist begin to analyze the implications of the observational result.

62. **Which situation calls might best be described as involving an ethical dilemma for a scientist?**
    *(Rigorous) (Skill 2.2b)*

    A. Submission to a peer-review journal of a paper that refutes an established theory

    B. Synthesis of a new radioactive isotope of an element

    C. Use of a computer for modeling a newly-constructed nuclear reactor

    D. Use of a pen-and-paper approach to a difficult problem

**Answer: B**

Although answer A may be controversial, it does not involve an inherently ethical dilemma, since there is nothing unethical about presenting new information if it is true or valid. Answer C, likewise, has no necessary ethical dimension, as is the case with D. Synthesis of radioactive material, however, involves an ethical dimension with regard to the potential impact of the new isotope on the health of others and on the environment. The potential usefulness of such an isotope in weapons development is another ethical consideration.

63. **Which of the following theories can be best described as the result of a scientific revolution in physics in the early decades of the twentieth century?**
    *(Easy) (Skill 2.3c)*

    A. String theory

    B. Classical electrodynamics

    C. Quantum theory

    D. Galilean relativity

**Answer: C**

The early part of the twentieth century is well-known as the time during which quantum theory was largely developed. This theory provided the foundation for the development of many modern technologies, including lasers, computers and various types of instrumentation. The other three responses were either largely developed prior to (B and D) or later than (A) this time period.

64. **Which of the following theories may be said to have had the largest technological impact on human culture?**
   *(Average Rigor) (Skill 3.3a)*

   A. The Standard Model

   B. General relativity

   C. Quantum mechanics

   D. String theory

   **Answer: C**

   Although general relativity (B) and string theory (D) are, to some extent, "buzz words" with a certain level of popular fame, they have not had any extensive technological impact. The Standard Model (A) also has questionable technological significance for truly extensive technological value. Quantum mechanics (C), however, can be credited as the theoretical foundation for semiconductor technologies (such as computers), lasers and numerous types of instrumentation for chemistry and physics.

65. **Which of the following experiments presents the most likely cause for concern about laboratory safety?**
   *(Average Rigor) (Skill 3.4a)*

   A. Computer simulation of a nuclear reactor

   B. Vibration measurement with a laser

   C. Measurement of fluorescent light intensity with a battery-powered photodiode circuit

   D. Ambient indoor ionizing radiation measurement with a Geiger counter.

   **Answer: B**

   Assuming no profoundly foolish acts, the use of a computer for simulation (A), measurement with a battery-powered photodiode circuit (C) and ambient radiation measurement (D) pose no particular hazards. The use of a laser (B) must be approached with care, however, as unintentional reflections or a lack of sufficient protection can cause permanent eye damage.

# TEACHER CERTIFICATION STUDY GUIDE

## Free Response Questions: Sample Responses

1. A 2 meter square loop of wire, connected to a resistive load, is arranged near a power line carrying 100 Amperes of current at 60 Hertz, as shown below. Assuming that the load is negligible in size, calculate the voltage amplitude across the load.

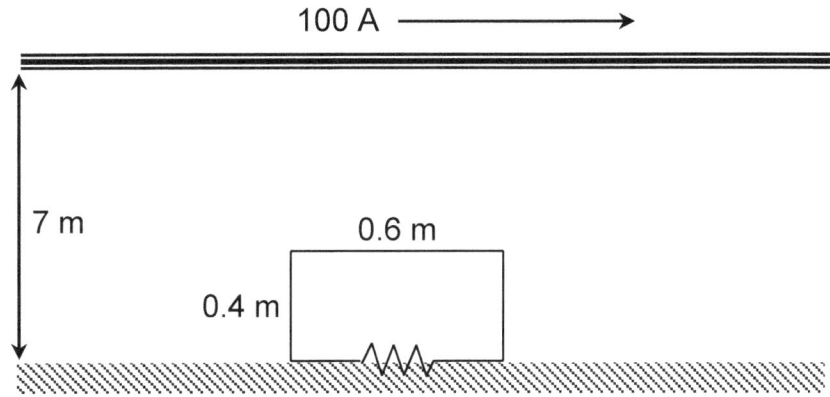

**Answer:**

Varying magnetic fields produce an electromotive force (EMF) in a closed loop of wire (a circuit). This EMF, in turn, can supply current to a load in the circuit. In the diagram above, energy is linked from the power line (a current-carrying conductor) to the wire loop through the time-varying magnetic field. The problem, as stated, involves calculating the magnetic flux through the loop and then the resulting EMF across the load.

First, it is necessary to calculate the magnetic field as a function of distance from the wire. It is safe to assume that the power line is long, and therefore it may be treated approximately as an infinitely long line of current. Using the cylindrical symmetry of the wire and applying Ampere's circuital law, the magnetic flux density B may be calculated as a function of distance from the wire. It is assumed that the flux density does not vary in the horizontal direction (along the length of the wire).

$$\oint_C \mathbf{B} \cdot \mathbf{dl} = \mu_0 I$$

where I is the current through the wire and $\mu_0 = 4\pi \times 10^{-7} \, N/A^2$ is the permeability of free space.

Choosing a circular path C of radius r centered on the power line, and noting that the flux density is invariant along the path, yields:

$$2\pi r B = \mu_0 I$$

$$B = \frac{\mu_0 I}{2\pi r}$$

By the right-hand rule, the flux is directed into the page at all points in the plane of the wire loop. Next, calculate the total flux $\Psi$ through the loop:

$$\Psi = \iint_S B\, dS = 0.6m \cdot \int_{7-0.4}^{7} \frac{\mu_0 I}{2\pi r}\, dr$$

$$\Psi = \iint_S B\, dS = 0.6m \frac{\mu_0 I}{2\pi}[\ln(7) - \ln(6.6)]$$

Calculating the numerical value yields:

$$\Psi = 7.06 \times 10^{-7}\, \text{Wb}$$

Note that the EMF induced is proportional to the derivative of the flux with respect to time. This may be derived from Maxwell's equations using Stokes' theorem.

$$\text{EMF} = -\frac{d}{dt}\Psi$$

Since power lines involve sinusoidally varying currents, the induced EMF should simply be the flux through the wire multiplied by the angular frequency, $\omega = 2\pi f$.

$$\text{EMF} = 2\pi(60\,\text{Hz})(7.06 \times 10^{-7}\,\text{Wb}) = \boxed{2.66 \times 10^{-4}\, \text{V}}$$

This is the voltage (EMF) induced in the wire due to the presence of the power line, and, therefore, it is also the voltage across the load. Since the direction of induced current flow is not relevant to this problem, the absolute value of the EMF is given as the solution.

2. **A 2,000 kg space vessel is designed to be accelerated away from the Sun using radiation pressure exerted on a sail of area 100 m² that has 95% reflectivity. (Assume that the sail absorbs the rest of the photons.) If the photon flux is assumed to be uniform over the space of interest, and if it has nominal average values of about 3.8x10²¹ photons m⁻² s⁻¹ and 5.5x10¹⁴ Hz frequency, what is the acceleration of the space vessel?**

**Answer:**

Radiation pressure is the force exerted on an object due to the absorption or reflection of photons. Typically, this force is not noticeable, since it is generally very small. The lack of air resistance in space, combined with the large photon flux produced by the Sun, makes radiation pressure a potential source of propulsion for space travel.

To calculate the acceleration of the space vessel, first notice that the photons have momentum p. This momentum, according to the following expression, can be calculated based on the wave properties of light.

$$p = \frac{h}{\lambda}$$

Alternatively:

$$p = \frac{E}{c} = \frac{h\nu}{c}$$

The force on the space vessel is due to the absorption or reflection of photons. The momentum of the massless photons is imparted to the vessel (through the sail) when absorption takes place, and twice the momentum is imparted to the vessel when reflection takes place. Thus, 95% of the flux incident on the sail will impart twice its associated momentum, and 5% of the flux will impart simply the single value of its momentum. The average total momentum imparted to the sail, per second, is then:

$$\Delta p = \left[ 0.95 \times 2 \frac{h\nu_{average}}{c} + 0.05 \frac{h\nu_{average}}{c} \right] \frac{1}{photon} \left( 3.8 \times 10^{21} \frac{photons}{m^2} \cdot 100 m^2 \right)$$

Here, the photon flux is multiplied by the distribution of momentum for reflected and absorbed photons and by the area of the sail. Using the values for h, c and $\nu_{average}$ yields the following result:

$$\Delta p = 7.41 \times 10^{23} \frac{(6.626 \times 10^{-34} J \cdot s)(5.5 \times 10^{14} Hz)}{3.00 \times 10^8 \frac{m}{s}} = 9.00 \times 10^{-4} \frac{kg \cdot m}{s}$$

The force is the time rate of change of the momentum:

$$F = \frac{\Delta p}{\Delta t}$$

The product of the acceleration and the mass of the space vessel may then be equated to the force. This yields the final answer when the numerical calculation is performed.

$$F = ma = \frac{\Delta p}{\Delta t}$$

$$a = \frac{\Delta p}{m \Delta t}$$

Since Δt is simply 1 second here, and the mass of the space vessel is 2,000 kg, the final answer is:

$$a = \frac{\Delta p}{m \cdot 1\,s}$$

$$a = \frac{9.00 \times 10^{-4}\, \frac{kg \cdot m}{s}}{(2,000\,kg)(1\,s)} = \boxed{4.50 \times 10^{-7}\, \frac{m}{s^2}}$$

This is an extremely small value, which implies that either the sail must be made much larger, or the design must be abandoned due to a lack of realistic propulsion power from radiation pressure.

# TEACHER CERTIFICATION STUDY GUIDE

**3. A 4 kg sphere, having a radius of 0.25 m and a uniform density, is rotating at f = 3 Hertz. If this sphere is dropped into a 2 liter, thermally isolated container of water at 25° Celsius, what is the final temperature of the water when the sphere (and water) stops rotating?**

**Answer:**

The rotating sphere will lose mechanical energy due to friction, eventually leading to complete transfer of kinetic energy to heat energy. Applying the first law of thermodynamics, the amount of kinetic energy that is lost to friction must be equal to the amount of heat energy added to the water. It is necessary, then, to first calculate the amount of kinetic energy in the rotating sphere.

The rotational kinetic energy of the sphere can be found by first determining the rotational inertia, I, of the sphere. To do this, use the following definition:

$$I = \int \rho^2 dm$$

Here, ρ is the distance from the axis of rotation and dm is the differential element of mass. Since the mass is uniformly distributed throughout the sphere, the density σ is constant. The integral for I is most easily evaluated in spherical coordinates. Thus:

$$I = \int_0^\pi \int_0^{2\pi} \int_0^R \sigma (r\sin\theta)^2 r^2 \sin\theta \, dr \, d\phi \, d\theta$$

Here, ρ has been expressed in terms of the radial distance r (the sphere rotates around a diameter – the identity of the diameter is not relevant to the problem). R is the radius of the sphere. Noting that σ is simply the mass of the sphere divided by the volume of the sphere, the integral may be evaluated as follows:

$$I = \frac{4\,\text{kg}}{\frac{4}{3}\pi R^3} \int_0^R r^4 \, dr \int_0^{2\pi} d\phi \int_0^\pi \sin^3\theta \, d\theta$$

$$I = \frac{4\,\text{kg}}{\frac{4}{3}\pi R^3} \left[\frac{R^5}{5}\right][2\pi]\left[-\cos\theta + \frac{\cos^3\theta}{3}\right]_0^\pi$$

$$I = 4\,\text{kg}\,\frac{3R^2}{10}\left[\frac{4}{3}\right]$$

$$I = 4\,\text{kg}\,\frac{2R^2}{5}$$

$$I = 0.1\,\text{kg}\cdot\text{m}^2$$

PHYSICS

The rotational kinetic energy is the following:

$$KE_{rotational} = \frac{1}{2} I\omega^2$$
$$KE_{rotational} = 2\pi^2 \, I f^2$$
$$KE_{rotational} = 17.8 \, J$$

This is the energy that is transformed, through friction, to heat energy. The specific heat (c) of water is 4190 J kg$^{-1}$ K$^{-1}$. The density of water is about 1,000 kg m$^{-3}$. The mass of 2 liters of water is:

$$m = \rho V = 1000 \frac{kg}{m^3} \cdot 2L \cdot \frac{1 m^3}{1000 L} = 2 \, kg$$

The following equation expresses the relationship of the initial temperature ($T_i$) and final temperature ($T_f$) of the water with respect to the heat energy added (Q).

$$Q = 17.8 \, J = mc(T_f - T_i)$$

This equation may now be solved, once the initial temperature has been converted to Kelvins:

$$17.8 \, J = 2 \, kg \cdot 4190 \frac{J}{kg \cdot K} (T_f - 298 \, K)$$
$$0.002 \, K = (T_f - 298 \, K)$$
$$T_f = 298.002 \, K = 25.002°C$$

Thus, although the change in temperature is slight, it can be seen that the rotational energy of the sphere is transferred to heat energy in the water, resulting in a temperature that is higher by 0.002 Kelvins.

CPSIA information can be obtained
at www.ICGtesting.com
Printed in the USA
BVHW07s2234280718
522828BV00021B/474/P